Literacy and learning through talk

Literacy and learning through talk

Strategies for the primary classroom

Roy Corden

Open University Press
Buckingham · Philadelphia

Open University Press
Celtic Court
22 Ballmoor
Buckingham
MK18 1XW

email: enquiries@openup.co.uk
world wide web: http://www.openup.co.uk

and

325 Chestnut Street
Philadelphia, PA 19106, USA

First Published 2000

A catalogue record of this book is available from the British Library

ISBN   0 335 20450 3 (pb)   0 335 20451 1 (hb)

Library of Congress Cataloging-in-Publication Data
Corden, Roy, 1948–
    Literacy and learning through talk : strategies for the primary
classroom / Roy Corden.
        p.   cm.
    Includes bibliographical references (p.   ) and index.
    ISBN 0–335–20450–3 (pbk.). – ISBN 0–335–20451–1 (hard)
    1. Children–Language.   2. Oral communication.   3. English
language–Spoken English–Study and teaching (Elementary)–Great
Britain.   4. Listening.   I. Title.
LB1139.L3C642   2000
372.62′2–dc21   99–44708
                                                                    CIP

Typeset by Graphicraft Limited, Hong Kong
Printed in Great Britain by St Edmundsbury Press Ltd, Bury St Edmunds, Suffolk

Contents

Acknowledgements

The author would like to thank colleagues and children he worked with in the National Oracy Project. The support and cooperation of teachers and children in Derbyshire, Nottinghamshire and Staffordshire is gratefully acknowledged. In particular, he would like to thank Allan Ahlberg for not 'setting the cops' on Rashmi; Kate Fox for her invaluable contribution; David Westgate for his support and mentorship; and Jim Johnson for his knowledge, inspiration and friendship.

The classification of grouping arrangements (Table 4.3) is reproduced from *Group Work in the Primary Classroom* by Maurice Galton and John Williamson, by permission of Routledge Publishers. Some of the ideas for classroom activities in Chapter 3 first appeared in the Summer 1998 and January 1999 issues of *Literacy and Learning*, and are reproduced by permission of The Questions Publishing Company.

In case of failure to obtain permission to include copyright material in this book the author and publisher apologize and undertake to make good omissions in subsequent printings.

○ Introduction

The term 'oracy' was first coined by Andrew Wilkinson (1965) who called for speaking and listening to be given much more prominence and to be included in our conception of literacy. In the 1970s, projects led by linguists and educationalists, such as Halliday *et al.* (1964) and Rosen and Rosen (1973), illustrated the importance of classroom talk, and the work of Barnes *et al.* (1969) and Tough (1977) drew particular attention to aspects of teacher–pupil discourse. Three major National Curriculum development projects took place between 1987 and 1993: the National Writing Project, the National Oracy Project and the Language in the National Curriculum Project. These were all government approved and funded initiatives undertaken by thousands of teachers working in schools throughout the UK and supported by regional coordinators. The projects were unique in bringing together teachers, local education authority (LEA) advisers, Her Majesty's Inspectors and academics. Collectively, the projects constituted collaborative action research on an impressive scale and should have had a major impact on educational policy and classroom practice. A recurring message was that talk has a central role to play in developing children's knowledge and understanding.

Classroom research, conducted by teachers themselves, therefore confirmed the theoretical stance of socio-cultural psychologists, such as Vygotsky (1978), Bruner (1986) and Wood (1988), and supported the call by educationalists such as Britton (1987) and Wells (1987b) for speaking and listening to be an essential part of the National Curriculum for English. Successive HMI surveys and reports also consistently highlighted the importance of spoken language in learning. Plowden (Central Advisory Council for Education 1967) echoed Wilkinson's call for more emphasis to be placed on spoken language, and Bullock (DES 1975) stressed the need for more collaborative group work and the use of exploratory language. The Assessment of Performance Unit (APU 1988) encouraged the development and evaluation of talk for a variety of purposes and audiences. The introduction of an oral component in GCSE examinations was hugely significant and, as Frater (1988: 36) states, 'secured an irreducible place for the spoken word in the English Curriculum'. The inclusion of speaking and listening as a distinct National Curriculum attainment target seemed to confirm the importance of spoken language as an integral and essential part of *literacy*. It is somewhat alarming, therefore, to find that despite heavy financial investment, current educational theory and 30 years of classroom research, speaking and listening is excluded from a recent major initiative, the National Literacy Strategy Framework (NLSF) (DfEE 1998b). Ironically the NLSF recognizes the importance of speaking and listening as 'an essential part of it [literacy]' (DfEE 1998b: 3), but does not address the issue or include speaking and listening in the planning of work for literacy.

The NLSF states that the most successful teaching is 'discursive – characterised by high quality oral work' (DfEE 1998b: 8) but offers no practical examples, no exemplification and no real demonstration of what this means. A searchlight model of teaching is presented, where reading strategies are taught in context and through the shared reading and investigation of texts. Proponents of the National Literacy Strategy (NLS) argue that the teaching approach includes major elements of constructivist learning, such as modelling, demonstrating and scaffolding. However, speaking and listening (interactive discourse), which is the very essence of constructivist learning, is not dealt with. The NLSF training pack for schools (DfEE 1998b) offers suggestions for teaching but the accompanying videos present some dubious examples of teacher–pupil interaction, more redolent of the asymmetric discourse pattern so soundly condemned by educationalists as being ineffective and inefficient. When I attended a regional Teacher Training Agency Literacy Strategy conference in 1998, I asked why speaking and listening had been excluded from the NLSF. I was told that 'the framework cannot include everything'. One third of the National Curriculum for English, 30 years of substantial classroom research and three expensive National Curriculum development projects is quite a significant exclusion.

The NLS is a paradox. It promotes scaffolded learning within the kind of apprenticeship approach advocated by Holdaway (1979) but is, at the same time, prescriptive. Use of the term *levels* indicates a hierarchy of reading strategies, while a framework which so clearly differentiates and demarcates specific aspects of English and locates them within years and terms, appears mechanistic and designed to reduce teaching to a crude instructional process. This is regrettable, since the NLS is supposedly 'underpinned by research and related evidence from a variety of disciplines' (Beard 1998: 6), and the NLSF is derived from the National Literacy Project and 'successful initiatives in the USA and Australasia' (Beard 1998: 4). The concept of dedicating time to the teaching of literacy follows the 1994 Dearing recommendations, and in fact meets only the *minimum requirement*. However, this point needs to be flagged by LEAs and literacy consultants, who should ensure that schools see the literacy hour as a part of teaching English and not a replacement for it.

I do not intend to dwell on the drawbacks of the NLS but to explore its potential, and to offer teachers ways of developing systematic and structured work which is also stimulating and enjoyable. My major aim is to explore some of the theoretical issues relating to speaking and listening and to reassert the central role of talk in learning. More specifically, I examine the concept of 'interactive discourse' and look at ways of ensuring that the teaching of literacy does not become an arid daily ritual, but is something which truly does encourage exploratory talk and the dynamic investigation of texts.

In Chapter 1 I show how the role of spoken language has become more prominent with the ascendance of Vygotskian theory. In Chapter 2 I examine the concept of literacy and show how children use spoken language to develop their knowledge and understanding. Chapter 3 is devoted to issues of policy and planning. I offer suggestions for whole school policy development and provide examples of how speaking and listening can be incorporated into literacy work plans. Group work forms a major element of the literacy hour and in Chapter 4 I look at ways to develop successful collaborative learning. Scaffolding is a major feature of constructivist learning, and in Chapter 5 I discuss the role of the teacher and identify strategies for intervention. The development of interactive discourse in whole class and small group work relies heavily on the quality of teachers' questions and questioning techniques. In Chapter 6 I address this issue and look at how exploratory talk can be encouraged. In Chapter 7 I examine the importance of story and story-drama and explore the potential for developing speaking, listening and learning. Each chapter is self-contained and examines separate aspects of talk and literacy. However, the issue of teacher–pupil interaction is a central and recurring theme throughout the book.

① ○ Talking, learning and literacy

The shameful neglect of spoken language

There is now a substantial body of research which demonstrates the relationship between talk, academic empowerment and achievement (Johnson *et al.* 1981; Slavin 1983b; Webb and Cullian 1983; Wells and Chang 1988; Sharan and Shaulov 1989; Wells *et al.* 1990). However, until the latter part of the twentieth century spoken language was largely ignored as an important facet of the school curriculum in the UK. It was not until the work of Wilkinson (1965) and Barnes *et al.* (1969) that spoken language received any real prominence within the field of educational research. Wilkinson described it as an area which had been 'shamefully neglected' and his call for a redefinition of literacy to include oracy gained recognition. Wilkinson (1965: 59) argued that:

> Where children are . . . placed in situations where it becomes important for them to communicate – to discuss, to negotiate, to converse – with their fellows, with the staff, with other adults . . . This is basically how oracy grows: it is to be taught by the creation of many and varied circumstances to which speech and listening are natural responses.

Schools Council projects headed by Halliday *et al.* (1964) and Rosen and Rosen (1973) helped to promote an interest in spoken language and literacy in primary schools. Tough's (1977) work, although receiving criticism for its emphasis on teachers' frames of reference and definitions of meaning, drew attention to the importance of effective teacher–pupil interaction. Tough showed that, given adequate and appropriate teacher support, even children in the nursery and infant age range were able to engage in exploratory discussions. Through her communications-skills project and the establishment of action research groups, Tough encouraged teachers to scrutinize their current practices and to consider how their use of language served to inhibit or facilitate children's talk for learning. Participation in the project certainly made me look very carefully at how my language encouraged or inhibited children's talking, thinking and learning.

The Bullock Report (DES 1975) was an authoritative document which confirmed the importance of oracy in the curriculum. The fundamental importance of talk at every stage of schooling was emphasized, the interaction of talking, reading and writing highlighted, and exploratory talk recognized as a powerful means of learning. In the secondary sector, English examining boards, in making use of group discussion and in requiring that all candidates undertake a form of oral assessment, underlined further the importance of spoken language. Research in the USA, Australia, New Zealand and the UK (Barnes 1976; Barnes and Todd 1977; Webb and Cullian 1983; Cambourne 1988; Corson 1988) continued to emphasize the role of talk in learning. After studies (Flanders 1970; Edwards and Furlong 1978) had illustrated the sterile and unproductive discourse that characterized formal whole class teaching, the concept of collaborative working gained prominence. Various forms of cooperative group work were pioneered in Israel (Sharan 1980); Australia (Reid *et al.* 1982) and the USA (Slavin 1983a; Johnson *et al.* 1988).

Ultimate recognition of the importance of spoken language in learning came with the establishment of the National Oracy Project (1987–93). This was a major curriculum development initiative involving 35 LEAs in England and Wales, including primary, middle and secondary schools and covering a wide geographical and cultural range. Teachers, supported by regional coordinators, investigated teaching, learning and spoken language within their classrooms. Their work has provided a body of classroom-based research evidence to demonstrate how talk is valuable in helping children to grasp new ideas, understand concepts and clarify their thoughts. Latham (1992: 257) suggests that the work of the National Oracy Project provided a necessary counterbalance to the 'top-down' model of curriculum planning of the National Curriculum, and Wells (1992: 283) claims that it was the work of the Project which finally led to the centrality of talk in education being recognized.

The National Oracy Project achieved much in promoting an understanding of the value of speech in the learning process. Its work was reflected in the English in the National Curriculum (DES 1989) programme of study attainment target 1, which stated that children should learn to express viewpoints and opinions, to discriminate between fact and opinion, relevance and irrelevance and to speculate and hypothesize, taking into account the views of others. The Order also made it clear that pupils should be given opportunities to engage in whole class and small group discussions in all areas of the curriculum. The National Curriculum for English (DfEE 1995a: 11) recommended that children be given opportunities to talk for a range of purposes and audiences and in a range of contexts. It stated that this range should include making exploratory and tentative comments when ideas are being collected together and making reasoned, evaluative comments as discussion moves to conclusions or action.

Social constructivism and interactive discourse

Wells (1992: 288) argues that the belated recognition of the importance of spoken discourse in education is surprising when one considers how large a proportion of time is spent talking and listening in every classroom. One reason he suggests is that the predominant model of communication and learning in western societies has been one of information transfer. Barnes (1976: 144–5) identified two major pedagogical styles: transmission and interpretation. The transmission teacher puts great emphasis on pupils' ability to reproduce information, while the interpretation teacher is more concerned with interactive discourse and cognitive processes. The two approaches are summarized in Table 1.1.

A simple transmission theory, Wells (1992: 289) argues, is completely incompatible with the theory of knowledge construction or constructivist learning:

> Thus while it is true that one function of a text is to enable the listener to reconstruct the speaker's meaning as accurately as possible, there is a second and equally important function, which is to provide the occasion for the generation of new meaning as the listener makes sense of what the speaker says by responding to it in terms of his or her existing knowledge and current purposes. It is in this second 'dialogic' function that a text acts as what Lotman (1988) calls a 'thinking device ... since traditionally, it has been the transmissional function which has dominated discourse in the classroom, the balance now needs to be rectified with much more attention being given to the dialogic function.

Table 1.1   Transmission and interpretation teaching

Transmission	Interpretation
Children seen as empty vessels	Children's existing knowledge is recognized
Teacher determines what is taught	Children's learning needs determine what is taught
Teacher transmits information	Teacher and children engage with information
(Asymmetric discourse pattern established)	(Interactive discourse pattern established)
Children passively receive information	Children interpret and actively evaluate information

The influence of Vygotsky and Bruner

Psychologists and educationalists, influenced particularly by Vygotsky (1978), have called for a pedagogy where discourse plays a central role in the formulation of meaning (Bruner 1986; Wood 1988; Barnes 1992). They emphasize the interrelationship between spoken language and learning and claim that discourse can enhance thinking and learning. Vygotsky made the point that thought is not merely *expressed* in words – it comes *into existence* through them. How or why talking facilitates our understanding is not clear but probably has something to do with that mysterious ability we all discover from time to time when, in trying to talk about something not yet clear to us, we find that we clarify it for ourselves and say things that we did not know we knew. As E.M. Forster is often alleged to have said, 'How do I know what I mean until I hear what I say?'

Talk is a distinctly human characteristic. It begins as an unfettered chattering voice: a constant stream of consciousness inside our heads which offers an ongoing commentary and critical evaluation of life around us. When we sit quietly watching a film, or reading a book, or listening to a speech, our minds talk to us. The mind does not passively receive messages and images, it engages with them, it wrestles with them, it challenges assertions and ideas. The fact that our mouths do not always transmit our thoughts does not mean that we are not actively engaged in intellectual discourse. It is the internal voice that allows humans to go beyond the here and now, to think in abstractions, to dig out memories and project future events. This private talk was studied in the early twentieth century but largely dismissed. Behaviourist psychologists saw private speech and thinking aloud simply as inappropriate verbal behaviour that eventually disappears. Piaget (1970) referred to children's inner thoughts or private talk as 'egocentric speech' and he distinguished this from socialized speech whose function is to communicate with others. Vygotsky, on the other hand, considered all speech to be socialized or to have a communicative function. Unlike Piaget, who considered that egocentric speech disappears as children mature, Vygotsky argued that speech turns inwards and becomes inner speech or internal language, both interacting with and influencing the thinking and learning process. He believed egocentric speech in infancy to be a precursor to internalized speech and a direct antecedent of thinking at a later stage. He claimed that, rather than disappearing as Piaget suggested, private speech continues to operate as an inner consciousness or verbal thinking. Vygotsky suggested that this internal voice enables children to comment on and explain their actions and is an essential part of their thinking and feeling. Britton (1987: 24) comments, 'It was a brilliant insight on Vygotsky's part to realise that when speech for oneself becomes internalised it is in large part because the child, in handling the freer forms of speech that constitute that mode, begins to be capable of carrying out mental operations more subtle than anything he or she can put into words'.

For Vygotsky (1978: 57), 'every function in the child's cultural development appears twice: first on the social level and later on the individual level'. This contrasts sharply with the Piagetian model of learning, where, as Bruner (1985: 26) says, 'a lone child struggles single-handed to strike some equilibrium between assimilating the world to himself or himself to the world'. Rather than seeing the child as a lone scientist, Vygotsky (1978: 26) proposed that language and thought combine to create a cognitive tool for human development and that 'children solve practical tasks with the help of their speech as well as their eyes and hands'. In focusing attention on the interaction between speech and the child's social and cultural experiences, Vygotsky provides us with a model of learning which emphasizes the role of talk and places social discourse at the centre. Most significant is the notion that children can learn effectively through interaction with a more knowledgeable other (which may be a peer or an adult). Vygotsky's influence can be seen in the work of Barnes (1976: 22), who says that 'classroom learning can best be seen as an interaction between the teacher's meanings and those of the pupils, so that what they take away is partly shared and partly unique to each of them'.

Central to Vygotsky's theory of learning is the zone of proximal development (ZPD), defined as 'the distance between the actual development level as determined by independent problem solving and the level of potential development as determined through problem solving under adult guidance or in collaboration with more capable peers' (1978: 86). It should be remembered that the ZPD is an attribute of each learning event and not an attribute of the child. Mercer and Fisher (1992: 342) point out that 'children do not carry their ZPDs with them'. Each new task will generate a different ZPD and key factors in determining children's learning 'potential' will be the nature of the discourse and the quality of teacher intervention (see Figure 1.1). Bruner (1985: 24–5) offers a useful summary of the concept:

> If the child is enabled to advance by being under the tutelage of an adult or a more competent peer, then the tutor or the aiding peer serves the learner as a vicarious form of consciousness until such time as the learner is able to master his own action through his own consciousness and control. When the child achieves that conscious control over a new function or conceptual system, it is then that he is able to use it as a tool. Up to that point, the tutor in effect performs the critical function of 'scaffolding' the learning task to make it possible for the child, in Vygotsky's word, to internalise external knowledge and convert it into a tool for conscious control.

The work of Bruner has been of great importance in developing our understanding of the relationship between spoken language and learning. Bruner, like Piaget, suggests the learner passes through mental development phases but argues that learning is facilitated through the provision

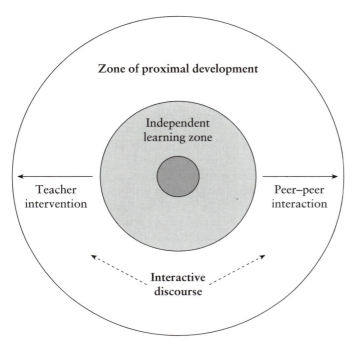

Figure 1.1   Independent and potential learning zones

of organized and structured learning experiences and opportunities for children to extend their current understandings. For Bruner, speech is a primary instrument of thought and the process of talking through ideas is an essential part of children's ability to handle information and make sense of new ideas and concepts. Bruner refers to this as a learner's 'channelling capacity' and argues that language helps children to code information so that cognitive restructuring can occur and a learning experience be made to fit into and extend an existing model of the world. In his later work, Bruner (1986: 127) acknowledges the importance of social interaction, negotiation and shared learning:

> Some years ago I wrote some very insistent articles about the importance of discovery learning . . . my model of the child in those days was very much in the tradition of the child mastering the world by representing it to himself in his own terms. In the intervening years I have come increasingly to recognise that most learning in most settings is a communal activity, a sharing of the culture. It is not just that the child must make his knowledge his own, but that he must make it his own in a community of those who share his sense of belonging to a culture. It is this that leads me to emphasise not only discovery and invention but the importance of negotiating and sharing.

Bruner, like Vygotsky, believed that learning takes place most effectively through the provision of appropriate social interactional frameworks, which he called 'scaffolding'. Bruner illustrates this concept by looking at the way parents, through interactive discourse, support their children in undertaking tasks, initially providing substantial scaffolding and gradually withdrawing it as the child becomes increasingly proficient. In sharing a book with a child, a parent might initially look through the whole text and discuss the illustrations. The parent might then draw the child's attention to one illustration, point to the words beneath it and read them aloud. The child might then be invited to read the text along with the parent. Alongside the withdrawal of support is a gradual handing over of responsibility from parent (expert) to child (learner). Quite simply, therefore, scaffolding is a process that enables 'novices' to undertake tasks they would be unable to do independently and unaided (see Wood *et al.* 1976). The metaphor is particularly appropriate because an important feature of scaffolding is that it is gradually removed as the learner demonstrates increased competence and finally independence. Scaffolding is also highly interactive, with an onus on constant interplay between teacher and learner in the joint completion of a task, and dialogue is crucial to the process because this is how support is provided and adjusted. Interventionist techniques for developing comprehension skills and metacognition, such as reciprocal teaching, are based firmly on Vygotskian theory and notions of scaffolding, 'proleptic' teaching and the anticipation of eventual competence. Interactive discourse is a crucial element, where 'a novice is encouraged to participate in a group activity before she is able to perform unaided, the social context supporting the individual's efforts' (Palinscar and Brown 1984: 123).

Social constructivism and teacher intervention

The theories of Vygotsky and Bruner therefore focus attention on the *interactive* process of teaching and learning and are particularly concerned with social discourse, collaborative learning and the joint construction of knowledge. They highlight the importance of effective teacher intervention and scaffolding strategies, such as:

- *Modelling:* showing children examples of work produced by experts.
- *Demonstrating:* illustrating the procedures experts go through in producing work.
- Supporting children as they learn and practise procedures.

The child is seen as an apprentice learner, initially requiring a great deal of support (scaffolding) as a novice but gradually becoming more proficient and finally being able to operate independently (see Table 1.2).

Table 1.2 From novice to expert: scaffolded learning

| Observer | | |
Context	Teacher	Child
Whole class	Shows examples of letters by reading extracts from *The Jolly Postman* (Ahlberg and Ahlberg 1986) and *A Letter to Father Christmas* (Impey and Porter 1988). Draws children's attention to specific aspects of organization and language features.	Watches, listens, responds to questions, poses questions, discusses.

| Novice | | |
Context	Teacher	Child
Small group	Reads selected letters from *The Jolly Postman.* Discusses audience (who to?) and purpose (what for?). Draws attention to aspects of layout, vocabulary, punctuation, register. Asks children to compose a letter of complaint to Big Bad Wolf. Acts as scribe.	Listens to teacher reading. Reads with teacher. Rereads parts aloud. Discusses the purpose of letters, layout and language. Composes letter orally for teacher to write.

| Apprentice | | |
Context	Teacher	Child
Small group/ individual	Conferences child. Guides, advises, informs, encourages, collaborates in the writing, acts as a response partner.	Plans, drafts, discusses and gains response from peers. Discusses work with the teacher and responds to advice.

| Expert | | |
Context	Teacher	Child
Small group/ individual	Acts as a fellow expert and offers critical evaluation.	Plans, drafts and redrafts a letter for a specific purpose and audience.

The concept of scaffolding is important and particularly useful because it neither places teachers firmly within an instructional, transmission role, nor marginalizes them, but 'represents both teacher and learner as active participants in the construction of knowledge' (Mercer 1995: 74). This conception of the shared construction of knowledge marks a major development from the Piagetian notion of children as lone scientists making meaning for themselves within the constraints of maturational stages.

The implications of Vygotsky's ideas for teaching and learning are immense. The notion of children constructing meaning within a social context and through discourse with both peers and teachers is particularly useful in helping us to move beyond the kind of polarized perspectives that have hindered pedagogic development in the UK. As Edwards and Mercer (1987: 164) put it, 'the value of Vygotsky's and Bruner's approach is to see the dichotomy [between transmission and progressive education] as false'. The notion of a ZPD denoting a difference between the child's independent and supported problem solving performance implies that effective teaching requires teachers to be able to define these levels in children's development, to plan appropriate tasks and to intervene appropriately and effectively. This is what Vygotsky (1982: 121) called 'properly organised instruction, designed to bring into being a series of developmental processes in the child which would not be possible without such intervention'. Vygotsky's view of human biological development being shaped through societal and historical factors also challenges the concept of individualized learning. While accepting that each child is unique, it recognizes that children share common traits, based on common culture, traditions and experiences. Thus, rather than attempting to provide individualized learning programmes for a class of 30 pupils, teachers can work productively with small groups and the whole class, differentiating in terms of planned intervention and support.

Learning in the NLSF

Psychologists and educationalists have made a strong case for the centrality of spoken language in the learning process and have supported Wilkinson's (1965) claim for it to be included in our conception of literacy. Barnes, in particular, has been a powerful contemporary voice in advocating such a constructivist model of learning: 'When a teacher "replies" to his pupils he is by implication taking their view of the subject seriously, even though he may wish to extend and modify it. This strengthens the learner's confidence in actively interpreting the subject matter; teacher and learner are in a collaborative relationship' (1976: 111). It is this interactive, collaborative relationship that lies at the heart of constructivist learning and which underpins major features of the NLS. The concept of dedicated structured time for the direct teaching of literacy is based on sound theory and empirical research (though this has been disputed: see Galton *et al.* 1999: 137; Stainthorp 1999: 5). However, the research underpinning the NLS has been reviewed by Beard (1998: 6), who concludes:

The inclusive nature of the Review is a testimony to how the National Literacy Strategy is underpinned by research and related evidence from a variety of disciplines. The complementary nature of much of the evidence is a clear indicator that, if it is widely and sensitively implemented, the National Literacy Strategy offers a major promise of significantly raising standards and of improving the life chances of thousands of children.

The evidence suggests that literacy is enhanced by children being part of a community of practitioners where:

- they experience literary activity around them and see literacy skills being used by experts;
- they are offered literary models;
- skills and processes are demonstrated;
- they examine, critically evaluate and deconstruct texts;
- they are encouraged to participate and to monitor their own progress;
- participation occurs within a positive, structured and secure environment;
- there are opportunities to work in a variety of learning situations such as individually, with peers and with teachers;
- there is a repertoire of learning contexts to support a variety of learning styles;
- independence is achieved through a gradual withdrawal of expert support.

Shared reading and writing

The concept of shared reading is nothing new or revolutionary to parents who have had their offspring snuggle up to them for a bedtime read. In this most intimate and secure of contexts, a child will be absorbed, eager to join in and certainly ready to intervene should parents make a mistake, fail to read with the desired intonation or, worst of all, attempt to omit part of the text. The translation of this domestic practice to the classroom can be traced to Martin (1976) who argued for a more 'deliberate' provision of literary models in the classroom, and Holdaway (1979), who highlighted the 'corporate experience' of shared reading as a powerful mode of learning. Holdaway argued that a shared examination of texts could be used by teachers to model and elucidate reading strategies, and to stimulate independent individual and small group reading and writing activities. Holdaway's developmental approach shows how children and teachers can be presented with such models and engage in a secure but challenging and productive apprenticeship approach to learning (see Table 1.3).

Modelling is most effective when the learner:

- feels able to succeed;
- perceives that the task is purposeful;

Table 1.3 The developmental approach to learning

Observation of demonstrations	Participation	Putting into practice	Performance
Undertaken by competent other such as parent, teacher, peer.	The child is invited to participate and collaborate.	Novice is given opportunity to practise without direction.	Novice now feels confident enough to present.
The learner is a spectator (novice) with no pressure to perform.	Genuine interest exists in acquiring the skill.	Self-regulation, self-correction, self-direction.	Expert now becomes the audience.
Modelled reading/writing.	Expert welcomes novice and explains, instructs, demonstrates.		Novice is given approval and acknowledgement.
Enlargement of texts/use of overhead projector.	Shared reading/ writing.		

- feels confident enough to take risks;
- respects and trusts the demonstrator/expert.

The elements not present in modelling are:

- competition;
- exclusion;
- criticism;
- coercion.

While the elements present are:

- cooperation;
- acceptance;
- approval;
- invitation to join in.

Guided reading and writing

The National Oracy Project endorsed the Bullock Report (DES 1975: 10–11) recommendation that 'the teacher's role should be one of planned intervention'. The Report suggests that teachers should have clear teaching and learning objectives in mind and should interact with children to support, guide and use language in an exploratory way. Most certainly, teachers in the National Oracy Project found it much more productive to remain with one group for a prolonged period of time rather than flitting constantly between groups. Guided reading offers teachers an opportunity to interact with a small group of children, to intervene and to support their learning.

Through discussion and the sharing of adverse ideas or the clash of perspectives, children may be brought to new levels of understanding and their intellectual horizons extended. Such 'creative conflict' can occur in whole class shared reading sessions or during guided and independent group work. The point is that focus, direction and teacher intervention does not have to result in 'instruction' or the establishment of learning contexts that encourage passivity and unquestioning acceptance. As the DfEE (1998b: 8) points out, 'literary instruction is not a recipe for returning to some crude or simple form of "transmission" teaching'.

Independent group work

Some people have argued that this aspect of the literacy hour is unrealistic and too demanding, particularly for children at Key Stage 1. This is surprising since, for many years, most primary classrooms have been organized with children seated in small groups working individually and independently on a range of activities (see Croll and Hastings 1996: 19–20). Indeed, it was the diversity of activities and the subsequent demands made on teachers that led to criticism from Alexander (1992: 29), who said that 'group work may quickly become counter-prod   )o many groups of pupils within the same   ; on too many different activities or subjec

As National Oracy Project coor   ervising students on teaching practice, I ca   y school where children were not seated in   ariety of different tasks. So what is differe   kind of independent group work required   lies, not in the seating arrangement or the   teacher and the expectations of the pupils. Substantial research (Croll and Moses 1985; Galton *et al.* 1980; Mortimor *et al.* 1988; Bennett and Dunne 1992; Galton and Williamson 1992) has shown that primary teachers spend very little time engaged in quality interaction with children. In discussing the follow-up survey to the original ORACLE study, Galton *et al.* (1999: 67) conclude that 'the present-day primary teacher has continued to engage in the same kinds of exchanges with their pupils as their predecessors did two decades ago'. The primary teacher's role has tended to be a supervisory one, where they have acted as 'overseers' and children have demanded, and expected, an instant response to their needs. This is an undesirable and exhausting *modus operandi*. It does not allow teachers to make effective use of their time and it creates pupil dependency rather than encouraging initiative and independence. Bennett *et al.* (1984) found that primary classrooms were characterized by teachers attempting to provide instant solutions to a constant stream of problems.

A basic tenet of the NLSF is that children's learning will be enhanced through well-focused, uninterrupted interaction with a teacher who can offer support and guidance and can scaffold the learning. In order to provide this quality time, teachers need to ensure that the rest of the class is engaged in worthwhile but self-maintaining and self-directed activities. Children working in independent groups need to be responsible, self-sufficient and to have a clear understanding of ground rules and expectations. Teachers in the National Oracy and Literacy Projects found that, once strategies have been learned and ground rules established, children are able to work efficiently and effectively without having to make constant, and often trivial and unnecessary, demands on the teacher. Moreover, the literate potential of peer–peer interaction in small groups has been well documented, with Wells and Chang (1988) arguing that such a learning milieu both enables and empowers learners. Issues related to independent group work and strategies for developing successful peer–peer interaction are explored in Chapter 4.

Talk in the NLSF

For many years there has been concern over children's knowledge about language (DES 1988). English in the primary school has tended to occupy a peripheral place in the planning of schemes and topics. Other subjects with more easily identifiable 'content' have provided the focus for work. English has tended to remain implicit rather than being made explicit; it has often been assumed to be going on as children are engaged in other areas of the curriculum. Teachers have taken for granted that as children work, for example, on a Vikings or mini-beast topic they will be speaking and listening, reading and writing. However, there has been little detailed evaluation of the range of speaking and listening skills being developed, the kinds of reading being experienced or the forms of writing undertaken. Linguists such as Perera (1987) have argued for children's implicit knowledge about language to be made explicit through an examination of the literary models that surround them in the form of books, poems, newspaper and magazine articles, manuals and so on. A major aim of the NLS is to place literacy at the centre of the primary curriculum and to secure time for focused language study. The NLSF:

- offers a cohesive and consistent approach to teaching literacy within the primary school;
- provides a systematic breakdown of the knowledge and strategies children need to develop in order to become independent readers;
- demands dedicated teaching and learning time;
- directs the teaching and learning focus during this dedicated time.

The crucial interplay between speaking, listening, reading and writing is recognized (albeit succinctly) in the NLSF: 'Literacy unites the important skills of reading and writing. It also involves speaking and listening, which although they are not separately identified in the Framework, are an essential part of it' (DfEE, 1998b: 3). However, it is regrettable that having emphasized the centrality of talk, the DfEE chose to exclude speaking and listening from the NLSF. Given the theoretical models of Vygotsky and Bruner and the vast amount of empirical research conducted over a 30-year period, much of it state funded and approved (National Oracy Project) if not officially published (Language in the National Curriculum Project), the exclusion is disappointing. It is what Andrew Wilkinson (1965), over 30 years on, may well have described as *shameful neglect*.

Although the DfEE claims that talking is inseparable from reading and writing, there is a danger of speaking and listening becoming marginalized. In an educational climate where target setting and league tables are dominant, although lip-service may be paid to spoken language, it may remain tangential. Collaborative discourse does not explicitly enhance crude statistical data derived from standard assessment tasks (SATs) that test children's individual and independent response to texts. This instrumental emphasis may result in the kind of asymmetrical discourse pattern which is a major characteristic of the instructional teaching the DfEE claims it wishes to avoid. One can only hope that the glaring omission of speaking and listening from the NLSF will be recognized and the anomaly rectified.

Those people at the sharp end of the NLS, whose task it is to implement government policy and transform theory into practice, are understandably anxious when politicians embark on personal crusades. Most teachers care passionately about what they do and want to get it right. Unfortunately, the establishment of a punitive inspection service does little to support teachers or facilitate creativity and flair. Rather than encouraging the development of imaginative and exciting literacy plans, the fear and distrust generated by the Office for Standards in Education (Ofsted) seems designed to engender a slavish adherence to a tightly structured, prescribed national scheme. In their anxiety to meet nationally imposed targets, determined by SAT results, schools may adopt an instrumental approach and focus on surface rather than deep learning, and whole class *interaction* may be nothing more than teachers taking *at* rather than *with* children, as noted by Galton *et al.* (1999: 189): 'Currently, the distinction between terms such as "direct teaching" and "interactive whole class teaching" are not well defined and teachers appear, therefore, to be responding to OFSTED's pressure by doing more of what they already do'.

The NLSF presents a major challenge to many schools, both in its practical application and in its philosophical/psychological demands. It requires a great deal of effort, energy and thought. It requires schools to reorganize timetables and to rethink current practices and long-held beliefs. Nevertheless, many teachers have found that the benefits of a dedicated literacy hour far outweigh the problems. The following case study describes how one school has adapted the NLSF to meet the needs of the staff and children.

Implementing the NLSF: a case study

As a deputy headteacher in a large primary school (Long Row School, Belper, Derbyshire), Kate Fox's role in implementing the literacy hour was twofold: not only did she have to get to grips with the strategy within her own classroom, but she also had to play a major part in presenting it to the staff as a positive initiative which would enhance teaching and learning in the school. After one year, she felt that the general feeling within the school was one of buoyant optimism. There were problems to overcome but staff had shown a willingness to adapt current practices to ensure that the literacy hour worked for them and for the children.

The staff did not perceive the NLS as some kind of pedagogic strait-jacket, but saw it as a useful tool to help alleviate the onerous and time-consuming task of constantly having to invent and reinvent work schemes. They found that having the NLSF freed them from this task and gave them more time to discuss 'how' to teach, creatively, through the careful choice of high-quality texts and the provision of stimulating activities.

Collaborative planning

The staff spent the first year with the NLSF evaluating what had gone well and what needed to be improved. As the school is organized into vertically-grouped classes, the first major challenge was to plan a system which would incorporate the needs of two year groups in a class. Teachers found that the best way forward was to cut and paste teaching objectives, matching similar statements, while still being clear which were directed at Year 1 and which at Year 2. They then organized the objectives into groups of statements to teach over a number of weeks. These medium-term literacy plans were mapped onto a half-termly overview plan, along with other subjects. Finally, and most importantly, the statements were transformed into weekly plans of activities for the children. Figure 1.2 illustrates the weekly plan of work based on *The Rainbow Fish* (Pfister 1995).

It became very clear that this kind of collaborative whole school planning was crucial. Without such collaboration, the result can be an unnecessary and time-consuming replication of resources and a lack of consistency. Monitoring progression and achievement can become problematic and the concept of a structured, spiral development in the children's learning may be undermined. At Long Row School the teachers share the burden of planning and preparation by working very closely in teams. Teachers who work in small schools, or who don't have the support of team teaching, may find this

CLASS: YEAR 1/2 Term: Summer Week beginning: 19.4.99.	BOOK(s) The Rainbow Fish by Marcus Pfister (1995).	EVALUATION				
Whole class shared reading and writing	**Whole class phonics, spelling and grammar**	**Group 1**	**Group 2**	**Group 3**	**Group 4**	**Plenary**
1. Reread *The Rainbow Fish* and enjoy. Discuss the fish's character and associated language – adjectives. Distinguish between adjectives for appearance and character.	Recap on vowel phonemes. Introduce phonemes of the week with blank paper. Teacher scribes children's suggestions for words.	Children draw the Rainbow Fish in literacy books – ten minutes. Around the edge they write adjectives to describe it – both appearance and character, including how the character changes.		Handwriting linked to blends of the week focusing on correct letter formation and distinguishing tall and small letters.	Group reading (GR) preceded by five minutes of handwriting instruction with G3. Text is *Meg's Eggs* (Nicholls and Pienkowski 1972). Focus on reading strategies and book structure.	G3 letter formation. Get the children to demonstrate. Is formation correct?
2. Explore the characters of the other sea creatures. Teacher models mapping as children did yesterday for other characters.	Look at yesterday's lists. Look at 'ai'. Do all words have 'ai' in correct position? Recap on known rules – 'ai' usually in middle and 'ay' usually at end. Children bring words home to add to lists.	Children take yesterday's work and recap the character/adjectives. They use this to write a character description, including reasons why, i.e. the fish is selfish in the beginning because…		GR – Text is *Barty's Scarf* (Chambers 1998). Focus as G4.	Handwriting as G3, Lesson 1.	G1 and G2 read out character descriptions. Have they made explicit the reasons for their statements?
3. Read tenses and pronouns. Read through extracts from the book putting Post-its over tense words and pronouns. Put wrong ones on Post-its and get children to correct them and say why.	Play the shopping game. Each child contributes a 'sh' word – lists it in order with others' contributions. Compile a shopping list by reading 'ai' words from class list begun on Monday. Focus attention on 'ai', 'ay' digraphs.	Handwriting – focusing on revising diagonal join using 'ai' vowel phonemes and associated spellings as basis.	GR preceded by five minutes of instruction with G1. Text is *The Day the Smells Went Wrong* (Sefton 1995). Focus – scanning text for information, character and descriptive language. Point out that C. Sefton is really M. Wadell.	Children plan the story of *The Rainbow Fish* in pictures, focusing on the structure. G3 could put a connective word on the top of each picture.		G1 – children model handwriting blend. Is it correct? G2 watch and comment. Remind G3 and G4 that this is what they're aspiring to.
4. Shared writing – model a story plan and the sorts of things we might find on it.	Hangman using 'ai' and 'sh' phonemes. Children must say if their letter is vowel or consonant.	GR – *The Worst Witch* (Murphy 1978). Focus as G2 Lesson 3 plus responding to inferential questions re: character.	Handwriting as G1 Lesson 3.	Children take yesterday's work out using word banks, following their plan and focusing on structure.		G3 and G4 read out their stories. Compare to plans. Have they got a sense of structure/followed plan?
Writing — Shared writing. From yesterday's plan, teacher rewrites the beginning of the story, introducing the key words. Children provide the key words.	Children plan and write their own Rainbow Fish adventure (G4 write straight away). Have discussion about what sort of things may happen to the Rainbow Fish (pirates, shipwrecks, etc.). Remind the children about the work done on settings last week and characterization this week. G1 and G2 need to be bringing all the elements together now, including punctuation. Remind children about targets. Give children time on G3 at planning stage. Remind G4 that they're 'having a go', but to make use of the word cards on the table to look up the basic words they know. As children finish, check through work on a one-to-one basis. Early finishers do 'sh' activity.					

Figure 1.2 Week plan for *The Rainbow Fish*

CLASS: YEAR 1/2 Term: Summer Week beginning: 17.5.99.	BOOK(s) Camille and the Sunflowers by L. Anholt (1999).	EVALUATION				
Whole class shared reading and writing	Whole class phonics, spelling and grammar	Group 1	Group 2	Group 3	Group 4	Plenary
1 What kind of book is it? Do we know anything about Van Gogh? List kinds of questions we might ask to gain information. Don't read book today.	Exploring the 'Q' mark. Why it is used. What kinds of questions can we ask (e.g. time, directions etc.)?	Record the questions they would want to ask to find out about Van Gogh and his life. Children choose how to do it, e.g. in list form (with comma), in speech bubbles with pictures of them in centre. Focus on questions and the 'wh' phoneme.		Handwriting (HW). Exploring the differences between small and tall letters focusing on 'wh' phoneme.	GR preceded by five minutes of HW instruction with G3. Text is Level 1 non-fiction. Focus on reading strategies and looking for information.	G1 and G2 share the questions they have come up with. Do they serve a purpose? Are they relevant?
2 Read the story and enjoy!	Explore the phoneme that begins Q words, e.g. 'wh'. Which words can we spell?	Recapping spellings of vowel digraphs. Under given headings children write lists of words they can spell correctly using rules they have learned to help them. Teacher to use as assessment. Children reminded about use of comma.		GR Level 2 non-fiction book focusing on reading strategies and extracting information.	Write about something they have learned following yesterday's GR session. Children to choose how to present it.	G4 read to others about what they have learned from non-fiction book that they didn't know before.
3 Which of our questions have been answered? What do we know about Van Gogh now that we didn't know before?	Recap on 'Q' mark – use and purpose. Introduce 'ed' and 'er' phonemes for G1 and G2.	Phonics activity for 'er' and 'ed' endings.		Handwriting activities using A Hand for Spelling (Cripps 1990) book.	GR Level 2 non-fiction book focusing on reading strategies and extracting information.	G3 read to others about what they have learned from non-fiction book that they didn't know before.
4 Read the fact page at the end. Compare and contrast to the story part. List differences.	Play 'hangman'.	Bearing in mind the sorts of questions they have asked and the information they have learned during the week, children devise a contents page for a fact book about Van Gogh. Explain that this is part preparation for extended writing where they will produce an illustrated book.		Write about something they have learned following yesterday's GR session. Children to choose how to present it.	Handwriting as G3 Lesson 1.	General consolidation – feedback from groups on information gleaned about Van Gogh.

Writing: Extended writing (possibly over two or three days). With the teacher as a guide, children will produce group books. Each child will provide a page of information with an illustration. On completion, children work on phonic games or non-fiction research from Discovery World Levels 1/2.

Figure 1.3 Week plan for *Camille and the Sunflowers*

aspect of the strategy daunting. One solution is for small schools to work in clusters to share plans and ideas. There are tremendous benefits to be gained from this kind of cooperation. Planning needs to be much more detailed and carefully 'thought thorough' if teachers are doing it, not just for themselves, but for colleagues from other schools to interpret and to use.

Moving out of the NLSF: making cross-curricular links

The school attempted to link the choice of text and objectives to other areas of the curriculum and, as a result, teachers found that the children were exposed to a stimulating and varied range of texts over the year. More poetry and non-fiction reading and writing were included than ever before. Teachers also moved out of the literacy hour framework occasionally. During these extended reading and writing periods, they provided opportunities for children to apply their skills and knowledge in order to produce a book, a pamphlet or a factsheet. One such project, which began with a book called *Camille and the Sunflowers* by Lawrence Anholt (1999) (see Figure 1.3), involved children using as many sources as possible to collate information about Vincent Van Gogh. Then, with appropriate teacher support, the children had to produce an information book, complete with illustrations, contents page and book blurb. The children drew up a list of questions to help guide their investigations (see Figures 1.4 and 1.5). The work, along with illustrations and clay sunflowers that the children had made in art, produced a stimulating, multifaceted display.

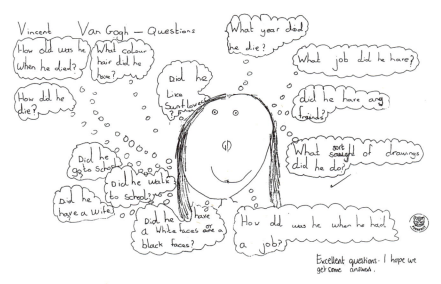

Figure 1.4 Abigail's question sheet

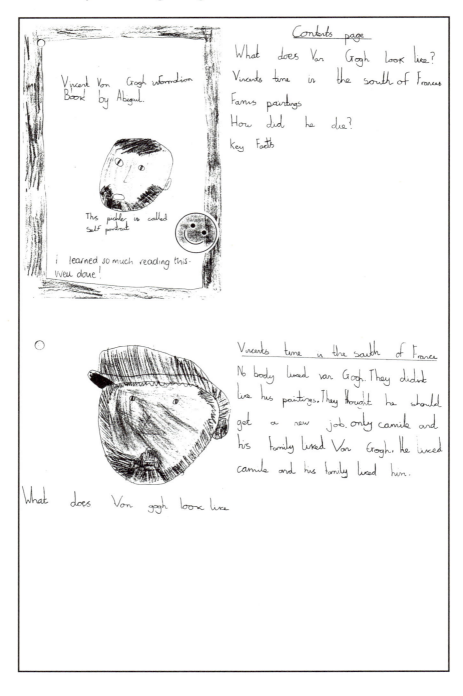

Vincent Von Gogh information Book' by Abigail.

This picture is called Self portrait

i learned so much reading this. well done!

Contents page
What does Van Gogh look like?
Vincents time in the south of France
Famus paintings
How did he die?
Key Facts

What does Von gogh look like

Vincents time in the south of France
No body liked van Gogh. They didnt like his paintings. They thought he should get a new job. only camile and his family liked Van Gogh. He liked camile and his family liked him.

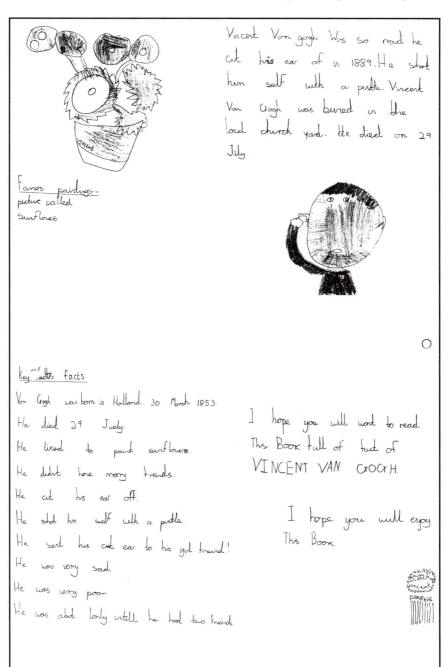

Vincent Von gogh Wos so mad he cut his ear of in 1889. He shot him self with a pistle. Vincent Van Gogh was buried in the local church yard. He died on 29 July.

Famos paintings - picture called Sunflowes

Key facts facts

Van Gogh was born in Holland. 30 March 1853.

He died 29 Jualy

He liked to paint sunflowers.

He didn't have marry freinds.

He cut his ear off.

He shot him self with a pistle.

He sent his cut ear to his gul frend!

He was very sad.

He was very poor

He was abot lonly untill he had two freinds.

I hope you will wont to read This Book full of fact of VINCENT VAN GOGH.

I hope you will enjoy This Book

Figure 1.5 Abigail's book

At the end of what had undoubtedly been an anxious and tiring year, the staff were still extremely enthusiastic about the opportunities that the NLS had provided for the children and for the staff. They had found it stimulating and rewarding to evaluate their practice: to celebrate what they had done well and to look at how they could change some aspects of teaching and planning to encourage still further those independent learning skills from which the children had so obviously benefited.

This case study demonstrates that, to imaginative and enthusiastic teachers, the NLS can be a liberating and innovative force. However it also shows how, because of its omission from the NLSF, speaking and listening is in danger of being marginalized. Although spoken language is an integral part of the weekly work planned by the school, it remains implicit. This is hardly surprising since, despite claiming that quality oral work is essential, the NLSF provides no place for speaking and listening on its recommended planning formats. Interactive discourse between pupils and between teachers and pupils lies at the very heart of a constructivist model of teaching and learning. Just like reading and writing, it needs to be planned for and shown explicitly on literacy work plans. This issue is explored in Chapter 3.

Exploratory talk

The linguist Halliday (1969) makes a huge contribution to our understanding of the relationship between spoken language and learning. Halliday's work is especially important for teachers in the way that it identifies the learning potential of *exploratory* talk. This *heuristic* function of spoken language has been the focus of a great deal of classroom research. The Assessment of Performance Unit (APU 1988: 5) identified a number of purposes for talk in schools and recognized the learning potential of collaborative discussion where children evaluate, speculate, expound and hypothesize. Barnes (1976) makes the point that not all talk is of equal value in helping children to construct meaning. He differentiates between 'process' and 'presentational' talk which are related to the speaker's sense of audience and purpose. Presentational talk is prepared, rehearsed and polished. It is well-structured and its fundamental purpose is to impress or influence an external audience. In presentation talk it is the needs of the audience which are paramount. Giving a speech or a prepared talk on a favourite pastime or hobby, or reporting on work are examples of presentational speech. Here some 8-year-olds are presenting their mustard seed experiment to the rest of the class:

Bridie: Well first we got a box and we got some cotton wool and we soaked the cotton wool under the tap.

Ros: We put a bread wrapper down so's the water won't go through.

Bridie: Yes, so the water won't go through the bottom of the box and then we cut a hole, just a little hole, a square little hole in one side of the box.

Ros: Then we put the seeds in on the cotton wool and we closed the box and put some Sellotape on to keep it closed.

Bridie: Then when we'd done that we put the box on the table by the window.

Ros: We waited for five days and then we opened the box and had a look.

Bridie: And it was growing up towards the little hole we had cut out.

Exploratory or process talk is not for an external audience but is more concerned with working things out. Such talk is unrehearsed, untidy and characterized by false starts, repetition, backtracking, pauses, overlaps and interruptions. Here are the same children using process talk as they actually conduct the experiment:

Ros: Put them [the seeds] on this paper . . . put them on here first.

Bridie: No . . . on cotton wool's best they'll be best on cotton wool not . . . [interrupted]

Ros: Who says cotton wool? . . . We haven't been told cotton wool . . . Mrs . . . [interrupted]

Bridie: I know but it's best I think . . . for keeping the water . . .

Ros: Yeah but hang on . . . We've got to wet it next haven't we or . . . [interrupted]

Bridie: Oh yeah or else they won't . . . [interrupted]

Ros: And after that . . . after we've wet 'em they'll grow then.

Bridie: Grow . . . no . . . so the cotton wool's got be soaked first . . . so's the seeds [interrupted]

Ros: They can drink then . . . they can drink then . . . from the cotton wool 'cos . . . [interrupted]

Bridie: Can live off the cotton wool . . . off the water in the cotton wool.

In this kind of exploratory talk it is the learning needs of the speakers which are most important. Barnes (1976: 126) describes such talk as 'often hesitant and incomplete; it enables the speaker to try out new ideas, to hear how they sound, to see what others make of them, to arrange information and ideas into different patterns'. What is also interesting about the short discussion of mustard seeds is the way the children are 'verbally framing' a procedure, using temporal connectives such as *first, then, after.*

In the classroom children use talk to:

- relate new information to existing experiences and knowledge;
- investigate, hypothesize, question, negotiate;

- argue, reason, justify, consider, compare, evaluate, confirm, reassure, clarify, select, modify, plan;
- demonstrate and convey understanding, narrate, describe, explain;
- reflect upon and evaluate new perceptions and understandings.

Conclusion

The NLSF with its emphasis on interactive whole class discourse, guided group reading, direct teaching and explicit intervention has posed a challenge to current orthodoxy and ideology. Piagetian psychology, endorsed (intentionally or not) by the Plowden Report (Central Advisory Council for Education 1967), has exerted inordinate influence over primary education and shaped the philosophy and practice of thousands of teachers. However, the work of theorists such as Vygotsky and Bruner and the findings of substantial classroom research into spoken language and learning show the necessity for changes in primary practice. The introduction of the NLSF has major implications for school planning, classroom organization and, most particularly, for the quality of teacher–pupil interaction.

2 ○ The discourse of literacy

Spoken language and literacies

Bruner (1990) has described literacy as an essential part of one's cultural toolkit. However, socio-linguistic studies have shown that language is used in different ways and that literacy can mean many things to many people. As Meek (1992: 226) points out, 'Literacy isn't the same in North Peckham, North Westminster, North Harrow'. Luke (1993: 4) suggests that people's freedom to use literacy as a cultural toolkit is influenced by 'the institutions, ideologies and interests operant in these societies', while Freire (1972) argues that institutions manipulate literacy materials to persuade the poor to accept their socio-political situation without question. Some research in classroom literacy has examined the ways in which working with texts through reading and writing activities is determined by institutional imperatives and preferences with 'classroom literacies' being designed for schooling. For example, Michaels (1985) shows how teachers' conceptions of literary competence is determined by children's ability to participate in a certain form of institutionally contrived discourse, or what Willes (1983) describes as the rituals of classroom discourse. It could be argued that the DfEE, in producing the NLSF with prescribed programmes of study and specific learning objectives, has provided teachers with the necessary documentation for evaluating children's competence within an idealized white, middle class, middle England conception of literacy. Teachers are required to match children against this ethnocentric conception of literary competence and accredit that competence through achievement in SATs. Gee (1990) supports Labov's (1972) criticism of a WASP (white, Anglo-Saxon middle class) perception of literacy and argues that 'the ability to talk about school based sorts of tasks is one way in which Western-style schools empower élites; they sound like they know more than they do' (cited in Baker and Freebody 1993: 279).

The DfEE's ideological stance and conception of literacy is strongly influenced by the belief that a modern democratic technological society requires a literate workforce to ensure economic growth and prosperity. Barber (1997) has warned of the economic consequences of low literacy levels, while Beard (1998) points to the cost of illiteracy in terms of remedial provision, lost business, unemployment benefits and crime. Graff (1994: 158) however, having reviewed the history of literacy in the western world, questions these assumptions: 'major steps forward in trade, commerce, and even industry took place in some periods and places with remarkably low levels of literacy; conversely, higher levels of literacy have not been proved to be stimulants or springboards for "modern" economic developments'.

By 'literate', we can mean that someone is able to read and write at a very elementary level, or we can mean that someone is well-read and capable of critical literary analysis. Literacy is a problematic concept, dependent on a number of factors and what a particular culture or society deems to be important and relevant. For example, Heath (1983) found that what counts as reading and writing is often specific to situations and cultures. She discovered major differences between the values placed on aspects of literacy in white and black working-class communities. In the former, children were frequently praised for reading; in the latter, the practice of reading was rarely mentioned. Philips (1983), in her study of North American Indians, also notes significant cultural differences in communicative practices with, for example, Indians displaying far more tolerance of prolonged silences during conversation. In *Sign of the Beaver* by Elizabeth George Speare (1983), a North American Indian boy named Attean has to attend a white school and finds that within this environment he is semi-literate. He befriends a white boy named Matt and invites him to spend the vacation with him on the Indian reservation. The white boy, literate in his own world, suddenly finds himself illiterate in a different environment:

> Matt began to feel uneasy. If Attean should take himself off suddenly, as he had a way of doing, Matt was not sure he could find his way back to the cabin. It occurred to him that Attean knew this, that perhaps Attean had brought him so far just to show him how helpless he really was, how all the words in a white man's book were of no use to him in the woods.
>
> (Speare 1983: 54)

When I read this book, I was reminded of the time I taught a secondary special needs class in a rural school. I would take them out into the countryside on field trips where 'they' would teach 'me' about trees and plants, berries and fungus, crops and fungicide, birds and animals, husbandry and farm machinery.

In 1956, the United Nations Educational, Scientific and Cultural Organization (UNESCO) adopted a definition of functional literacy based on the

degree of reading and writing skill required for individuals to function effectively in their own society. However, this definition diminishes the importance
of oracy and fails to recognize the oral culture of some societies. Indeed,
spoken language has certain advantages. Books can be burned, as in Nazi
Germany, or distorted, as in Stalinist Russia, and it can be argued that written
accounts of historical events are merely the interpretations of the powerful
or victorious. The writers of Ofsted reports are not without their critics in
this sense (see Galton *et al.* 1999; Stainthorp 1999) and it is interesting to
note that in a supposedly free and democratic society the Language in the
National Curriculum (LINC) Project materials were not officially published.[1]
The burgeoning of women's studies, with an emphasis on previously little-
known women authors, is testimony to the fact that literature has been
male dominated. Literacy undoubtedly confers power and prestige in our
society but we should be wary of seeking absolute or unchanging conceptions
of what it means to be literate.

In providing a national framework based on a particular conception of
literacy fixed in time, place and culture, the DfEE is in danger of imposing
an instrumental, ethnocentric and static model of literacy in schools. Comber
and Cormack (1997: 29) suggest that 'if literacy is "constructed" then
teachers can choose to change the construction of literacy in their setting
– if they find it is not currently working for their students'. The literacy
hour has drawn criticism from some who see it as being too rigid and not
allowing ideas to be extended or themes developed. Others, following the
example of teachers involved in the National Literacy Project, have used
the dedicated time to introduce and focus on aspects of literature which
are then developed beyond the literacy hour and across curriculum areas.
Stannard (1998) makes the point that teachers can use the literacy hour
with a degree of flexibility and treat the time as approximate. He suggests
that initially teachers might adhere closely to the structure of the literacy
hour, but move into a more flexible approach as they gain confidence.
He advises teachers to 'maintain the balance but have good reasons for
changing from that structure to something else related to particular tasks'
(1998). Moreover, teachers need to recognize that the literacy hour forms
only a part of the teaching of English. This is made clear in the NLSF which
states that: 'The Literacy Hour is intended to be a time for the explicit teaching of reading and writing. Teachers will need to provide opportunities
for practising and applying new skills in independent work at other times'
(DfEE 1998b: 14). Thankfully, there are signs that imaginative teachers,
aided by literacy consultants and supported by positive LEAs, are developing exciting and imaginative practices which reflect the truly diversionary
nature of literacy and are using the NLSF as an aide to planning rather than
a blueprint for it.

The inclusion of speaking and listening as a distinct National Curriculum
attainment target officially sanctioned its importance. However, it would

be a mistake to see spoken language in splendid isolation or as operating discretely from reading and writing. Meek (1991: 13) argues that all societies are fundamentally oral and that any understanding of literacy must begin with a recognition of that orality. Literacy, she says, 'is about language, and the primary form of language is, of course, speech'. Bruner (1972) describes literacy as a 'cognitive amplifier' and Wells (1989) uses the term 'literate thinking' where real or imaginary worlds, created through words, may be explored through literate thinking in speech as well as in print. The NLSF recognition of the crucial interrelationship between speaking, listening, reading and writing echoes the work of researchers who have used the term 'literacy event' to describe the complex socio-cultural interaction of people with print.

Literacy events

Studies of literacy events have shown that different social situations demand the use of particular sorts of text used in particular ways, using appropriate language. Discourse analysts have attempted to explain how and why kinds of language are used in different contexts and refer to the 'discourse of situations', by which they mean the rules, rituals and expected interaction associated with a particular context. Research has shown that preschool children develop some understanding of the forms and functions of literacy, and Heath (1986) suggests that those children who grow up in a literate community have opportunities to participate in literacy events before they begin formal education. Most adults have internalized the etiquette of discourse situations but children, often to the embarrassment of parents, are still learning. I recall a school inspector pompously asking a 5-year-old child if she knew what two plus two equalled. 'Don't you know!' answered the little girl in a disgusted tone.

The discourse of the classroom figures large in the lives of children, and the rules and rituals of literacy events have to be learned. Heath (1986: 168–70) refers to literacy events as 'genres of language use' and identifies six such events in school:

- *Label quests:* these are language activities in which adults either name items or ask for their names.
- *Meaning quests:* within this language activity, adults either infer for the young child what he or she means, interpret their own behaviour or that of others, or ask for explanations of what is meant or intended.
- *Recounts:* within this genre, the speaker retells experiences or information known to both teller and listener. As children retell, they may be questioned by the listener who wants to scaffold the telling in a certain way.

- *Accounts:* unlike recounts which depend upon the power differential, where one party asks another to retell or perform for the sake of performance, accounts are generated by the teller. Accounts provide information that is new to the listener or new interpretations of information that the listener already knows.
- *Eventcasts:* in this genre, individuals provide a running narrative on events currently in the attention of the teller and listeners or forecast events to be accomplished in the future.
- *Stories:* this is perhaps the most familiar genre, because of our customary associations with the written stories read to children and requested of children's imagination. The mould of these fictional accounts is such that they must include some animate being who moves through a series of events with goal-directed behaviour.

In perceiving reading as a social event, Heath takes a Vygotskian stance which highlights the fact that children's interactions with texts are often mediated through oral language practices. In their examination of reading as a social event, Maybin and Moss (1993) support this view and argue that it is through talking about text that children share what they know about reading and about how it gets done. For example, it is through talk that children explore the imaginary world created by the words of the writer and relate it to their own experience.

Literacy and metalanguage

The importance of metalinguistic knowledge has been stressed by a number of researchers such as Downing and Valtin (1984). This knowledge ranges from what Clay (1972) called concepts about print, to more complex knowledge about genre, form and style. The NLSF identifies the metalinguistic knowledge that children in the primary years need to develop, and the various components are categorized as 'word', 'sentence' and 'text' levels:

- *Word level:* phonological and alphabetic knowledge; word recognition.
- *Sentence level:* knowledge of spelling strings and patterns; punctuation.
- *Text level:* knowledge of text structures, organization and literary devices.

This is unfortunate nomenclature since *levels* implies differentiation and the existence of a hierarchy, which subsequently implies a teaching and learning priority. The emphasis on word level work at Key Stage 1 reinforces this notion. *Strands* is a more appropriate term because:

- fluent independent reading requires an orchestration of the full range of strategies;

- developing readers do not learn to read by using any one strategy in isolation;
- the linguistic components are interdependent and do not operate discretely.

There is convincing evidence that young children benefit from an early development of phonological awareness (Bryant 1989; Adams 1990; Goswami and Bryant 1990). However, the fact that children learn to read words like 'McDonalds' from the age of 3 serves to illustrate the importance of words being placed within a meaningful context. 'McDonalds' (word level) is located within a semantic setting (text level). If we extend the word and place it in a sentence such as 'Have your party at Ronald McDonalds', we can see how, in reality, all three metalinguistic strands combine to support the developing reader by offering multiple cues. These cues are most effectively synthesized through spoken language. The child sees and recognizes the semantic field or text of McDonalds – for example, the symbol, the bright colours, the general ambience of a fast-food outlet. The child hears the word 'McDonalds' within a syntactic unit or sentence, as in 'Shall we go to McDonalds for something to eat?'

The development of metalinguistic awareness (knowing terms) and a metalanguage (understanding and using the terms) allows children not only to order their thoughts and to express feelings but also to question, explore and interpret the words of others. Spoken language helps to develop higher order thinking because, as Vygotsky suggests, learning occurs initially on a social plane and is then internalized – that is, spoken language is not used simply to express thoughts, it is used to create them. To write is to make this internal private language visible, both to oneself and to a wider audience. This visibility allows and invites scrutiny and a search for meaning from readers, who also bring their own language to the written text during the interrogation. In proficient readers, this interrogation most often occurs individually, internally and silently. With young children, it manifests itself in speech; children like to hear what the writer has said. Not only do children want to listen to the words that have been written, they also seek the interpretations of others (when in the company of peers) in addition to reassurance (when in the company of adults). Reading activity should be seen as a busy, bustling act of social collaboration, drawing heavily on the *orality* of language. Barnes (1992: 125) talks about the importance of children being able to work on understanding. He suggests that at the centre of working on understanding is the idea of trying out new ways of thinking and understanding and that 'the readiest way of working on understanding is often through talk, because the flexibility of speech makes it easy for us to try out new ways of arranging what we know'. This dynamic process of learning is demonstrated in the following snapshots of children working collaboratively on various literacy activities.

Year 1

In the first snapshot, two Year 1 children are looking at a book which tells the Russian folk tale, *The Great Big Enormous Turnip*. Although there is a simple written text on each page, the children decide to 'read' the illustrations, to draw on their semantic understanding and to 'tell' themselves the story. What is particularly interesting is the way that Shelley (S) and Asimar (A) talk their way into narrative mode. Asimar begins the process (A6) by accentuating *won't*. Shelley (S7) follows Asimar's initiative and this marks the onset of a cumulative and collaborative story making/storytelling venture. The children demonstrate their existing literary knowledge and their understanding of repetition in books. In substituting the word *out* for *whoosh*, Shelley (S20) displays an awareness of pattern in story and her understanding of the pattern change that often occurs on the final page.

1	S:	He's in his garden.
2	A:	He's giving his plants some water . . . my granddad's got a watering can like that.
3	S:	He's growing a big turnip [points to the title and reads] The big Turnip . . . turn over . . . look . . . he's pulling it up now.
4	A:	He's pulling it . . . but it's stuck . . . won't come out.
5	S:	So . . . along comes his wife.
6	A:	And along comes Mrs Farmer and they pull and they pull but it *won't* come up . . . so come and help me.
7	S:	So *come and help* they shout and along comes the little girl and . . .
8	S/A:	And they pull and they pull but it *won't* come up.
9	S:	So all together they shout . . . *come and help*.
10	A:	Come and help to pull the turnip . . . come and help us pull this great big turnip.
11	S:	And along comes the little boy.
12	S/A:	And they pull and they pull but it *won't* come up.
13	S/A:	So all together they shout . . . *come and help*.
14	S:	And along comes the puss.
15	S/A:	And they *pull* and they *pull* but it *won't* come up.
16	S/A:	So all together they shout . . . *come and help*.
17	S:	And along comes a teeny weeny little mouse.
18	S/A:	And they *pull* and they *pull* and it comes out.
19	A:	And they *pull* and they *pull* and *out* it comes.
20	S:	They *pull* and they *pull* and *whoosh*, out it comes.

Years 2 and 3

In the following snapshot, Year 2 and 3 pupils are discussing the making of a puppet theatre, in which they intend to perform the story of *Jack and the Beanstalk* for the rest of the class. It provides a simple illustration of young children developing their awareness of the difference between story and scripted dramatization. This snapshot shows the children clarifying their understanding of textual differences and, in particular, the need for a narrator, standing outside the plot and the participating characters and adopting the stance of third person. They realize that this role is crucial in order to ensure cohesion and continuity for their audience.

1   *S:* So me . . . I'm Jack . . . and . . .
2   *P:* And me . . . I'm the giant . . . I'll be the giant.
3   *T:* What about . . . his . . . wife . . . we need a voice for Mrs . . . giant.
4   *P:* Yeah and for Jack's mum . . . so . . . you be her . . . Jack's mum and N . . . you can be the giant's wife.
5   *S:* OK then . . . so I'm on first . . . mine . . . my puppet comes on and says . . .
6   *T:* But . . . but before that . . . what about before that?
7   *P:* Oh yeah . . . how will people know what it's about?
8   *S:* 'Cos of what it's called.
9   *P:* Yeah but we need another voice don't we?
10 *S:* Another puppet?
11 *T:* No not . . . or yeah . . . it could be a puppet . . . but not . . . but not in the story.
12 *N:* Yeah like . . . the one who's telling the story.
13 *S:* Oh I get you . . . like who says . . . who talks to the people who're watching and . . .
14 *N:* Who says this is the story of Jack and the Beanstalk . . .
15 *P:* Once upon a time there was this boy . . .
16 *S:* Oh I get you . . . then I come on . . .
17 *T:* Or you could already be on but you don't say anything yet . . . 'till N's finished.
18 *P:* Then you start talking.
19 *N:* And I say things like . . . one day Jack's mother sent him to . . .
20 *S:* Oh yeah . . . I get you . . . so . . . so it's not a part . . . it's just like a voice.
21 *N:* Telling the bits we can't say.
22 *P:* Talking to the class.
23 *T:* Yeah.

Year 4

In the next snapshot, Year 4 pupils demonstrate their awareness of the language features of different genres, in particular the differences between narrative and report writing. The discussion begins with A(1) offering the traditional narrative opening, *One day*. This opening establishes a narrative genre and the other members of the group begin to develop the text according to its parameters until B(8) feels that something is wrong and challenges the mode. She does not say that the text doesn't 'look' right, but that it does not 'sound' right. On reaching the conclusion that the opening has seduced them into writing in a particular genre which is inappropriate to their needs, they identify, in quite precise terms, what the problems are, demonstrating aspects of knowledge about language: tense, the need to write in reported speech, to avoid direct speech, passive rather than active verbs, being specific rather than general – as when they indicate the exact day and name the characters involved. They are using spoken language to bring to bear a particular way of thinking about a particular genre (Christie 1988; Barnes and Sheeran 1992).

1	A:	One day a girl was walking through the woods.
2	B:	A girl was walking through the woods when . . .
3	B:	When she stopped 'cos she was hungry . . . wanted . . .
4	A:	Something to eat . . . wanted some food.
5	D:	Along came a wolf and sat down.
6	A:	A wolf came and sat down beside her . . .
7	D:	'Hello little girl' he said, 'where are you going?'
8	B:	This isn't right . . . it doesn't sound right.
9	C:	[reads through what has been written]
10	B:	It sounds like a story.
11	C:	Yeah . . . it's like make believe . . . like we've made it up.
12	A:	Yeah and a report is supposed to be real . . . not made up.
13	B:	What happened . . . like in the news.
14	C:	OK . . . so . . . like it's not happening now . . . it's happened.
15	A:	It's in the past and we're telling people what happened.
16	C:	Right . . . so one day [starts to write].
17	B:	We need to say which day . . . give the exact day and about what time it was.
18	C:	Yeah like . . . on Saturday November first.
19	D:	At ten o'clock.
20	A:	A little girl, whose name was . . .
21	C:	Little girl . . . by the name of Riding Hood.
22	A:	Riding Hood . . . was walking through the woods . . . when . . .
23	B:	We need to say which woods . . . not just any woods . . . have a name.
24	C:	Is walking through Bradley Woods.
25	D:	Should be was . . . was walking.
26	A:	Along came . . . no . . . a wolf . . . as she was sitting a wolf came along.
27	C:	The wolf sat down beside her and said . . . 'Hello little girl' . . .
28	D:	No . . . it's like a story again . . . that bit is.

Year 5

The following snapshot illustrates the importance of spoken language in the creation of written narrative. Two Year 5 children have brainstormed and made a bone pattern for storytelling. They are now discussing how they might write the story. P and J are developing their sense of cohesion and the use of cohesive ties. Connectives such as 'and', 'but', 'because', 'so', 'when', 'until' and 'finally' are used to expand the text from simple into compound and complex sentences. Cohesive devices such as the use of the pronouns 'he', 'him', 'his', 'they' and 'who' are used to hold the text together in a meaningful way and make it easier to read. Undesirable repetition is recognized and 'one day' is avoided by the use of 'until'. In opening the story, the determiner 'this' (king) is changed for the more appropriate indefinite article 'a' (king) and the timeless 'once' establishes the genre of a traditional tale. The pupils are seeking to give their text global coherence. They are displaying an awareness of audience and an empathy with the reader; that is, being able to move in and out of the roles of writer and reader, an indication of developing literary sophistication.

1	P:	There was this king.
2	J:	Once there was a king.
3	P:	There was once a king . . . and . . . and once . . . and one day . . .
4	J:	He was bored . . . he was rich and everybody did everything for him and he didn't have anything to do.
5	P:	There was once a king who was bored.
6	J:	Yeah . . . there was once a king who was bored 'cos he was rich and everything was done for him.
7	P:	Was done for him . . . by his servants . . . they did it all.
8	J:	Yeah . . . and everything was done for him by his servants.
9	P:	So . . .
10	J:	So one day the king couldn't stand it any more.
11	P:	When he couldn't stand it any more.
12	P:	So one day when he couldn't stand it any more he screamed . . .
13	J/P:	'I'm bored!' [the boys laugh].
14	P:	And his scream could be heard throughout the land.
15	J:	Yeah . . . that's good . . . his scream could be heard throughout the land . . . but . . .
16	P:	Yeah . . . but nobody knew what to do until one day an old woman . . .
17	J:	We keep saying 'one day'.
18	P:	OK . . . nobody knew what to do until an old woman that . . . who lived in the forest . . .

19   J: In a cottage in the forest . . . so the scream couldn't be
            heard for ages . . .
20   P: Who lived in a cottage deep in the forest finally heard the
            scream.

Year 6

In this final snapshot, Year 6 children are engaged in a silent reading, group discussion activity. Having silently and independently read three different newspaper reports of a Stoke City versus Luton Town football match, they set about interrogating the texts.. Individual hypotheses are verbalized, as ideas are exchanged and offered for consideration and evaluation. There are marked differences between individual comprehension and this cooperative venture. Rather than merely answering questions posed by someone else, the pupils are establishing questions for themselves; they are flagging tentative thoughts and exploring possibilities in a dynamic and active manner, and engaging in active rather than passive reading. There are linguistic mode markers to indicate the kinds of language being used. C's opening, 'I reckon' offers a hypothesis to the group. M(2) responds with an evaluation of the utterance and a challenge which contains an implicit demand for C to provide some kind of justification and elaboration. C(3) demonstrates a level of thinking which is beyond the literal level of comprehension. He interrogates the text and concludes that the report is factual by drawing on his contextual knowledge of current football players and league positions. The children M(8), S(9/11) and J(12) look beyond the actual words and draw conclusions that are based on implied textual evidence. C(17) again suggests bias and indicates tentative support (18), but offers an alternative viewpoint for consideration. Their talk explores the text, probes, justifies and expands ideas; the pupils deconstruct the text in their search for linguistic evidence of bias.

1   C: I reckon they're both for real.
2   M: How come . . . they could be both made up.
3   C: 'Cos it's got the teams . . . the names are right and that, and it
            tells you Luton are near the bottom . . . well they are aren't they?
4   J: I think they are for real but I think this one's one-sided.
5   C: Yeah it's . . . like you can tell whose side he's on.
6   M: Mmm . . . yeah 'cos the way he says things like . . .
7   S: Whose side is he on then do you reckon?
8   M: Luton . . . he's on Luton's side 'cos he says things like 'Stoke
            left in a foul mood'.
9   S: Er . . . yeah and he says the Luton crowd was good doesn't he?
10   J: Where's that [looks at the text]?
11   S: [reads from the text] 'The Luton crowd were a decent
            fair-minded lot'.

12   J: And he says the Luton manager is good.
13   C: They were outplayed for forty-five minutes . . . Stoke were
        outplayed it says.
14   M: This one [referring to a different account] isn't as biased is it?
15   J: I can't understand half the words in that.
16   S: Yeah . . . [reads from the text] 'Stoke City, that odd mixture
        of' . . . I dunno what this means . . . 'cudgels and
        call . . . is . . . then . . . ics . . . are capable of producing
        football of balletic grace'.
17   C: That's biased though isn't it? It's saying Stoke are skilful.
18   S: Or is he saying . . . right . . . Stoke players are like
        women . . . play like girls?
19   M: No I don't think so, 'cos he says here Hudson had complete
        control . . . and at the end it's saying if anyone lost they
        would feel as if they'd been robbed.
20   C: Yeah, but you can tell that's more biased than that by the
        headlines I think . . . don't you think? [reads from the text]
        'Stoke feel like victims of a mugging' . . . 'Things looking up
        at Luton'.

These snapshots of children of various ages, working in a variety of
contexts, illustrate the point that spoken language does more than help
children to become literate; it forms an integral part of what it means to
be literate. Literacy is a living dynamic process, constantly responding to
and reflecting cultural, socio-economic and political contexts. Rapid technological advances and changing social practices over the last 40 years have
resulted in significant changes to our vocabulary, initiated a new metalanguage, required new proficiencies and demanded an acquisition of new
literary skills, knowledge and understanding. Hoggart (1970) drew attention to the need for an extended perception of literacy to encompass media
texts, Hood (1975) spoke of visual literacy and Masterman (1980) argued
for the need to develop 'teleliteracy'. The term 'computer literate' has now
entered our language, revolutionizing reading habits and introducing new
writing processes and formats. Teletext, CD-ROM, interactive video, modem,
email, the Internet and 'spamming' are not only additions to our vocabulary; they have enormous implications for our conception of what it means
to 'be literate' within our society. Meek argues that reading needs to be
redescribed because the notion that it is an unchanging activity is wrong.
She goes on to say:

> If we are to redescribe reading, we have to begin with how people
> do it, and what they do it for. A description of literacy always has to
> include its uses, so we make lists of social texts. But the poems in the
> Underground sit next to the advertisements. They aren't read in the
> same way. So we need to know more about how, in our multilingual,

multicultural society, people read for dialogue and desire, before they go to school, while they're there and afterwards. Schooled literacy is only part of the picture.

(Meek 1992: 231)

Literacy as empowerment

Nevertheless, in any society, however pluralistic, there exists a politically dominant conception of literacy. We can distinguish between being able to read and write (which is the ability to decode and encode text), and being literate, which is the ability to critically evaluate and to act upon knowledge and experience. Wells (1987a: 110) argues that literary behaviour is 'simultaneously both a mode of language use and a mode of thinking'. People who are literate have an enriched control over their lives and environments. Literacy strengthens their capacity for rational thought and critical evaluation, and allows them to participate fully in social and intellectual practices. However, others, such as Friere (1972), argue that being able to read merely creates an illusion of achievement and is a way of preserving the sociopolitical status quo. From this perspective, literacy is presented as a consumer item and parents can estimate consumption through their children's achievement in SATs: that is, their children's ability to demonstrate conformity to a dominant institutional definition of what it means to 'be literate'. What we need to ask is whether the dominant institutional definition of literacy, as prescribed by the NLSF, promotes active, critical, 'potentially disruptive' participation, which empowers all people to contribute to the cultural, political and economic life of society, or promotes passivity, conformity and acceptance of a dominant social and political ideology. Is it empowering or debilitating?

What are the consequences of illiteracy for the individual? The Bullock Report (DES 1975: 95) identified the inability to read and understand information as a major problem for people in a modern society, while Cope and Kalantzis (1993: 7) point to the social, economic and political benefits of being able to read and write in a range of genres. Failure to achieve competence in literacy limits people's capacity for achievement in most other areas of school learning. Stanovich (1986) refers to this as the 'Matthew effect' (after the biblical analogy) where the rich get richer and the poor get poorer. I agree with the Kingman Report (DES 1988: 4) that 'there is no advantage in ignorance'. I believe that people have the propensity to resist or adapt *systems* in order to humanize them and make them workable and relevant. Teachers, supported by school governors, can make professional judgements and use their expertise to ensure that the NLSF is not an educational strait-jacket but a source of liberation and empowerment: a means of overcoming exploitation or exclusion. To be illiterate in our society is to be disempowered, to be vulnerable, to be devoid of an effective voice. Neil Kinnock, cited in Jackson and Stockwell (1996: 162) makes this point most eloquently:

> Why am I the first Kinnock in a thousand generations to be able to get to university? Was it because all of our predecessors were thick? Did they lack talent? Those people who could sing, and play, and recite poetry; those people who could make wonderful, beautiful things with their hands; those people who could dream dreams, see visions; those people who had such a sense of perception as to know in times so brutal, so oppressive, that they could win their way out of that by coming together? Were those people not university material? Couldn't they have knocked off their A levels in an afternoon? But why didn't they get it? Was it because they were weak – those people who could work eight hours a day underground and then come up and play football? Weak? Those women who could survive eleven child bearings, were they weak? Those people who could stand with their backs and legs straight and face the great – the people who had control over their lives, the ones that owned their workplaces and tried to own them – and tell them, 'No, I won't take your orders'. Were they weak? Does anybody really think that they didn't get what we had because they didn't have the talent, or the strength, or the endurance, or the commitment? Of course not. It was because there was no platform on which they could stand.

Neil Kinnock's words evoke childhood memories of my own father: frustrated, often angry and impotent in the face of less intelligent but more powerful others, not because he did not have a platform but because he did not even have access to a platform. Literacy was the access and he did not have it. I am in agreement with Meek (1992: 226) when she says that 'the continuous debate about how reading should be taught is not about method but about whether or not the kind of reading which has traditionally been the privilege of a limited number of children in school should become the entitlement of all'. The NLS is, perhaps, a step towards that entitlement.

Arguments about literacy and literacy teaching will undoubtedly continue and opinions will be divided. However, if we accept that literacy is about empowering individuals to take part effectively in society – and by take part I mean to contribute but also to be critical and potentially disruptive – then it is essential that people are equipped to do so. A ninth-century Chinese proverb says 'The world cheats those who cannot read'. The Kingman Report (DES 1988: 2.17) reiterates this simple truism: 'A democratic society needs people who have the linguistic abilities which will enable them to discuss, evaluate and make sense of what they are told, as well as to take effective action on the basis of their understanding . . . Otherwise there can be no genuine participation, but only the imposition of ideas of those who are linguistically capable'.

In order to critically evaluate something we must first understand it. In order to understand it we need to be able to decipher it – to read it – to deconstruct it. Then, if we are dissatisfied, we need to have the wherewithal to do something about it. By literacy, therefore, I refer to the ability to:

• decode text (in its various forms) in order to read fluently and independently (being able to read);
• detect bias, prejudice, satire, irony;
• differentiate between fact and fiction;
• critically evaluate, analyse and make judgements about texts;
• challenge texts and offer alternative viewpoints and interpretations;
• reject the philosophical (epistemological foundations) of texts (being literate).

Whatever our conception of literacy may be, spoken language should be seen as an integral and important ingredient. As Andrew Wilkinson (in Wilkinson *et al.* 1990: 6) says, 'this is what oracy is about – about not being manipulated, about negotiating as equals, about standing up and speaking the truth as we see it'. Throughout the following chapters, I will explore opportunities for developing talk for learning and examine ways of integrating speaking and listening activities within a structured approach to the teaching of literacy.

Note

1 LINC (1992) *Language in the National Curriculum Materials for Professional Development.* The materials were not published by the DfEE but are obtainable from the LINC Secretary, Department of English Studies, University of Nottingham, NG7 7RO.

3 ○ Planning for talk

Talk across the curriculum

The removal of statutory requirements for schools to follow programmes of study in the non-core subjects has led to concern about the marginalization of some curriculum areas such as history and geography. However, a revision of the National Curriculum presents an ideal opportunity for schools to develop an approach to learning which recognizes the value of talk in learning across all curriculum areas. This importance has been emphasized by the School Curriculum and Assessment Authority (SCAA) (1997a: 7): 'Talking with children has a central role in assessing their understanding, and it is often through talk that a fuller picture of what a child can do is gained'. The booklet and videos produced by the Qualifications and Curriculum Authority (QCA), *Gathering Evidence of Children's Reading Through Talk* (1998) support this view and provide examples of children demonstrating achievement through oral discourse. In planning the curriculum, therefore, as well as taking into account the programmes of study for English and the NLSF learning objectives, it is important to look carefully at the requirements for learning through talk in each subject. In its publication *Use of Language: A Common Approach* (1997b), the SCAA examines some of the ways this may be achieved and indicates that when revising policies and developing new practices schools should be aware of the broad learning potential of talk.

Working towards an effective talk policy

Although the Bullock Report (DES 1975) emphasized the importance of schools developing whole school policies for language development, the HMI (1985: 5) survey found that, in oral work, 'good practice more often depended on the initiatives of individual teachers than on the existence of agreed school policies'. HMI (1990) criticized schools for giving too little time to oracy and HMI (1998) reported that the recording of progress in speaking and listening in schools was generally weak. For any practice to be successfully implemented, it needs to emanate from an agreed policy and a corporate, whole school commitment. The National Oracy Project (Norman 1990: 13) suggests that 'if talk is to be valued as a tool for learning and a means of communication of educational worth equal to reading and writing, its status may have to be improved in the eyes of everyone concerned with the children and the school'. A useful way for schools to initiate policy development is to examine their existing policies and audit current classroom practices.

Conducting a talk curriculum audit

Select a particular term or year's work: look carefully at particular elements within that work in order to identify the opportunities that exist. Observe if children are encouraged/required to use talk to:

• explore what they already know;
• ask and answer questions;
• work collaboratively on tasks;
• review and reflect on work.

Observe the opportunities for teachers to monitor and evaluate learning through talk by:

• checking whether assessment, recording and reporting procedures include space for comments that reflect children's understanding and ability by what they say;
• reviewing medium-term plans and increasing the range and variety of spoken language opportunities.

Collecting evidence of learning through talk

Each teacher can tape-record or video one example of classroom talk and provide a short piece of transcript. These examples can then be discussed at a year/team/school meeting in terms of:

• What kinds of task were the pupils doing?
• What was the audience and purpose?
• How successfully did they tackle the task?
• What influenced the way they talked and worked?
• In what ways could the task be changed to improve the quality of talk and learning?

Undertaking a pupil-pursuit

One or more teachers might 'follow' one pupil over the course of a week in order to log talking and listening opportunities and experiences before reporting back to a year or school meeting.

Organizing practical talk workshops

It is useful to find time, either at a regular year/staff meeting, or during professional development days, to experience particular strategies at first hand. Teachers who have been consciously building talk into their literacy plans might run sessions in which particular strategies are introduced and based on materials and tasks from schemes of work. Teachers can then reflect on their experiences and consider ways of applying the strategies to other areas of the curriculum and across different age groups.

Planning for talk

Planning for talk means thinking about the opportunities that arise from schemes of work. In examining talk policies within their own schools, teachers I have worked with identified a number of concerns. They considered the issues and emerged with some suggestions for colleagues (see Table 3.1).

Developing talk for learning: some strategies

Teachers working in the National Oracy Project developed a framework for evaluating their current school policy and practice. They examined the issue from five different perspectives (see Figure 3.1). A useful way of evaluating and transforming a paper policy into a successful action policy is to see how it will impact on major aspects of teaching and learning.

Table 3.1   Identifying issues: dealing with concerns

Issue or concern	Suggestions
Organization	Try different group work techniques such as jigsaw (see Chapter 4).
	Plan groups to account for friendship, gender, interest, multicultural and ability variables.
	Match groups to nature and purpose of tasks.
	Develop pupil responsibility by giving them roles such as observer, chair or scribe.

Table 3.1 Cont'd

Issue or concern	Suggestions
Climate	Adopt different teaching roles to suit learning contexts and pupils' needs. Be prepared to move out of the expert role (see Chapter 5). Offer a non-evaluative forum where the pupils can make tentative suggestions, explore, probe and so on.
Resources	Experiment with different room layouts. Negotiate for use of other areas/rooms. Develop a talk display board/area, stimulus material, recordings for headphone use. Look at existing stock of tape recorders – are they battery operated, easy to use, portable?
Pupil involvement	Develop positive attitudes and mutual understanding from Year R. Start with pair work and build up to group discussion gradually. Use drama and role play to build strategies. Consider pupils' contributions in different subject areas.
Discipline	Structure lessons and consider time, pace, working process and product. Establish individual responsibility and accountability in group work. Evolve rules collaboratively with pupils. Encourage pupil self/group-evaluation. Differentiate activities to allow for quality teacher intervention with focused groups.
Talk not valued by pupils, other staff or parents	Develop ethos of valuing purposeful talk from Year R. Encourage learning through talk across the curriculum. Plan a cross-curriculum oracy day with evidence of 'good talk'. Display 'talk at work' through photos, tapes and so on. Refer explicitly to National Curriculum requirements concerning talk and communication. Invite parents and others to observe and take part in discussion sessions.
Assessment	Develop self-assessment formats and procedures. Practise listening/observing with small groups. Compare and discuss standards with other staff and pupils through watching video recordings. Encourage pupil awareness of criteria. Build into work plans opportunities for observing and recording speaking and listening. Examine existing methods of recording and assessment and evaluate if they are functional, formative, easy to use and meaningful.

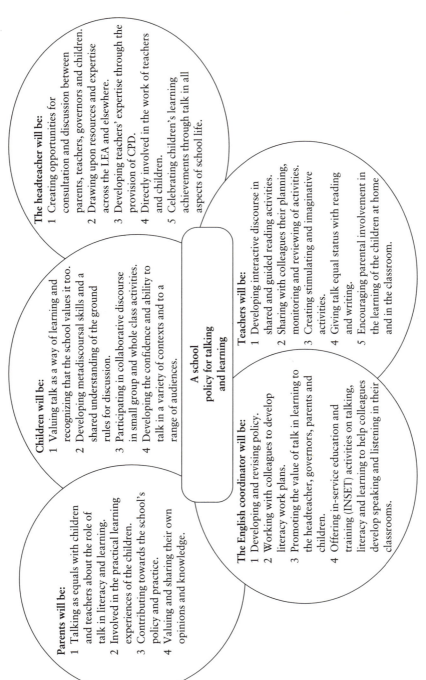

The headteacher will be:
1 Creating opportunities for consultation and discussion between parents, teachers, governors and children.
2 Drawing upon resources and expertise across the LEA and elsewhere.
3 Developing teachers' expertise through the provision of CPD.
4 Directly involved in the work of teachers and children.
5 Celebrating children's learning achievements through talk in all aspects of school life.

Children will be:
1 Valuing talk as a way of learning and recognizing that the school values it too.
2 Developing metadiscoursal skills and a shared understanding of the ground rules for discussion.
3 Participating in collaborative discourse in small group and whole class activities.
4 Developing the confidence and ability to talk in a variety of contexts and to a range of audiences.

A school policy for talking and learning

Teachers will be:
1 Developing interactive discourse in shared and guided reading activities.
2 Sharing with colleagues their planning, monitoring and reviewing of activities.
3 Creating stimulating and imaginative activities.
4 Giving talk equal status with reading and writing.
5 Encouraging parental involvement in the learning of the children at home and in the classroom.

Parents will be:
1 Talking as equals with children and teachers about the role of talk in literacy and learning.
2 Involved in the practical learning experiences of the children.
3 Contributing towards the school's policy and practice.
4 Valuing and sharing their own opinions and knowledge.

The English coordinator will be:
1 Developing and revising policy.
2 Working with colleagues to develop literacy work plans.
3 Promoting the value of talk in learning to the headteacher, governors, parents and children.
4 Offering in-service education and training (INSET) activities on talking, literacy and learning to help colleagues develop speaking and listening in their classrooms.

Figure 3.1 School policy

Table 3.2   Making talk work

	Teaching role	Learning tasks	Classroom	Whole school
	Teaching approach/roles/ expectations/ responses etc.	Nature and organization of tasks etc.	Physical aspects/ organization/ groups/ climate etc.	Policy/ethos/ organization etc.
Encourage				
Discourage				

Activity

Use Table 3.2 to help you discuss how aspects of your school policy might encourage or discourage talk. An overarching principle, that has emerged from numerous professional discussions, workshops and seminars, is that oracy is something which needs to permeate the whole school and to be an integral part of learning in all curriculum subjects.

Putting policy into practice

The constant criticism of teachers by the press, fed by Ofsted's 'deficit' inspection approach and negative style of reporting, is hardly designed to encourage professional conscientiousness and commitment. Disaffection and anxiety in teachers may result in arid, instrumental teaching. Lessons that should be 'discursive, interactive and characterised by high quality oral work' (DfEE 1998b: 8) are more likely to resemble transmission lessons, characterized by teacher-dominated discourse and low-order questions. In their revised Observational Research and Classroom Learning Evaluation (ORACLE) survey, Galton *et al.* (1999) suggest that although the proportion of whole class teaching has increased, what teachers do when they are teaching the class is rarely stimulating. In arguing against Ofsted's simplistic concept of teaching and learning, Galton cites the work of Alexander *et al.* (1991: 324), who identify different types of knowledge which they categorize under three broad headings:

- *Construction or procedural knowledge:* Concerned with the acquisition of information – knowing about something or how to do something. It also includes *conditional knowledge:* knowing when to apply such information.

- *Conceptual knowledge:* Concerned with knowing and understanding ideas and principles. It includes *domain* and *discipline* knowledge: the ability to process and categorize information; and *discourse knowledge*: knowing about language and its uses.
- *Metacognitive knowledge:* Concerned with knowing one's own cognitive processes. It includes *strategic* knowledge: understanding what it means to think scientifically, or historically and so on; and *self* knowledge: knowing ourselves as learners and being able to monitor our thinking.

It should be recognized that, although there may be an emphasis on one type of knowledge during a particular activity, knowledge *in action* cannot be neatly compartmentalized. There will invariably be fluid and dynamic interaction occurring. Nevertheless, it is important for teachers to be aware of the kinds of knowledge and understanding they wish to develop during a lesson. The purpose of an activity and the teaching objective should determine the classroom layout, the resources and the nature of the teacher–pupil and pupil–pupil interaction. An effective language policy needs to encompass all types of knowledge. The following examples (see Figures 3.2–3.8) of planning work at Key Stages 1 and 2 illustrate the integral part of *talk* in a vibrant literacy programme.

Literacy teaching with one class: a case study

The following case study explores work undertaken with a Year 6 class in a large primary school serving an economically and culturally diverse community. It shows how speaking and listening form an important part of literacy activities and demonstrates the centrality of talk in learning. The teaching of English comprised five literacy hours and two one-hour writing workshops per week. This approximates to Dearing's recommendation of 25 per cent dedicated teaching time for literacy at Key Stage 2. Aspects of other curriculum areas, particularly history and geography, were also covered within the literacy sessions. The range of texts used and some of the activities and outcomes are discussed. Work emanating from one particular text is then examined in detail.

A literacy hour

Shared reading

Each session began with the teacher reading extracts from literary texts to the whole class. Children's attention was drawn to particular aspects such as:

- setting, character, plot, style;
- standard and non-standard English;

Week	Texts and activities	Comprehension and composition	Grammar and punctuation	Phonics, spelling, vocabulary
1	*The Jolly Postman*	Listen and respond to the story. Discuss favourite parts and characters. Notice difference in main text (rhyme) and letters. Begin noticing different features of different kinds of texts.	Read aloud using expression. Understand full stops and capital letters and their effect on meaning. Understand the difference between a sentence and a line of writing.	Initial consonant clusters: bl, cr, dr, st, tr. Rhyme, see-tea-knee, told-sold, hot-spot-got, say-away, blue-too, tell-bell-well. Alliteration: big broom/new newt. Vocabulary: postman, people, palace, wicked witch, giant, grandma, Goldilocks.
2	*Little Red Riding Hood* *Three Little Pigs*	**Character** (*focus*) Identify and discuss kinds of characters, in fairy tales, e.g. heroes, villains, giants, ogres, witches, princes, princesses etc.	Use grammatical knowledge (of spoken language) to predict text. Predict words from preceding words. Identify types of words – word families – words that 'fit' in a sentence. Identify nouns and recognize their function.	Initial consonant clusters. High frequency and special interest words. Rhyme and rhythm. Spelling words with 's' for plurals. Handwriting.
3	*Cinderella* *Little Red Hen*	**Character development** (*focus*) Identify and discuss appearance, behaviour, qualities of different kinds of characters. Identify and discuss predictable qualities and behaviour.	Identify adjectives and recognize their function.	Final consonant clusters. High frequency and special interest words. Rhyme and rhythm. Spelling words ending in ng, ck. Handwriting.
4	*Jack and the Beanstalk* *Billy Goats Gruff*	**Plot** (*focus*) Recognition of conventions in story openings and endings. Identification of main characters and key events. Recognizing links between characters and events. Predicting behaviour/actions. Resolutions, themes, morals.	Identify verbs and recognize their function. Order and reorder sentences.	Final consonant clusters. High frequency and special interest words. Rhyme and rhythm. Spelling words ending in ss, ff, ll. Handwriting.
5	*Goldilocks* *Ginger Bread Boy*	**Language** (*focus*) Identify the key language features of narrative (focus on fairy stories). Dialogue in narrative.	Identify phrases and sentences of significance or interest from reading. Begin to use story structures and features in own writing.	Critical features of words. High frequency and special interest words. Rhyme and rhythm. Spelling common irregular words. Handwriting.
			Speaking and listening Telling and retelling stories, ordering events, taking turns to speak, listening to others. Read with variety, pace and emphasis, express views, consider characters and plot. Enact story, listen to story, tape, exchange ideas and explain views. Explore the language of storytelling. Participate in drama activities and role play. Distinguish features of standard and non-standard English.	

Extension work (in and beyond the literacy hour)
History of the postal service/modern postal service.
Writing variety of letters for audience/purpose (see Figure 3.3).
Celebration cards (multicultural).

Figure 3.2 Medium-term plan, Key Stage 1, Year 1

	Whole class shared reading and writing	Whole class word and sentence work	Guided group work	Independent group activities	Plenary
M	Introducing the book **Speaking and listening** Listen and respond, participate appropriately, e.g. read aloud, clap to rhymes. Read with variety and pace. Role play.	Consonant clusters. Read on sight familiar words from the text. Read with expression. **Speaking and listening** Make relevant contributions. Ask and answer questions. Explore words and meanings. Read aloud with intonation – stress syllables.	G1 Graded texts. G2 Graded texts. **Speaking and listening** Follow instructions. Take turns to speak. Express view about texts. Share ideas and listen to others' views.	*Group Activity* 1 Full stops (to) guided reading. 2 Guided reading (to) handwriting. 3 Sequencing story strips. 4 Character words. 5 Spelling patterns.	Common letter patterns.
T	Predicting and sequencing.	Predict text from grammar. Investigate words that 'fit'. Identify sentences – use term appropriately.	G4 G5 Continue with work on graded texts.	G1 Activity 3. G2 Activity 4. G3 Activity 5. G4 Activity 1 (to) guided reading. G5 Guided reading (to) Activity 2.	Review sequencing activity.
W	Character analysis.	's' for plurals.	G1 G3 Continue with work on graded texts.	G1 Guided reading (to) Activity 2. G2 Activity 3. G3 Activity 1 (to) guided reading. G4 Activity 5. G5 Activity 4.	Review characters and 's' spelling.
Th	Comparing stories.	Irregular words.	G2 G4 Continue with work on graded texts.	G1 Activity 5. G2 Activity 1 (to) guided reading. G3 Activity 4. G4 Guided reading (to) Activity 2. G5 Activity 3.	Recall/recap on sequence of *Jack and the Beanstalk.*
F	Make own class book.	Recognize and spell high frequency words in the text.	G3 G5 Continue with work on graded texts.	G1 Activity 4. G2 Activity 5. G3 Guided reading (to) Activity 2. G4 Activity 3. G5 Activity 1 (to) guided reading.	Read and review the class book. Draw attention to specific points.

Figure 3.3   Week plan for Key Stage 1, Year 1 (text/s: *Jack and the Beanstalk* and graded group texts)

Shared reading and writing

Texts and additional resources

Jack and the Beanstalk, flip chart, adhesive stickers, felt pens, pointer, cassette recorder. Prepare story structure frame for flip chart. Prepare adjective and synonym webs and rhyme.

Learning objectives

T2 predict by looking at blurb, cover, title, illustration etc.
S1 read aloud using expression appropriate to the grammar of the text.
W3 discriminate read and spell words with initial consonant clusters.
W5 read on sight familiar words.

Teaching sequence and activities (first 15 minutes)

Show the cover and ask children about title, author and illustrator.
Turn to first page and ask children what they think the story will be about – who is Jack/Giant?
Read the story and ask the children to predict what will happen at key stages.
Get the children to read the rhyme aloud (fee fi fo fum) loudly and with expression.

Teaching sequence and activities (second 15 minutes)

Write selected consonant blends on the flip chart, e.g. br, fr, st, sm, gr.
Tell the children you are going to read some sentences out of the book and ask them if they can hear any words that start with the sound, e.g. gr.
Tell the children you are going to say some words and they are to tell you which blend the word begins with, e.g. friend, smoke, great, brick, freeze, frost, grip, green, smile, stop, smooth, grass, still.
Tell the children you're going to pick out some words for them to learn – go through the process of look-trace-cover-write-check (boy, man, woman, five, ten, fifteen, twenty).

Guided group reading and writing

Group 1	Group 2
Texts and additional resources Group set of a graded reader, e.g. *We're Going on a Bear Hunt* (Rosen and Oxenbury 1989).	**Texts and additional resources** Group set of a graded reader, e.g. *Animal Homes* (Root and Hughes 1994), Ginn All Aboard scheme.
Learning objectives T7 discuss incidents in stories. T10 identify and compare basic story elements, e.g. beginnings and endings. S2 grammatical awareness to predict words.	**Learning objectives** T21 understand the purpose of contents pages, index. Begin to locate information by page numbers and words of initial letter. T25 assemble information from own experience, e.g. how to care for pets. W11 handwriting.
Teaching sequence and activities See NLSF Module 4 Guided Reading, Teacher's Notes pp. 42–4. 1 Introduce the book. 2 Independent reading. 3 Focus on story structure and prepositions.	**Teaching sequence and activities** See NLSF Module 4 Guided Reading. Teacher's Notes pp. 42–4 and Guided Writing pp. 44–51. 1 Introduce the book. 2 Independent reading. 3 Focus on organizational features of text.

Independent work

Group 1	Group 2	Group 3	Group 4	Group 5
Resources Photocopied illustration from text.	**Resources** Story-writing frame.	**Resources** Word wheels.	**Resources** Cripps: *A Hand for Spelling* (1990).	**Resources** Frame.
Activity Making a 'Giant' picture model.	**Activity** My story.	**Activity** Work on consonant clusters.	**Activity** Handwriting and spelling work.	**Activity** Shopping list.
Learning objectives T22 write labels for drawings.	**Learning objectives** T16 use some elements of known stories in own work.	**Learning objectives** W3 phonemes and consonant clusters.	**Learning objectives** W11 practise handwriting and spelling.	**Learning objectives** W11 practise handwriting. T25 write lists.

Plenary focus   G3 to share work on consonant clusters – reinforce work from shared reading.

Figure 3.4   Day plan Key Stage 1 (learning objectives from NLSF Year 1, Term 2)

Letter form	From	To (audience)	Purpose	Language and organizational features
Note	Giant	Children	Offer of reward for information on Jack and the gold	
Letter	Children	Giant	Offering information	
Postcard	Jack	Giant	Joke – mocking Giant	
Invitation	Cinderella	Ugly Sisters	Invitation to wedding	
Letter	Goldilocks	Three Bears	Apology	
Birthday card	Baby Bear	Goldilocks	Greeting	
Letter	Grandma	Riding Hood	Asking Riding Hood to visit	
Summons	Three Pigs' solicitor	Wolf	Statement of legal proceedings	
Letter	Wolf	Editor of newspaper	Claiming innocence	
Computer printout	Pig community	Listing Wolf's misdemeanours	To make a case against Wolf	
Leaflet	Securifor House Security Systems	Pig community	Advertise Inform Persuade	

Opportunities for speaking and listening (class/group/pairs)
Reading and writing letters

• Discussing purpose, language and organization of letters.
• Sharing ideas, insights and opinions.
• Presenting to audience, live or on tape.
• Performing in drama/adapting language to roles.

Writing a 'Securifor' leaflet advertising ways of protecting your home against wolf attack

• Listening as the teacher reads from advertising leaflets.
• Exploring, developing and clarifying ideas.
• Discussing possibilities – taking turns to speak.
• Making explanations of choices.

Figure 3.5   Fairy tale letter-writing grid

Week	Texts	Comprehension and composition	Grammar and punctuation	Phonics, spelling, vocabulary
1	*Fair's Fair*	Examining and evaluating literary style, use of language and literary devices. Figurative language, e.g. simile and metaphor. Reading for information – making inference, drawing conclusions. Characters – roles and relationships.	Examination of punctuation as a cohesive and stylistic device. Punctuation of direct and reported speech. Tense. Noun phrase/expanding noun phrases. Word functions (adjectives).	Develop understanding and use of technical terms for describing and discussing texts. Spelling polysyllabic words. Recognition of unfamiliar words. Synonyms.
2	*Fair's Fair* *Joe Burkinshaw's Progress* *Oliver Twist*	Style, mood, atmosphere, theme. Examining the centrality of character to plot. Examining how characters are portrayed through dialogue, action and description. Using a model from reading to draft and refine own writing.	Investigation of how dialogue is presented in narrative. Standard and non-standard English – subject – verb agreement. Colloquialism/idioms. Word functions (verbs and adverbs).	Regular verb endings. Words within words. Synonyms. Spelling polysyllabic words.
3	*Fair's Fair* *Smith* *Great Expectations*	Analysis of shape and structure of the plot – opening, setting, identification of main events, complication, climax, resolution. Using a model from reading to draft and refine own writing.	Developing understanding and use of compound and complex sentences. Use of conjunctions. Word functions (families).	Antonyms, homonyms. Prefixes and suffixes. Affect of context on vocabulary choice. Spelling polysyllabic words. Compound words.
4–6	*A Strong and Willing Girl* *Mouldy's Orphan* *The Batty Boy* *The Stolen Watch* *Street Child*	Comparison of different authors' styles, uses of language and literary devices. Similes, metaphors and imagery. Changes in language and conventions.	Apostrophe used for omission. Compound and complex sentences. Use of conjunctions/connectives. Use of semicolon and colon.	Alliteration. Phrases and clichés. Word origins. Old and new words. Words that are changing in meaning.
7–8	Use fiction texts (above) to explore aspects of Victorian life. Compare fiction with historical texts and primary documents. Examine range of non-fiction genre.	Language and organizational features of non-narrative texts, e.g. diary, newspaper article, work rota, will etc. Reading for information. Making notes. Distinguishing between fact and fiction.	Reported speech – past tense. Passive voice. Modal verbs, e.g. imperative form in instructional documents. Organization and layout, e.g. contents, index, subheadings, captions, lists, diagrams, glossary.	Field-specific words, e.g. technical words and terms, jargon, phrases. Word attack skills to read unfamiliar words. Spelling unfamiliar/unusual words.

Speaking and listening
Contribute to discussion and debate.
Present ideas, research findings and work to a wider audience.
Explore, develop and explain ideas – share insights and opinions.
Respond to and evaluate verbal contributions and written work.
Present poems aloud in small groups/to whole class.
Explore themes in the story – fears, hopes, dreams.
Hot-seat characters – change/extend story and perform play script.
Perform scenes for video/make into radio play and perform.

Extension work
Library/research skills – investigating life in Victorian times.
Reading information texts and making notes.
Writing 'A Guide to the Victorians' or 'A Child in Victorian Times'.
Writing prequel/sequel to stories.
Transforming narrative into play script.
Adapting a narrative for media production (film or radio).
Making a documentary about an aspect of life in Victorian times.

Figure 3.6 Medium-term plan, Key Stage 2, Year 6

	Whole class	Group Briggs	Group Dahl	Group Doughty	Group Fine	Group Pearce
M	Focus on imagery produced through the use of alliteration, simile, metaphor, personification.	T Critical reading. Text investigation (figurative language).	T Reading for information: going to school and work.	Thought tracking.	Investigative report.	Punctuation probe. Spelling/synonyms.
	Speaking and listening Listen and respond. Comment on/evaluate ideas. Question to clarify and extend. Justify views. Report/describe observations.	Speaking and listening Consider words. Explore how language varies/changes. Explore standard and dialect forms.	Speaking and listening Investigate, represent information and perspectives.	Speaking and listening Explore, develop explain ideas. Predict. Improvization/role play. Share insights and opinions.	Speaking and listening Explore differences in spoken/written language.	Speaking and listening Read aloud. Investigate text. Identify and discuss common features.
T	Focus on the use of speech marks and on how Garfield uses other punctuation marks and ellipses to create an oral storytelling style.	T Reading for information: going to school and work.	Punctuation probe. Spelling/synonyms.	T Critical reading. Text investigation (figurative language).	T Reading for information: going to school and work.	Thought tracking.
W	Focus on developing characters through description, action and dialogue. Punctuation, adjectives, verbs, adverbs.	T Reading for information: going to school and work.	Thought tracking.	Investigative report.	Punctuation probe. Spelling/synonyms.	T Critical reading. Text investigation (figurative language).
Th	Focus on developing characters through the use of expanded noun phrase.	Punctuation probe. Spelling/synonyms.	T Critical reading. Text investigation (figurative language).	T Reading for information: going to school and work.	Thought tracking.	Investigative report.
F	Focus on relationships between characters – thoughts, feelings, inner dialogue. Narrative voice and tense.	Thought tracking.	Investigative report.	Punctuation probe. Spelling/synonyms.	T Critical reading. Text investigation (figurative language).	T Reading for information: going to school and work.

Figure 3.7 Week plan for Key Stage 2, Year 6 (texts: *Fair's Fair*, using written sources in primary history)

Shared reading and writing

Texts and additional resources	Learning objectives
Fair's Fair, acetate sheets, overhead projector. Prepare extracts from the text on acetate sheets.	T1 describe and evaluate the style of an individual writer. S2 conduct detailed language investigations of proverbs and dialect. W7 experiment with language – creating new words, similes and metaphors.
Teaching sequence and activities (first 15 minutes) Ask pupils to identify special features of Garfield's writing style – list these on an acetate sheet. Read aloud various extracts from the story to demonstrate these features. Discuss whether other authors use similar devices. Identify any specific devices used by Garfield, or ones that are unfamiliar to the pupils. Discuss specific literary devices used by Garfield – illustrate by reading aloud and showing on the overhead projector.	**Teaching sequence and activities (second 15 minutes)** Discuss how Garfield creates an 'oral' style through the use of tense, punctuation and colloquial language. Read aloud selected extracts to illustrate various points. Show extracts from the text and ask pupils to identify interesting punctuation, colloquialisms, idioms. Pupils write alternatives to some expressions used in the text, e.g. spifflicating, stone the crows.

Guided group reading and writing

Group 1		Group 2	
Texts and additional resources	**Learning objectives**	**Texts and additional resources**	**Learning objectives**
Group sets of Fair's Fair. Extracts from Six Apprentices and The December Rose.	T5 To compare and contrast the work of a single writer.	Extracts about child workers and working conditions in the mines and mills.	T17 appraise a text quickly and effectively; to retrieve information from it; to find information quickly and evaluate its value.
Teaching sequence and activities Discuss and summarize stylistic features of Fair's Fair.	Pupils read extracts independently – highlight stylistic similarities with Fair's Fair. Group share ideas and discuss.	**Teaching sequence and activities** Pupils read texts independently. Discuss initial thoughts/feelings about working conditions.	Teacher poses questions/raises issues for debate. Pupils investigate texts to justify responses.

Independent work

	Group 1	Group 2	Group 3	Group 4	Group 5
Resources	Group set of Fair's Fair.	Extracts from non-fiction historical texts.	Set of texts or extract and thought-tracking frame.	Report-writing frame.	Set of texts or extract and punctuation probe sheet.
Activity	Critical reading/text investigation.	Reading for information.	Thought tracking.	Investigative report writing.	Punctuation probe.
Learning objectives	T7 annotate passages in detail in response to specific questions.	T18 secure the skills of skimming, scanning and efficient reading so that research is fast and effective.	Term 2: T2 revision, explaining how events might look from other points of view.	T20 secure control of impersonal writing, particularly the sustained use of the present tense and the passive voice.	Term 1 revision: S6, secure knowledge and understanding of more sophisticated punctuation marks.

Plenary focus
Feedback from G4. Discussion of language and organizational features of formal reports.

Figure 3.8 Day plan, Key Stage 2 (learning objectives from NLSF Year 6, Term 3)

- figurative language and stylistic devices;
- salient features of different narrative types.

Transparency sheets and an overhead projector were used to experiment with various aspects and to draft and redraft texts collaboratively with the children.

Group discussion

Following a whole class period of 20–30 minutes the children worked in small groups to interrogate texts. The class was organized in different ways depending on the nature of the task and the learning purpose (see Chapter 4). Sometimes the class would work in jigsaw groups, where different specialist groups were formed to investigate one aspect of a text and eventually returned to a home group where they shared information.

Plenary

Following group discussions, the children would come together as a whole class to discuss their findings. This provided the teacher with an opportunity to consolidate and reinforce the learning, and again use was made of an overhead projector to illustrate and illuminate various aspects of language and use of literary devices.

Writing workshops

> The literacy hour is intended to be a time for the explicit teaching of reading and writing. Teachers will need to provide opportunities for practising and applying new skills in independent work at other times.
> (DfEE 1998b: 14)

A main teaching objective was to encourage the children to use the knowledge they had gained from reading and interrogating texts when composing their own writing through the drafting and redrafting process. For writing workshops the classroom furniture was rearranged to provide children with an opportunity to work alone but also to seek peer responses and to work collaboratively when necessary. In a writing workshop pupils can read each other's work, comment and share opinions. By asking questions and making suggestions the children as readers are able to alert their peers as writers to the needs of a real audience. Moreover, writing workshops provide teachers with an ideal opportunity to interact with children during the drafting process, to offer support and to scaffold their learning.

Organization of writing workshops

The classroom was arranged so that children had an opportunity to work individually or collaboratively. This was not easy with 32 children in a classroom designed for a maximum of 25. However, it was possible to arrange the tables so that some children were in a small group situation while others worked either in pairs or individually. Situations in schools will vary and some planning and experimentation will be required before the most suitable seating arrangement can be found.

- The class was organized so that each child had two response partners to consult.
- There would be a teacher–child conference after a writer had received at least one partner response.
- The proceedings were occasionally stopped to flag a child's work or demonstrate a feature.
- Time was spent at the end of each workshop to share, consolidate, reinforce and reflect.

The National Writing Project (1989) illustrated the value of children gaining responses from their peers and many teachers are now familiar with the concept of response partners. However, just as children need to learn the ground rules for group work, so they need to understand what is expected of them during a writing workshop. Each child needs to be aware of the general working procedure, and specifically, how to undertake the role of response partner. This was established by the provision of response partner cards. These cards clarified the roles and responsibilities of both the writer and response partner.

Card 1 (writer)
When you have finished drafting:
- Read it aloud to yourself.
- Ask yourself: am I pleased with it?
- Is there anything I want to change or add?
- Now read your writing to a partner.
- Listen to what she or he says.
- Has she or he got any good ideas to help you improve your writing?
- Now ask the teacher to read your work.
- Listen to what she or he says.
- Has she or he got any ideas to make your work even better?

Card 2 (response partner)
When you respond to work:
- Listen carefully as work is read to you.
- Say what you like about the writing. Try to find at least two good things to say.
- Think about how the writing might be improved.
- Is there anything missing or unclear?
- Is the work well organized?
- Is the language and style suitable?
- Is there any part that could be developed?
- Can you make any useful suggestions?
- Could anything be taken out?

Children had two named response partners to whom they could go for consultation and feedback during the drafting process. Once children had

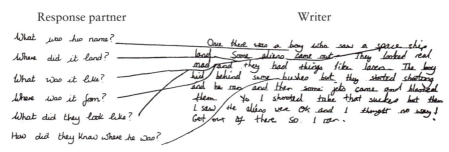

Figure 3.9 Drafting and response partner feedback

gained feedback from partners and modified their work according to any suggestions, they would request a conference with the teacher to discuss their work. Having two partners helped reduce potential disruption because if one partner was engrossed in her or his own work another option was available. However, there needed to be flexibility in the system and if movement around the classroom became intrusive or the request for responses was likely to cause inordinate disruption, the teacher would interject to redirect children or to act as a response partner and provide necessary feedback. Whole class attention was focused on particular strategies or devices that children had used in their writing. Extracts from children's work were read aloud and aspects of their writing displayed on an overhead projector or chalkboard. Children drafted on one side of an A3 sheet of paper and left one side clear for comments from response partners and the teacher (see Figure 3.9). This approach provided the opportunity for:

- concentrated individual work;
- peer collaboration and interrogation of texts;
- explorative small group discussion and debate;
- teacher intervention and encouragement;
- drafting, redrafting and responding to critical evaluation;
- interactive whole class discourse;
- consolidation and reflection, self-assessment and evaluation.

Interactive whole class work

Within the literacy hour teachers are required to teach the whole class for approximately 30 minutes each day. The National Curriculum for English (DfEE 1995a: 13) states that at Key Stage 2 children should 'be encouraged to respond imaginatively to the plot, characters, ideas vocabulary and organisation of language in literature'. This may be a matter of concern for some teachers, especially those with classes that contain two or more year groups and a very broad ability range. There is no doubt that this offers a real challenge and requires careful planning and preparation of resources to ensure that all children have an opportunity to participate. However, through effective questioning and sound scaffolding, teachers can ensure that genuine interactive learning occurs in whole class teaching (see Chapters 5 and 6). The teacher began each session by reading short texts or extracts from longer texts to the whole class and focusing on particular aspects of language such as:

- setting, character, plot, style, theme;
- the language and organizational features of different narrative genres;
- the literary devices used by a range of authors;
- standard and non-standard English;
- aspects of figurative language (adjectives, adverbs, simile, metaphor, personification);
- grammar and punctuation.

Relevant parts of a text were highlighted, questions posed and critical debate encouraged. For example, on one occasion the teacher wanted to draw children's attention to Roald Dahl's general style and especially to his method of developing characters. The teacher opened the session by reading extracts from *Matilda* (1989) to demonstrate how Dahl uses direct action and dialogue description to develop characters. This can be done through photocopying and cutting and pasting onto paper as handouts but an overhead projector proved to be an invaluable piece of equipment. Selected extracts can be copied and enlarged and drawings can be used to stimulate debate. In one session the teacher used an illustration of Miss Trunchbull from *Matilda* and asked the children to create a description web by thinking of suitable words and phrases. Most of the words the children came up with described Miss Trunchbull's physical appearance and provided an excellent direct description. Over the year each child developed a character portfolio. This was a book that contained profiles of characters and lists of words to describe them. For example:

Character: Miss Trunchbull
Book: *Matilda*
Author: Roald Dahl

awesome	loathsome
barbaric	mammoth
bossy	mean
blobby	mountainous
cruel	muscular
ferocious	macho
fierce	spiteful
formidable	strict
gigantic	terrible
grumpy	terrifying
grotesque	ugly
hideous	vicious

Table 3.3 Adjective frame for *How Tom Beat Captain Najork and his Hired Sportsmen*

Fidget Wonkham Strong	*Captain Najork*	*Tom*	*Bundlejoy Cosy Sweet*
Suitable adjectives:	Suitable adjectives:	Suitable adjectives:	Suitable adjectives:

On other occasions the children and teacher made adjective charts after reading a book. For example:

- teacher and pupils brainstormed a list of adjectives for describing people;
- an overhead transparency was used to show a frame containing the names of the main characters;
- the frame was completed by selecting suitable adjectives to go in each column (at this point the children were encouraged to use their character portfolios) (see Table 3.3).

The teacher was able to expand on the idea of 'direct' description and introduce the concept of 'action' and 'dialogue' description by copying relevant extracts from books down one side of an overhead transparency. With these models as an explicit visual reference, the teacher was able to work with the class on drafting and redrafting action and dialogue descriptions using the blank half of the transparency sheet. On other occasions the teacher and children would repeat this procedure by taking characters from stories the children were writing themselves. The class would make a description web and from this create a dialogue and develop some action. In Figure 3.10 the dialogue is based on characters from a story being written by one of the children.

Looking at how authors develop character through action and dialogue enabled the teacher to focus children's attention on verbs. For example, in the children's draft the words *hissed*, *whimpered* and *sneered* tell us more about the characters. Children can sweep a text and search for vibrant verbs. For example, in *Stone Age Magic* by Brian Ball (1989), the word *said* is used infrequently. It is replaced by a whole variety of more evocative verbs such as:

demanded, croaked, soothed, whimpered, shrieked, snarled, sneered, sobbed, cried, whispered, shouted, screamed, wailed, bellowed, barked, stammered, reported, hissed, murmured, stormed, sighed, announced, assured, retorted, groaned

Personification was explored by examining *Beware the Killer Coat* by Susan Gates (1994). In the story the coat becomes a living character through the author's use of this literary device: 'The coat scowled back at me with

Text model of dialogue description	Children's draft

"I want those filthy pigtails off before you come back to school tomorrow!" she barked. "Chop 'em off and throw 'em in the dustbin, you understand?"
 	
    Amanda, paralysed with fright, managed to stutter, "My m-m-mummy likes them. She plaits them for me every morning."
 	
    "Your mummy's a twit!" the Trunchbull bellowed. She pointed a finger the size of a salami at the child's head and shouted, "You look like a rat with a tail coming out of its head!"
	I'd better not see you in my place again or you're for it," hissed Monica. "L-l-leave me alone or I'll tell on you," whimpered Gina." She started to cry. "Go on and blub you little whimp, you're nothing but a weasel," sneered Monica.

Text model of action description	Children's draft
"My m-m-mummy thinks I look lovely, Miss T-Trunchbull," Amanda stuttered, shaking like a blancmange. "I don't give a tinker's toot what your mummy thinks!" the Trunchbull yelled, and with that she lunged forward and grabbed hold of Amanda's pigtails in her right fist and lifted the girl clear off the ground. Then she started swinging her round and round her head faster and faster … Soon Amanda Thripp was travelling so fast she became a blur, and suddenly, with a mighty grunt, the Trunchbull let go of the pigtails and Amanda went sailing like a rocket right over the wire fence of the playground.	"I'll tell on you", cried Lisa. "Oh you will eh!" shouted Monica and with that she pushed Lisa back against the wall. "Well here's a taste of what you'll get if you do." Monica grabbed Lisa's hair and pulled her head down. She got a can of coke and tipped it over her hair. Monica shouted to everybody. "Look here everybody I've got a wet weasel here!

Figure 3.10 Drafting using texts as models

its rows of little metal teeth. The flaps on the front were wicked green eyes glinting at me'.

    Looking at how an author has created and developed characters in a story can lead to the question of reader response. The teacher encouraged children to think about this by:

- showing a character chart to the whole class on an overhead transparency;
- getting the children to work in pairs or groups to complete the chart;
- sharing the findings of pair/group work and making a class character chart;
- transferring the chart onto large paper for display (along with other work) (see Table 3.4).

Table 3.4   Character chart for *The Eighteenth Emergency*

Character	Role	Age and appearance	Makes me feel	What I like	What I dislike	Behaviour
Mouse						
Ezzie						
Mr Casino						
Hammerman						

Media and drama

> Pupils should be taught to compare and evaluate a novel or play in print and the film/TV version, e.g. treatment of the plot and characters, the differences in the two forms, e.g. in seeing the setting, in losing the narrator.
>
> (DfEE 1998b: 50.T1)

If a book has been made into a film or adapted for TV it can offer an excellent opportunity for critical evaluation. Children can examine aspects of setting, plot, characters and atmosphere and look at how the script differs from the original text. Alternatively, after reading a book or a chapter from a book, a useful activity is to select a scene and discuss how it might be dramatized. Most primary schools now possess VCR equipment and it is possible to make a storyboard, such as that shown in Figure 3.11, and to experiment not only with the language but also with media and drama production. The children discussed how they would adapt *The Eighteenth Emergency* (Byars 1976a) for TV or film.

Non-standard English

> Pupils should be taught to understand the basic conventions of standard English and consider when and why standard English is used.
>
> (DfEE 1998b: 44.S2/54.S1)

In some sessions children's attention was drawn to the use of non-standard English and the teacher would begin by reading a book such as

'His head was pounding with fear. He could not even swallow. He expected his legs to fold up at any moment like the legs of an old card table' (p. 33).

Scene	Directions	Dialogue/narration	Camera shot	Sounds/music
Deserted street, Hammerman is coming.	Mouse looks around in panic searching for a way to escape.	We've got to get off the street, and fast.	High angle of street. Cut to Mouse and Mr Casino.	Echoes/water dripping, low menacing music.
Mouse and Mr Casino frantic to escape.	Mouse goes through door, pulls Mr Casino with him, pushes Mr Casino back against the wall.	Here, in here, quick Mr Casino, please, come on quick before Hammerman sees us.	Long shot of street, cut to Mouse and Mr Casino, cut back to street.	Music gets louder and faster, slow footsteps gradually getting louder and closer.
Mouse and Mr Casino in entrance hall.	Mr Casino moves to the door, Mouse tries to stop him.			
Entrance hall to outside in the street.	Mr Casino pushes open the door, goes out into the street. Mouse is horrified but follows.			

- *Cut:* way of changing abruptly from one shot to another.
- *High-angle shot:* taken from high up to reveal a situation or to show the vulnerability of characters.
- *Long shot:* image that allows a panoramic or distant view of a scene.

Figure 3.11 Storyboard for *The Eighteenth Emergency* (Street Scene)

Wolf Pie by Andrew Matthews and Tony Ross (1989) or *Geordie Racer* by Christopher Russell (1990). A whole class discussion would follow and examples of non-standard English would be examined. Using a non-permanent pen enabled the teacher to write extracts from the book on an overhead transparency and to play around with the text. For example, some of the language in the book might be rewritten to represent the children's local dialect or it might be converted into standard English.

Geordie Racer

Text	'Ye're ganning t' the allotment then pet?' asked mam.
Local dialect	'You off up allotment then me duck?'
Standard English	'Are you going to the allotment my dear?'
Text	'Aye, t' wait for Blue Flash.'
Local dialect	'Arr, for wait on Blue Flash.'
Standard English	'Yes, to wait for Blue Flash.'
Text	'He'll not be home for hours yet, man.'
Local dialect	'He wunner be wom for hours yet lad.'
Standard English	'He won't be home for hours yet son' (or young man).

Such activity would lead to a general whole class discussion of accent, dialect and slang and eventually to small group work, where the children would examine special words and phrases, the origins of words, root words and derivatives.

Other forms of English

Reading books like *The Eighteenth Emergency* (1976a) and *The Midnight Fox* (1976b) by Betsy Byars led to an examination of American English. Photocopying extracts from the books onto overhead transparencies allowed the teacher to work with the whole class: to look at examples of American English and translate them into Anglo-English. The class then drew up a list of American words and matched them to their English equivalents.

drawing pin	thumbtack
lift	elevator
playground	schoolyard
holiday	vacation
cinema	movies
biscuit	cookie
petrol	gas
pry	snoop
dustbin	trashcan
wardrobe	closet

The children also looked at American words that had gained acceptance in the UK, such as nylon, burger, commuter, motel, drive-in, jeep, sweatshirt and phoney, and at borrowed words from North American Indian language such as moccasin, tobacco, tomato and canoe.

Reading stories by an American writer also led to discussion about differences in spelling. Many of the children found this an area of confusion because of their exposure to American commercial products, American TV

and computer games. The teacher was able to explain that during the nine-
teenth century so many people were emigrating to America from different
parts of the world that Noah Webster suggested many English words be
simplified. He wrote an American English dictionary in 1828 which contained such words as: color, woolen, plow, center, defense and gray.

Changing English

> Pupils should be taught to conduct detailed language investigations
> through interviews, research and reading, e.g. of proverbs, language
> change over time, dialect, study of headlines.
>
> (DfEE 1998b: 54.S2)

The children looked at how language changes over time so that some words
become dated while others are no longer used at all. An extract from *Oliver
Twist* where Oliver meets the Artful Dodger was used to demonstrate this.

> He was, altogether, as roystering and swaggering a young gentleman
> as ever stood four feet six, or something less, in his bluchers.
> 'Hullo, my covey, what's the row?' said this strange young gentleman
> to Oliver.
> 'I am very hungry and tired,' replied Oliver: the tears standing in his
> eyes as he spoke. 'I have walked a long way. I have been walking these
> seven days.'
> 'Walking for sivin days!' said the young gentleman. 'Oh, I see. Beak's
> order, eh? But,' he added, noticing Oliver's look of surprise, 'I suppose
> you don't know what a beak is, my flash com-pan-i-on.' Oliver mildly
> replied, that he had always heard a bird's mouth described by the term
> in question.
> 'My eyes, how green!' exclaimed the young gentleman. 'Why, a beak's
> a madgst'rate; and when you walk by a beak's order, it's not straight
> forerd, but always agoing up, and niver a coming down again.
> 'Was you never on the mill?'
> 'What mill?' inquired Oliver.
> 'What mill! Why, "the" mill – the mill as takes up so little room that
> it'll work inside a Stone Jug; and always goes better when the wind's
> low with people, than when it's high; acos they can't get workmen.'
> 'But come,' said the young gentleman; 'you want grub and you shall
> have it. I'm at low water-mark myself – only one bob and a magpie;
> but, as far as it goes, I'll fork out and stump . . .'

As well as examining the general vocabulary and style of the writer, sentences
such as *Hullo my covey, what's the row?* were discussed along with sayings
such as *I'll fork out and stump* and words like *bluchers, beak, grub* and *bob*.
The Anglo-Saxon poem *Beowulf* was used to illustrate the changing
nature of language and children compared extracts from the original with

revised versions. On other occasions the teacher would read chapters from historical fiction such as *A Strong and Willing Girl* by Dorothy Edwards (1993), or *Joe Burkinshaw's Progress* by Geoffrey Kilner (1979). This would be used to stimulate discussion about words that had emerged during the children's own lifetime, such as *interface, networking, smart-card, Glasnost* and *spamming*, and about words that were no longer used or words that had become old-fashioned but were still used by parents and grandparents, such as *wireless* rather than *radio*.

Invented language

Pupils should be taught to experiment with language, e.g. creating new words.

(DfEE 1998b: 54.W7)

How Tom Beat Captain Najork and His Hired Sportsmen by Russell Hoban (1974) is an excellent book for drawing attention to the special language of games. In addition to reading this story, the teacher took examples of playground rhymes from *Children's Games in Street and Playground* by Opie and Opie (1975) and displayed them on an overhead projector. This led to further discussion of the names and terminology associated with different games and pastimes, both old and new.

nibs	allies	puddies
bollies	bearings	dobbers
oners	*marbles*	clearies
twoers	pop allies	beaut
queenies	moonstines	pilots

On one occasion, the class made a list of words and considered all the slang terms that have been used to represent them.

grub	fills	scranner
tuck	*food*	bain
nosh	snap	chuck

Other word webs were made for other things such as *hands, mouth, face, nose, money, sausages, head*.

Group interaction

Pupils should be taught to contribute constructively to shared discussion about literature, responding to and building on the views of others.

(DfEE 1998b: 50.T5)

At the beginning of the year the teacher introduced a generic framework for literary evaluation to the whole class and this was discussed. The children kept a copy of the framework in their work folders and were able to refer to it throughout the year. The 'Framework for critical reading' ran as follows:

Opening

How does the story begin? Is someone telling the story? Is there dialogue between characters? How does the story opening make you want to read on? How does the author catch your interest? Is it possible to predict the kind of story/the plot/events/outcome?

Setting

Where and when is the story located: past, present, future, real or imaginary world? Why has the location been chosen? Is it suitable for the plot? What other locations might have been used? How does the period in which the story is set influence the plot (events, action, relationships)? How has the author created the setting? By telling the reader? By describing it? Through dialogue between characters? Has the author provided a strong visual/detailed image?

Plot

What are the main events? Which is the high spot of the story? Are there any unexpected events or twists in the story? How many problems (complications/challenges) are there? Is there one main problem? Are there other minor problems woven into the story? How does this make the story interesting? How is the main complication resolved? In a stereotypical manner, e.g. and then I woke up/she waved her magic wand/they all lived happily ever after? A more original and interesting way? Was the ending satisfactory or disappointing? Was the ending predictable or unexpected? How could the ending be improved? How could the story end with a twist?

Character

Who are the main characters? Who are the other characters in the story? Why are they included? Are there any heroes/heroines? Who are they? Are there any stock characters (stereotypical) goodie/baddie, e.g. wicked witch, school bully etc.? Do you empathize with any of the characters? Which ones? Why? How has the author gained your empathy? How are the characters described? Find examples which show their appearance/ personality. What do you think about the main characters? Do you like or dislike any qualities/mannerisms? Do any of the characters change during the story? How/what effect does this have on the story? What are the relationships between the characters? Show the relationships on a web or chart (sociogram). How important is each character to the story? Rank the characters in order of importance. Discuss what difference it would make if any of the characters were not in the story.

Style

Is there anything about the author's style that is distinctive/interesting/ unusual? Does the author use figurative language effectively (adjectives, adverbs, simile, metaphor, onomatopoeia). How does the author make use of other literary devices, e.g. narrative voice, formal or colloquial language, foregrounding, foreshadowing, flashback, sentence structures, repetition, connotation, punctuation?

Mood/atmosphere

How does the story make you feel (sad, happy, angry, surprised, sympathetic)? Do you have different feelings at different times in the story? How? Why? Do your feelings towards the characters change as the story develops? Why? What particular events or actions by the characters affect your feelings and make you feel sad, happy, angry, surprised, sympathetic? Find examples in the story.

Theme

What is the story about? Is it about relationships, fear, bullying, greed, selfishness, self-sacrifice, fairness, goodness, honesty, violence? Is it fiction, fantasy, bibliographic, realistic?

Responding to literature

> Pupils should be taught to articulate personal responses to literature, identifying why and how a text affects the reader.
>
> (DfEE 1998b: 50.T3)

Using the 'Framework for critical reading' for reference, children were encouraged to formulate their own questions for specific texts, and made question cards. For example, 'plot' questions for *The Eighteenth Emergency* were:

- What type of story is *The Eighteenth Emergency*?
- Is there a problem that triggers off events? What is it?
- What do you think are the main events?
- What is the high spot (climax) to the story?
- Do the characters have any unusual habits?
- Do any of the characters behave in predictable or unpredictable ways?
- Are there any surprises or unexpected events?
- Did the story end as you expected it to?
- Did you find the ending satisfactory or disappointing?
- Would you have changed the ending? Why? How?
- If you were rewriting the story what changes would you make to the plot that you think would make the story more interesting?

Style questions for *The Eighteenth Emergency* were:

- What do you think about Betsy Byars' writing style?
- Is there anything that you especially like?
- Is there anything about her style that you dislike?
- Do you find Betsy Byars' style of writing easy or hard to read?
- What is it about the style that makes it easy or hard/pleasant or unpleasant?
- Is there anything she does that you would like to do in your own writing?
- How well has Betsy Byars brought the characters to life for you as a reader?
- How do you think she has done this?
- Can you find any examples where she has used language in special or unusual ways?
- Can you find any good examples of alliteration, similes or metaphor?
- Make a list of interesting adjectives and adverbs that Betsy Byars uses and that you might use in your own writing.

On some occasions, there would be a broad evaluation of a text and all aspects would be examined, usually over a number of sessions. During other single sessions, the teacher concentrated children's attention on selected aspects such as setting, plot or style. For example, on one occasion *Piggybook* by Anthony Browne (1986) formed the basis for whole class and small group discussion. As a whole class and before reading the story the children:

- discussed and listed all the characteristics normally associated with pigs;
- listed any well-used phrases to do with pigs;
- made a descriptive web for a pig (identified words associated with a pig);
- discussed what is meant by calling someone a pig;
- examined the cover and talked about what a piggyback is;
- predicted from the cover and their understanding of a piggyback what the story might be about;
- discussed whether a different animal might be used instead of a pig.

During small group work, children reread the book and studied the text and illustrations. The pages had to be numbered for reference. The illustration of father and sons was page 1. The children discussed:

- who was giving the piggyback on the cover page and the significance of this;
- who they might give a piggyback to and why;
- why there are flying pigs on the title and dedication pages and what message Anthony Browne may be trying to convey to the reader;
- the significance of the photograph across pages 2 and 3;
- the images of the mother and the choice of colour on pages 4 and 5;
- the significance of the shadow on the wall on page 7;

- a comparison of the illustrations on pages 8 and 9;
- the significance of the cavalier and cat on pages 10 and 11;
- Mr Piggot's buttonhole on page 13;
- what the illustration across pages 20 and 21 was saying to the reader;
- the significance of all the characters smiling at the end;
- why Mrs Piggot is outside the family frame on pages 26 and 27;
- why Mrs Piggot is happy mending the car on page 28;
- the meaning of the saying 'pigs might fly' and investigated and listed other well-used sayings and their meanings.

They wrote:

- an inventory of all the images throughout the book to do with pigs;
- a list of all the words in the book associated with animal behaviour;
- a 'living together/family' charter;
- a list of stereotypical views about male/female roles;
- a work rota for mum, dad and the boys in *Piggybook*.

Narrative type

Pupils should be taught to understand aspects of narrative structure.
(DfEE 1998b: 52.T1)

Developing an awareness and understanding of the language and organization of a wide variety of narrative texts was a major objective. The teacher wanted to draw children's attention explicitly to the major language and structural features of different kinds of story. Over the year children composed their own literature files. These contained titles of books they had found in each category, book reviews and any examples of particular story types they had written. Story types identified were:

adventure	fable	historical	realist
anthropomorphic	fairy story	humorous	sci-fi
classical	fantasy folk tale	legend	detective
epistolary	ghost/horror	myth	

The children's knowledge about the language and organizational features of different kinds of story was developed through whole class examination of texts and small group discussions. The issue of readers' expectations was explored and the predominant characteristics of different texts were discussed. Children found the framework shown in Table 3.5 useful.

One particular kind of narrative the class examined in some detail was fairy tales. The children particularly enjoyed looking at the retelling of traditional stories and, using frameworks such as those shown in Table 3.6, investigated changes in the language and stylistic features of the different texts.

Table 3.5   Story feature framework

Setting/opening	Characters	Plot	Style/mood/theme
In what kinds of surroundings is this type of story often set? Does this kind of story often begin in particular ways?	What kinds of character do we often find in this type of story?	What problems, events, twists, resolutions do we often find in this kind of story?	Is this type of story often recognizable by the kind of language it uses (vocabulary) or by the way that language is used? Does this type of story create a certain atmosphere? Are there particular themes we associate with this type of story?

Table 3.6   Frameworks for examining fairy tales retold

Goldilocks and the Three Bears			
Traditional tale	Roald Dahl	Michael Rosen	Tony Ross

Three Little Pigs			
Traditional tale	Jon Scieszka	Eugene Trivizas	Raymond Briggs

Working with one text: Fair's Fair by Leon Garfield

Narrative style

Pupils should be taught to be familiar with the work of some established authors, to know what is special about their work, and to explain their preferences in terms of authors, styles and themes.

(DfEE 1998b: 50.T6)

Pupils should be taught to describe and evaluate the style of an individual writer [and] compare and contrast the work of a single writer.

(DfEE 1998b: 54.T1/T5)

Table 3.7 A 'word wall'

The *(definite* *article)*	*big* *(adjective)*	*black* *(adjective)*	*dog* *(common* *noun)*	*pulled* *(verb)*	*Jackson* *(proper noun)*
roughly *(adverb)*	*down* *(preposition)*	*a* *(indefinite* *article)*	*dark* *(adjective)*	*silent* *(adjective)*	*street* *(common* *noun)*

Looking at how successful writers of children's literature use language can be a potent strategy for learning. The teacher used *Fair's Fair* (Garfield 1981) to focus attention on some of the language choices and literary devices used by one author. Set in Victorian times, this is a story of two poor homeless children who are rewarded for their honesty, bravery and generosity. One way of developing children's syntactic knowledge and drawing their attention to language choice is to take characters from a story and make a 'word wall'. In the example (see Table 3.7), the head sentence contains a range of grammatical and lexical words that create a semantic unit: that is, words chosen and placed in a particular order to convey a certain meaning. However, although some choice has been made the writer does not have total freedom but is constrained by grammatical conventions. By adding suitable words to the boxes and creating similar sentences, children can develop their knowledge about the function of different groups of words. The activity, done as a whole class or in small groups, can also illustrate that it is what a word does (its function) which determines the kind of word it is in any particular context.

> Pupils should be taught to secure the basic conventions of standard English.
>
> (DfEE 1998b: 48/50.T1)

> Pupils should be taught to understand how writing can be adapted for different audiences and purposes, e.g. by changing vocabulary and sentence structures.
>
> (DfEE 1998b: 48.T2)

One language feature of narratives is the use of ellipsis. The teacher wanted to draw children's attention to this feature and to develop their understanding

Table 3.8 Ellipsis chart

Example of ellipsis	Words missed out
Hard to tell if they were on a road or a frozen river	It was

of its purpose. The class looked at how Garfield has used ellipsis in *Fair's Fair* and discussed the effect on the reader. The children concluded that Garfield uses ellipsis because it is what people do naturally when they talk. They realized that ellipsis is used to make the dialogue sound natural and to add dramatic effect, because the story is actually written to be told. The teacher again used the overhead projector to illustrate extracts from the text:

Dreadful weather, as hard and bitter as a quarrel.
Not a light in it, not a glimmer, not a twinkle, even.

The children discussed this in groups and then as a whole class. They decided that if Garfield had written *It was dreadful weather* and *There was not a light* it would not have sounded as dramatic or poetic. It is the *dreadful weather* and *not a light* that Garfield wants to emphasize. During group work the children examined the text to find other parts in the story where ellipsis has been used and they made a chart similar to that illustrated in Table 3.8. The children discussed which words had been left out and whether this made the language sound more natural. They tried putting in the words they thought had been left out, then read the text aloud to hear if it sounded less natural or had lost some of its dramatic or poetic effect.

Collaborative group investigation

The children became literary detectives where they investigated texts for examples of figurative language. They plotted their findings on charts (see Table 3.9).

Pupils should be taught to understand the need for punctuation as an aid to the reader.
(DfEE 1998b: 45.S6/51.S6)

Investigating texts as 'punctuation detectives' proved to be an interesting way for children to develop their awareness and understanding of punctuation marks (see Table 3.10).

Pupils should be taught to take account of viewpoint in a novel through . . . explaining how events might look from a different point of view.
(DfEE 1998b: 50.T2)

Table 3.9 Charts for investigating and plotting figurative language

Simile

Page	Simile	Image/illustration
35	like ghost children in the air	Eerie, pale, faces covered, cold, misty.
		(If there is no illustration children could draw one. Young children could draw their image rather than describe it in writing. Alternatively they could 'tell' their image to the teacher who could act as scribe.)

Metaphor

Page	Metaphor	Image/illustration
6	snow flakes fighting in the wind	Cold, windy, blustery, snowy day.

Alliteration

Page	Alliteration	Reason/effect/image
16	panels all over like a poacher's pocket	Sounds poetic and helps to make the simile more effective.

Table 3.10 Punctuation probe chart

Mark	Name	Example (from the text)	Reason for use
!	Exclamation mark	Hullo! You got a collar on. Hullo again! Stone the crows! You got a key!	To show more and more surprise and growing excitement.

Imagine that Mr Beecham-Chambers, Mr Chuter and Ede can see everything that is happening. Discuss what they might be thinking at different times in the story. Write their thoughts in the thought bubbles.

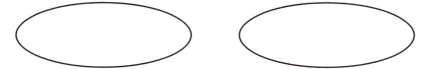

Dreadful weather, with snowflakes fighting in the wind and milk freezing in the pail. Jackson was out in it, sitting on his doorstep.

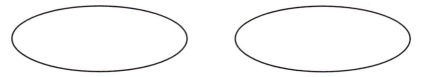

'Seeing as how,' says Jackson to the monster, 'I got time on me hands and no business in view, I'll spare an hour and take you home. All we got to do is find the door this key will fit.'

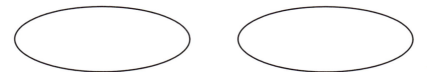

After breakfast Lillypolly swept the stairs and polished the bannisters while Jackson washed the dishes and fetched the coal. The dog did nothing at all. 'Fair's Fair,' said Jackson. 'He's only a dog after all.'

'Do you think,' said Lillypolly, 'they'll come home for Christmas?'

Figure 3.12 Thought tracking

Report

Confidential

Gender:	Female/male	
Name:	*Lillipolly*	Age:
Place of birth:		
Parents' names:	Mother	Father
Parents' occupations:	Mother	Father

Report (life history)

Reporter's name:

Figure 3.13   Investigator's report

'Thought tracking' is an excellent way of developing insight into various characters. The activity can be done independently but is much more effective when done collaboratively, in a group, where ideas can be exchanged, challenged and justified by reference to the text. The type of frame shown in Figure 3.12 can be provided by the teacher, or pupils can make frames for each other, again generating useful discussion.

Reading, writing and discussing non-fiction

> Pupils should be taught to secure control of impersonal writing, particularly the sustained use of the present tense and the passive voice.
>
> (DfEE 1998b: 55.T20)

Children can relate information gained from historical investigation and the reading of non-fiction texts to a narrative by writing imaginary reports on characters, as shown in Figure 3.13.

The NLSF emphasizes the need for children to develop skills in reading and writing non-fiction (DfEE 1998b: 3). It also makes the point that opportunities should be found for developing work beyond the literacy hour through extended reading and writing activities which are 'linked to other curriculum areas' (p. 14). It states that children should: 'develop skills of biographical and autobiographical writing in role, describing a person from different perspectives, e.g. police description, school report, newspaper obituary' (51.T14); 'develop a journalistic style' (51.T15); 'use the styles and conventions of journalism to report on, e.g. real or imagined events' (51.T16); 'write non-chronological reports linked to other subjects' (51.T17); and 'use IT to plan, revise, edit writing' (51.T18).

Fair's Fair can be used as a springboard into numerous writing activities, allowing teachers to introduce and explore the language features and organization of different kinds of text, and to develop children's competence in writing for a wide range of audiences and purposes. For example:

- autobiography;
- will (Mr Beecham-Chambers);
- diary (letter, postcard, Christmas card);
- recipe (menu, shopping list);
- work rota;
- advertisement (owner missing, lost dog found);
- newspaper article (rags to riches, plight of homeless children);
- police file and report (identikit, description, missing person);
- interview (questionnaire);
- riddle (cryptic message);
- board game (search for the house, matching the key);
- TV/radio phone-in;
- historical factsheets (town life, transport, working conditions, Victorian childhood).

The process of critical reading–group discussion (CRGD) is a central feature of guided and independent group work, both within and beyond the literacy hour. Children's ability to identify the features of a variety of texts, compare and evaluate arguments, locate and summarize information, investigate style and vocabulary, ascertain impact, appeal, honesty and bias, is best developed through collaborative discourse and cooperative activity. The reading of *Fair's Fair* provided the basis for an investigation into town life, working conditions and the role of children in Victorian times. The class was organized into jigsaw groups (see Chapter 4) and the work entailed:

- library research (using the Dewy system, contents, index, glossary, cross-referencing);
- locating information from the library (CD-ROM, websites, TV and radio);
- reading, comparing and making notes from primary and secondary sources;
- evaluating sources for accuracy and detecting bias;
- selecting, editing and summarizing information;
- planning, composing and presenting information along with evaluations and interpretations.

One group compared an official report of working conditions and an unofficial interview with a child worker. Another group examined two accounts, written by the same person, of working and living conditions in a mill town. The first of the two extracts that follow is taken from the official report and the second from the personal account. Both extracts are taken from Blyth and Hughes (1997).

Extract 1
Mr. C. employed sixty-seven power-loom weavers of cords and velveteens. The weavers generally superintended two looms each, several had three looms, and one or two had four looms, the latter being assisted by tenters (assistants who 'tended' the looms), whom they had to pay. A weaver of average ability, would earn, on two looms, from ten to twelve shillings per week; one with three looms, would get from thirteen to fourteen shillings; and one with four looms, would earn as much as fifteen shillings a week clear. A number of the hands lived in houses belonging to Mr. C., for which they paid from one shilling and sixpence, to two shillings and nine-pence per week, and their rent was settled every pay day.

I made excuses to enter some of the houses, and found them uniformly neat and clean, one tenement was beautifully clean; the walls were as white as lime could make them; the good housewife, who was up to the elbows in suds, gave me liberty to see their chambers [bedrooms], and I found the walls and the beds on a par with the house below; they were almost spotless, and the air was as untainted as the wind. This was one of a row of houses; several others which I entered were almost in as good condition; they had generally flowers and green shrubs in the windows, and before the doors were small gardens with flowers and a few pot herbs. The tenements consisted of a front room, a kitchen, and two chambers, and the front rooms were furnished with handsome fire-grates, ovens, and boilers, all as well burnished as black lead, a good brush, and a willing hand could make them. The rent of those dwellings was two shillings and nine-pence per week, clear of all rates.

Extract 2
Whilst my life at the bobbin-wheel was wretched on account of the confinement, my poor old aunt had generally a sad time with me. It was scarcely to be expected that a tall, straight, round-limbed young ruffian like myself, with bare legs and feet, bare neck and a head equally denuded, save be a crop of thick coarse hair, should sit day by day twirling a wheel and guiding a thread; his long limbs cramped and doubled under a low wooden stool.

. . . I accordingly at times from a sheer inability to sit still, played all kinds of pranks, and threw myself into all kinds of attitudes, keeping my wheel going the while lest my aunt should have it to say I was playing and neglecting my task. I generally sat near her at her work, and I must confess that I sometimes exhibited these antics from a wish to provoke rather than amuse my observant and somewhat irritable overseer. On these occasions I frequently got a rap on the head from a weaver's rod which my aunt would have beside her, whereupon I would move out of her reach and continue 'marlockin' [frolicking, or fooling about] until I got either more correction, or was dispatched on an errand, or banished into the 'loom-house' amongst the weavers.

The National Curriculum for English (DfEE 1995a: 13) states that 'pupils' reading should be developed through the use of progressively more challenging texts'. As well as being provided with challenging texts, children need to develop the confidence and ability to 'be challenging': to be able to analyse and evaluate texts and to pose questions rather than merely answer them. For the teacher in this case study, talking about texts, exploring, evaluating and discussing them constituted a major difference between conventional comprehension and critical reading.

Talk across the curriculum

A narrative text can provide the initial stimulus for work on various speaking and listening and reading and writing tasks across a range of National Curriculum subjects. For example, the reading of *Fair's Fair* can generate the following cross curricular work:

Art
- Quality of illustrations, portrayal of characters
- Puppets, face masks, animation of story
- Shadows and silhouettes
- Cartoons and caricatures
- Illustrating further books that are written such as sequels

Geography
- Maps (directions, town plans, routes)
- Victorian cities, towns, villages and urban development
- Trade and industry
- The British Empire in Victorian times

History
- Victorian buildings, clothes, transport and social conditions
- Occupations (chimney sweep, pie-maker, lamp-lighter, butler, maid)
- Games, pastimes, entertainment

Maths
- Measurement (scale, keyholes, model house, puppets, distances, volume)

Music
- Victorian music and musical instruments, entertainment, music-halls
- Victorian composers such as Elgar and Brahms

PSE
- Sharing, fairness
- Families
- Fear, loneliness and rejection
- Favourite foods and smells (cookery)
- Christmas, festivals/celebrations, multicultural
- Kindness, patience and honesty

Science
- Echoes, sound
- Snow, freezing, temperature changes, keeping warm, fire
- Food (steam from the meat pie)
- Light and shadows

Technology
- Lock mechanisms
- Design locks and keyholes
- Puppets (shadow theatre)
- Pop-up books (through the keyhole books, concertina books)

Conclusion

As the case study demonstrates, it is possible to plan stimulating activities where speaking and listening play a central rather than tangential role in the learning. Through effective teacher–pupil and peer–peer discourse, aspects of language and literature (fiction and non-fiction) can be investigated. Interactive whole class and small group discourse underpinned the work. Talk provided vibrancy and stimulated spontaneity and creativity. It allowed the teacher and pupils to probe, investigate, explore and hypothesize, to challenge, justify, reflect and evaluate a range of narrative and non-narrative texts. It enabled children to perceive and make sense of literary devices used by authors and to integrate these into their own writing repertoire.

Despite the dysfunctional role of Ofsted, teachers are developing enough confidence to assert their professional expertise and to use their professional judgement. They are drawing from the NLSF to devise medium- and long-term plans to meet the learning needs of their children. Teaching is exciting and learning is effective and enjoyable. There is a realization that direct teaching does not have to result in pupil passivity: that structured, systematic and well-focused learning can be fun. There are indications that we may be entering a 'new age' of investigative learning, where teachers are translating Vygotskian theory into effective practice in the classroom. Ways of maximizing the learning potential of group work are explored in Chapter 4.

4 ○ Group work

Sitting in groups and group work

British primary schools have, since the early 1970s, generally been organized with children seated around tables in small groups. The fostering of collaborative, investigative learning is often given as the prime justification for this arrangement. However, although group seating has been a prominent feature of classroom organization in primary schools, prior to the National Oracy Project, there was little evidence that teachers were planning for talk in any systematic way. Research on classroom organization has consistently confirmed the view that a great deal of group work in primary schools is either ineffective or inappropriate. The HMI survey (1978) of primary education made no mention of the kind of collaborative and expressive talk recommended by the Bullock Report (DES 1975), or the purposeful discussion described by researchers such as Johnson and Johnson (1990: 77), who state that cooperative learning is not:

- having students sit side by side at the same table and talk with each other as they do their individual assignments;
- having students do a task individually with instructions that the ones who finish first are to help the slower students;
- assigning a report to a group where one student does all the work and others put their name to it.

The ORACLE survey (1975–80) found that although grouping had become a major feature of classroom organization, collaborative work was rare (see Galton *et al.* 1980; Simon and Willcocks 1981). Of the 58 classes observed, 50 used an informal layout but throughout the observation period, 90 per cent never organized collaborative group tasks. The survey found that most children spent their time in school working alone, individually and silently. Only 18.6 per cent of the time was spent on interaction with peers and a meagre 1.5 per cent of time was allocated to group interaction. HMI (1982) stated that the aims, objectives and methods for promoting oral language needed to be more clearly defined and Alexander *et al.* (1992) recommended that teachers give more consideration to matching seating arrangements to teaching and learning purposes, rather than organizing classes into groups as a matter of course. Ofsted (1993) found that although classes were organized into small groups, children worked independently on individual work tasks. Galton *et al.* (1999) conclude that the organization within primary classrooms has hardly changed since the original 1976 ORACLE survey. Although teachers now appear to be spending more time in group and whole class teaching, the pattern of interaction has remained fairly constant and 'children still mostly sit grouped around tables, but still work mostly alone' (Galton *et al.* 1999: 105). What research and reports confirm is that we have been seduced by the colourful, bustling, busyness of the primary classroom, which has, in effect, masked a lack of quality teacher–pupil interaction.

Group work and learning

> Cooperation is working together to accomplish shared goals and cooperative learning is the instructional use of small groups so that students work together to maximise their own and one another's learning.
>
> (Johnson and Johnson 1990: 69)

Barnes and Todd's (1977) seminal work on collaborative learning illustrated its importance in the development of children's cognitive understanding. The National Oracy Project (see Norman 1992) highlighted the learning potential of peer group discussions which are reflective and hypothetical and where speech is tentative and exploratory. Des Fountain and Howe (1992: 146) suggest that children need 'worthwhile opportunities to work together in small groups, making meaning through talk'. In the USA the value of dialogue in scaffolding children's comprehension skills has been demonstrated by Palinscar and Brown (1984), while Rosenblatt (1989: 173) argues that teacher–pupil and peer–peer dialogue and interchange is a vital ingredient in helping children make connections between the reading and writing processes:

> Group interchange about the texts of established authors can also be a powerful means of stimulating growth in reading ability and critical acumen. When students share their responses and learn how their evocations from transactions with the same text differ, they can return to the text to discover their own habits of selection and synthesis and can become more critical of their own processes as readers. Interchange about the problems of interpretation and a collaborative movement

toward self-critical interpretation of the text can lead to the development of critical concepts and criteria of validity of interpretation. Such metalinguistic awareness is valuable to students as both readers and writers.

Achievement in group work

Researchers in the USA have made great claims for the effectiveness of group work in enhancing motivation, developing social skills and raising levels of academic achievement. Slavin (1983a) devised a number of structured approaches to competitive–cooperative group work such as TGT (team games, tournaments) and STAD (student-teams achievement divisions). The CLIP (cooperative learning implementation programme) (Robertson 1990) focused on collaborative learning and aimed to promote prosocial skills and academic achievement. In the UK, Mercer (1991) and Moore and Tweddle (1992) investigated the role of CAL (computer assisted learning) and explored its potential for pair and group work. Slavin reports that his methods can develop social relations, improve children's self-esteem and increase student achievement. Johnson and Johnson (1990: 71) make similar claims and offer evidence to suggest that group cooperative learning can promote higher achievement than an individual competitive approach. They argue that promoting positive interdependence and individual accountability in group work results in higher achievement, more positive relationships and higher self-esteem. Sharan (1980) also concludes, though rather more tentatively, that team learning methods result in enhanced academic achievement in comparison with a more traditional teaching approach. Sharan and Shaulov (1989) point particularly to benefits in terms of social development and motivation, arguing that cooperative groups typically generate devotion and application to a task. Sharan (1990: 182) concludes that group investigation: 'fosters more positive attitudes towards learning, more motivation to learn, and more cooperative patterns of behaviour among classmates in multi-ethnic groups, than does the typical presentation–recitation method'.

Despite these claims, there has been some debate over whether group work produces results superior to those obtained from individual or whole class teaching. Bennett and Blundell (1983) suggest that children are likely to spend more time on task when working in traditional rows than when working in groups. However, other studies (e.g. Hertz-Lazorowitz 1990) show that time on task is substantially higher during collaborative group work than in whole class activities.

Determining when and whether children are on or off task is highly problematic. As Hastings (1990) has pointed out, children can develop various ploys to give the impression of being on task when they are actually doing very little. Similarly, children can appear to be off task, when in reality they are thinking. Dyson (1987: 397) notes that 'off task behaviour may in fact contain some of the children's most intellectually skilful behaviours'. I have numerous examples of children making significant contributions to discussion following apparent off task behaviour. In one such example a group were discussing the Beatles song 'Eleanor Rigby'. They were investigating the meaning of the words 'Father Mackenzie wiping the dirt from his hands as he walked from the grave'. One group member appeared to withdraw from discussion. He leaned back in his chair and actually turned away from other group members. However, he suddenly turned back to face the group and said, 'no . . . no it means two things . . . it means he's wiping away the dirt . . . mud of burying her and he's wiping her away at the same time'.

It is extremely difficult to conclude whether group work is more academically effective than whole class or individual work because the measurement of achievement is not easy to determine. Moreover, there is a difference between product and process outcomes. The criteria for achievement will be different for investigative 'open tasks' that require higher order thinking than for closed 'information gathering tasks'. Bennett and Dunne (1992) found a difference in the amount of abstract talk during work on English and maths tasks, the former generating 20 per cent of the total and the latter almost zero. A low proportion of abstract talk was also found to occur in technology and computer tasks. Bennett and Dunne suggest that action tasks, which for example require children to make things, demand a different kind of activity than many English tasks, which require children to discuss issues and make decisions unrelated to action – that is, they do not have to produce something, a main learning outcome of such tasks being the *process* of discussion. The point is that group work should be just one of a whole repertoire of organizational arrangements within the classroom. As with any other arrangement it should be used only when it is appropriate to do so. If children happen to be engaged in a task that requires individual attention and concentration, the educational milieu should reflect this need. It is organizational lunacy to seat children face to face around a table if their learning need at that particular time requires a little peace and privacy. Attempting to compare academic results in whole class, individual or group work situations is a difficult and somewhat futile task. Effective teaching requires a variety of contexts, including whole class, small group and individual learning scenarios. Academic achievement is facilitated by a careful match between learning objective, classroom organization, task and teacher intervention.

Group work in a literacy hour

The literacy hour, organized into whole class and guided and independent working groups, provides opportunities for children and teachers to engage in purposeful interactive discourse to meet differentiated learning objectives. Managing independent group work is considered to be one of the most challenging aspects of the literacy hour by many teachers. Indeed the NLSF training pack devotes a section to this issue and many LEAs have advised schools to establish shared and guided reading sessions before attempting to introduce independent reading groups. At first glance this seems surprising, since most primary school classrooms have been organized into small groups since the early 1970s. Teachers' anxieties would appear to confirm research which shows that, while children have been organized into groups, they have rarely been engaged in cooperative or collaborative group work (Bennett 1985; Mortimore *et al.* 1988; Tizard *et al.* 1988). Research also suggests that children have been accustomed to working within a particular teaching and learning culture, where they can call for, and expect to receive, the teacher's attention on demand. As Bennett and Dunne (1992: 125) suggest, 'A central feature of the typical primary classroom is the atmosphere of "busyness" which is accentuated because the bulk of the interactions between teachers and pupils are on an individual basis, and to attend to different children's needs the teacher must continually move rapidly around the classroom'.

Teachers have found themselves having to respond to multitudinous demands, not only because the children have expected it but also because the structure necessary for supporting group work and encouraging independent, cooperative interaction has been inadequate. The classroom of one experienced and particularly gifted primary teacher I worked with in the National Oracy Project had the 'busy, bustling' milieu. It looked exciting, imaginative and highly interactive. After viewing video recordings of her classroom practice, the teacher concluded that, although she thought she was engaging in quality interaction with the children, she was merely 'putting out forest fires'. We rationalized her approach by:

- focusing on specific curriculum subjects;
- dealing 'collectively' with issues in groups;
- structuring tasks carefully;
- matching the type of group to the nature and purpose of the task;
- establishing ground rules for group work.

The result was dramatic. The classroom retained its busyness, but we described it as 'buzz with a purpose'. However, the most significant development was the increase in time the teacher was able to spend with a group of children in 'quality interaction', where she could scaffold their learning appropriately and effectively. This was in 1989, nine years before the introduction of a literacy hour and the current concept of guided and independent groups. Similar experience is noted by Bennett and Dunne (1992), who describe teachers' astonishment at the decline of demands from children following the successful implementation of cooperative groups.

Making group work work

Although the organization of students into small groups may increase the potential for meaningful discourse, it does not mean they will automatically engage in productive collaborative discussion. Evidence from some studies indicates that students working in groups interact cooperatively for only a small percentage of the time (Galton *et al.* 1980; Alexander 1992). Other studies show how the same tasks can generate different student responses in terms of the quality of talk and collaboration that emerge (Crook 1991; Jones and Mercer 1993). Moreover, McMahon and Goatley (1995) found that without specific instructions from the teacher, student-led reading groups tend to use an asymmetrical discourse pattern more commonly associated with formal whole class teaching.

Evidence from longitudinal studies (Norman 1992) and other empirical research (Hoyles *et al.* 1990; Mercer 1995) confirm the view that successful peer-group work depends on students having a shared understanding of the purpose of the task and a joint conception of what they are trying to achieve. However, some studies show how students' interpretations of the ground rules may differ in important ways from those of their peers and/or teachers (Rohrkemper 1985; Mercer *et al.* 1988). For example, while some students working in reading groups may see it as an opportunity to explore and interrogate texts collaboratively, others in the same group may see it as an opportunity to exhibit individual knowledge and demonstrate an ability to get the correct answers. There is evidence that when teachers bring ground rules for discussion into the open, it can lead to improved motivation and levels of performance among students (Prentice 1991; Dawes *et al.* 1992). However, a substantial body of research shows this practice to be uncommon and that students usually receive little help in understanding and appreciating the ground rules for group discussion (Mercer and Edwards 1981; Hull 1985; Phillips 1992; Elbers and Kelderman 1994). Moreover, some studies illustrate how students' traditional conceptions of school learning contexts can inhibit collaborative discussion (Edwards and Mercer 1987; Barnes and Sheeran 1992; McMahon and Meyers 1993). (This is discussed in more detail in Chapter 6.) Teachers in the National Oracy Project identified a number of key features of successful group work in reading and group discussion activities, where both process (the interaction) and product (the cognitive outcome) are important.

Features of successful group work are:

- use of hypothetical, explorative language;
- individual initiatives being accepted and developed by the group;
- participation of all group members;
- discussion developed through discourse rather than dispute, that is: through challenge, evaluation, reasoning and justification (based on evidence from texts) rather than through intuitive, unqualified personal feelings;

- absence of excessive diversion from the task (either external interference or internal disruptive behaviour);
- avoidance of premature and unsatisfactory consensus.

Teachers found that for these features to be encouraged, it was useful to consider a number of issue before, during and after the task. Before the task, the activity must be:

- well-planned and structured;
- carefully organized;
- thoroughly resourced;
- appropriate for the learning objective.

During the task, the teacher should:

- introduce the activity and establish a collaborative working climate;
- clarify expected outcomes (working process and end product);
- ensure children have a clear understanding of the ground rules for group work;
- ensure children have a clear understanding of respective roles and inter-dependency;
- intervene appropriately and effectively.

After the task, there should be:

- an evaluation of learning (group process and individual learning);
- reflection, reinforcement and consolidation of learning;
- an identification of key aspects for further development or investigation;
- a method of rewarding all participants.

Planning and structuring group work

Research has shown that collaborative interaction won't happen simply by seating children together and instructing them to work as a group. Children need to understand why they are being asked to work as a group and to see the relevance and usefulness of what they are doing. They also need to appreciate what it means to work in a group: to recognize individual and collective responsibilities. Getting children to discuss the benefits of collaborative learning and to negotiate the ground rules is an essential prerequisite to successful group work. Similarly, for group work to be successful it needs to be carefully matched to its intended purpose, and organized accordingly. Moreover, it should be remembered that pair or group work is only a suitable form of classroom organization if the task requires a cooperative response and the children's learning is likely to be enhanced by working collaboratively. The kind of group should be determined by the nature of the task and the purpose of the activity.

One particular primary school I worked with in the National Oracy Project developed a whole school approach to group work. The staff found they needed to:

- get children to value group work and establish ground rules;
- identify appropriate tasks for group work;
- recognize the social and cognitive demands of group tasks;
- organize different kinds of groups for different tasks and purposes;
- develop pair and group work techniques;
- develop children's metadiscoursal skills.

Successful group interaction depends on the cooperation of the children and their willingness to make it work. Children, like adults, are more likely to cooperate if they know why they are doing something and appreciate the benefits of what they are doing. The best way to do this is:

- To provide children with a task where they have to work cooperatively, pool knowledge and skills, and share information.
- Following the task, ask the children to talk about how it felt to work as a team. What benefits did they get? How was it more enjoyable than having to work alone?

Establishing the ground rules for group work

After conducting extensive research in primary schools, Kagan (1985) concludes that successful group work requires a degree of tolerance, mutual understanding and an ability to articulate a point of view. In collaborative work, children are expected to discuss, reason, probe and question. Such skills, argues Kagan, are not innate but have to be taught. Children need to understand the rules and expectations associated with this mode of working. The ground rules for group work need to be made explicit. The best way to achieve this is to engage the children in an activity which focuses their attention on the process of group interaction and encourages them to draw out their own list of rules. For example, explain to the children that they are going to design a 'rules for group work poster'. Organize the class into groups and get each group to:

- individually write a list of rules for when they are working in a group;
- share and discuss the individual lists;
- identify any common rules;
- draw up a group list of main rules;
- collect the group lists and from these, draw up a class list of common rules for group work;

- discuss the list with the class, suggesting modifications and additions;
- agree on a final set of rules.

The teacher should:

- display the rules where everyone can see them;
- ensure that everyone abides by the rules;
- ensure that the rules are enforced.

Primary age children will often identify the following rules:

- don't shout;
- don't all talk at the same time;
- listen to each other;
- give everyone a chance to say something;
- help each other out;
- share ideas;
- take people's ideas seriously;
- don't make anyone feel silly;
- everyone should join in.

It is important for children to develop their understanding of both negative and positive elements and to see what is and what is not useful. One useful strategy to use when introducing group work is to place a cassette recorder on the table and ask the children to switch it on when they begin a discussion and switch it off when they have finished. Replay the recording and ask the children to discuss what they hear. They will often identify for themselves many of the issues the teacher would want to address. Children I have worked with have said things like:

- there's too much noise;
- everyone's shouting;
- everyone's talking at once;
- you won't let anyone else say anything;
- you don't listen to other people;
- you don't say anything;
- we're not discussing, we're just arguing;
- we're supposed to listen to everyone's point of view.

Roles in groups

Having an explicit set of rules helps children to self-regulate. It can also ensure that all group members participate. Teachers in the National Oracy Project found that primary children rarely opt out of well-organized group activities (a feature also noted by Bennett and Dunne 1992). However, the American researchers Salomon and Globerson (1989) showed that some children can devise work avoidance strategies, and they identify what they call 'free riders', 'suckers' and 'gangers'. Free riding occurs when children opt out of work and allow others to complete a task. Low ability children may do this if the task is challenging and other members of the group are clearly more able. The low ability child can become marginalized and have no apparent use. High ability children may also free ride if they feel the task is too easy or is moving too slowly for them. The sucker effect can occur when children, who are usually motivated and enthusiastic, are allowed by others to do most of the work. They then feel they are being exploited and do not contribute effectively. Gangers are those children who may collectively reject a task and simply go through the motions of working. The ORACLE study (Galton *et al.* 1980) identified 'attention seekers', who tend to move around the classroom and interrupt other children, thus eliciting the teacher's attention. At the other extreme are 'hard grinders' (Galton and Willcocks 1983) or what Pollard (1985) describes as 'goodies'. These are children who conform to teacher's expectations and remain on task for extended periods of time. However, children who are 'eager participants' (Galton *et al.* 1999), keen to engage in whole class question and answer sessions, may be 'solitary workers' and prefer to work individually, rather than as collaborative group members. 'Intermittent workers' are perhaps the most difficult to spot because they tend to work when they feel they are being observed by the teacher but move off task whenever an opportunity arises.

In some activities, assigning key roles to children can be counter-productive and may inhibit the natural flow of ideas. However, in other tasks, cooperation can be facilitated by children having clear roles to play within an overall structure. This issue is discussed in some detail by Bennett and Dunne (1992: 147), who suggest the following key roles in a group of four:

- *Coordinator:* to keep the group on task, to ensure contributions from all, to guide discussion or activity.
- *Data gatherer:* to take notes or summarize ideas, to clarify ideas and to read aloud from some materials when appropriate.
- *Secretary:* to record group answers or materials, to act as spokesperson when reporting to the class.
- *Evaluator:* to keep notes on the group process (how well individuals in the group are working together), to lead any evaluation at the end of the session.

Stages in group discussion

From her work in the ORACLE study Tann (1981) identified three key stages in the discussion process:

- *The orientation stage:* involves children in defining problems, interpreting the task and setting limits on the activity.
- *The development stage:* involves children in generating ideas and using reasoning strategies.
- *The concluding stage:* is marked by increasing acceptance of each other's ideas and more progressive focusing on the specific strategies necessary for a successful resolution of the problem.

Robertson (1990: 195–6), reporting on the CLIP, suggests that children need time to develop group work skills and that they go through several 'naturally occurring' stages before operating at their most productive level. She discusses five stages of development:

- *The orientation stage:* where group members find out about one another and their place in the group.
- *The norm establishment stage:* where members develop shared expectations of behaviour and learn to organize themselves into an effective team.
- *The conflict stage:* where group members test one another and the teacher. This conflict is not necessarily a signal that something is going wrong and that groups should be changed. It is often a signal that groups are on track, moving towards productivity. Conflict will naturally happen and is an opportunity to learn problem solving and interpersonal skills.
- *The productivity stage:* which is generally the longest stage in the life of a group where group members focus both on the task and interpersonal relations.
- *The termination stage:* where group members look back at their experience together and deal with the problems of parting. They look toward experiences with a new group and consider what they have learned that they can take with them.

It should be noted that Tann's (1981) work was conducted under controlled conditions and recorded through systematic observation, and that Robertson's (1990) work took place in the USA and was concerned with cooperative learning in maths. My own observations of children working on English tasks in naturalistic classroom settings indicates that the interactive process is not quite so predictable or sequential. Successful group work in most literary activities is characterized by talk which is tentative and explorative. Interaction is dynamic and unpredictable, as children appear to go off at a tangent, leap ahead or backtrack. Discourse is characterized by the false starts, hesitations, rephrasing and changes of direction noted by Barnes (1976: 28). The group process is also, to an extent, determined by the nature of the task and the particular learning context created by the teacher and the task structure.

Group tasks

Mercer (1992: 221) argues that 'the education value of any classroom talk between children, with or without a teacher present, may hinge on how well a teacher has set up the activities and environment for generating and supporting suitable kinds of talk'. Lyle (1993: 195) points to the importance of teachers encouraging children to see themselves as responsible learners by designing activities which 'ensure children pose questions, make observations, contribute opinions'. However, this is no simple matter. Bossert *et al.* (1984) show that certain kinds of task organization are likely to create particular learning contexts, which will in turn influence the way that children interact. Barnes (1976) suggests that learning through discussion needs to be planned and carefully resourced by the teacher in order to provide the appropriate context for discussion. Teachers should organize and introduce tasks according to the intended purpose. Too little structure for some kinds of task may result in chaos and pupil anxiety; too much structure for investigative tasks may inhibit discussion. Barnes and Todd (1977: 84) refer to tasks which are *loose* or *tight* and show how this affects patterns of interaction. Their distinction reflects the difference between activities where the teacher has one particular solution in mind and those where alternative solutions are acceptable. They cite one particular group of girls who, despite assurances to the contrary, determined that a task was tightly directed, and as a consequence displayed anxiety and a frantic search for the one correct answer. Barnes (1992) explains that tasks requiring 'exploratory talk' do not require pupils to learn new information but to manipulate what they already know, and explore possibilities.

Cowie and Ruddock (1988) (cited in Bennett and Dunne 1992: 71) differentiate between:

- *Discussion tasks:* where there is an onus on process and the sharing of ideas. The subject matter is likely to be interpretative or controversial – for example, a poem, narrative text, magazine article or newspaper report. The outcome may be a group decision or consensus, or the development of individual interactive skills and cognitive understanding.
- *Problem solving tasks:* where a number of alternatives may be critically evaluated, for example a sequencing, prediction or deletion activity. The outcome may require a group consensus or individual decisions that are reached after group discussion.
- *Production tasks:* where children work collaboratively to produce a group response – for example, the dramatization of a text, or the adaptation of a text for a film. A jigsaw activity, where children work on different aspects of a topic to achieve a group goal (such as writing an information book about ancient Egypt), is an example of a production task.

Table 4.1 Organization of tasks

Loose	Intermediate	Tight
Discussing a controversial issue such as fox hunting.	Discussing a poem, chapter or short story and evaluating its literary quality.	Reading aloud accurately and with expression.
Free choice reading.	Reading and evaluating a variety of story openings.	Reading, discussing and answering literal-level comprehension questions.
Writing in a personal journal.	Writing in a particular genre or poetry form.	Reading and understanding key aspects of a non-fiction text and writing a summary.

Activity

Choose a text and plan three activities that could be located on the left, middle and right of the loose–tight continuum.

Bennett and Dunne (1992: 190) suggest that group work is particularly valuable for problem solving tasks, but show that the kind of abstract talk which is a feature of English tasks 'is more difficult for children to generate and is less fluent than talk relating to action'. Doyle (1983) and Galton (1989) also argue that ambiguous tasks are more challenging and much more likely to produce anxiety and uncertainty. Cohen (1994) suggests that exploratory tasks, which require higher-order thinking skills, depend more for their success on the quality of interaction than do routine information gathering or practical tasks. Imaginative teachers can plan interesting and flexible schemes of work to meet the learning objectives within the NLSF. The structure of the literacy hour, along with extended and cross-curricular work, provides an opportunity for children to work in a rich variety of ways and in different social and cognitive contexts. In planning work, the nature and ambiguity of tasks and the degree of children's personal sense of freedom and ownership needs to be considered. Table 4.1 exemplifies tasks that may fit within a loose–tight continuum.

A further distinction between tasks is made by Deci and Ryan (1985), who differentiate between those which are inherently interesting to children and those which may be less interesting but necessary for learning and development. This is an important point because the degree of inherent interest can impact on children's motivation and behaviour. Teachers need to be aware of potential differences in the level of children's intrinsic interest and motivation and to plan accordingly, thinking about such things as introduction,

Table 4.2 Analysis of group discourse: social and cognitive functions

Social	Utterance	Cognitive
Initiating	'What if say he's poaching and that's why he's out late and he's moving dead careful?'	Setting up hypothesis
Supporting and extending	'You might be right, yeah 'cos he he's got dogs hasn't he Jas?'	Evaluating and constructing a question
Contradicting	'No he hasn't . . . he hasn't got a gun . . . it doesn't say does it . . . anyway 'cos he's got dogs doesn't mean he's a poacher does it?'	Raising new questions and putting an alternative view
Relating to personal experience	'I went with me Uncle Ted once after rabbits and he didn't have dogs or a gun.'	Qualifying/reasoning
Eliciting	'Where does it say . . . it doesn't say anywhere . . . look it only says he moved stealthily.'	Using and advancing evidence from the text
Supporting	'No but like his wax jacket and leggings he's got on . . .'	Providing descriptive details from the text

timing, pace, groupings, activities and teacher intervention. For successful group learning to occur, teachers need to consider the relationship between the social, communicative and cognitive aspects of talking and learning and to structure tasks carefully in terms of social interdependence and cognitive demand.

Social and cognitive demands of group work

Group work places considerable social as well as cognitive demands on children. In discussing an issue or solving a problem they develop their understanding within a social context. Table 4.2 shows how children talk to explore, hypothesize and evaluate while simultaneously maintaining and developing the social framework.

Group discussion can deteriorate into what Mercer (1994) calls disputational talk, where group members simply argue their own viewpoint and don't consider those of others. To be of value, some kinds of group discussion need to be informed, where children bring to the task essential background experience and knowledge. This must be planned for and provided by the teacher in order to establish a productive context for talk. I once recorded a group of Year 6 children discussing the sale of the Mappa Mundi (it caused something of a storm when this famous medieval map of the world was put on sale some years ago). The children made an admirable attempt to discuss whether, as a 'board', they should sell or retain the map but after a short while a long silence ensued. It was suddenly ended by the comment, 'Oh let's flog the bastard!' Similarly a Year 3 class I was working with was engaged in an environmental topic using texts such as *The Iron Man* by Ted Hughes (1968) and *Dinosaurs and All that Rubbish* by Michael Foreman (1972). The teacher and I decided to jigsaw an activity and to place the children in different roles so they would argue a case from various perspectives: for example, a farmer, a local resident, an environmentalist, a local councillor. The task was a failure because we had expected the children to role play without knowing enough about the roles. We decided to try again but this time spent some time developing the children's knowledge and understanding of what it means to be an environmentalist who wants to protect land, or a farmer who wants to sell it. The activity was a huge success.

In designing tasks, teachers need to consider the cognitive demands and social skills required to undertake activities cooperatively. Devising activities that are appropriate for cooperative rather than individual outcomes is a challenge. However, once the learning purpose is determined, and it is clear that group work is appropriate, the necessary organization becomes clearer. Biot (1984) suggests that it is most appropriate to begin cooperative group work with simple, tight production tasks, where children are clear about the procedure and the expected outcome, before moving on to introduce collaborative problem solving activities with looser, more abstract discussion. Lyle (1993) found that structured activities with well-defined rules helped to keep pupils on task for extended periods of time. Certainly my own experience of working with teachers and children in the National Oracy Project would confirm the effectiveness of the two-stage approach advocated by Galton and Williamson (1992), where task and context demands are increased gradually as children develop their skills and confidence. Points to consider might be:

- What are the social and cognitive demands of the task?
- Is the task suitable for cooperative/collaborative working?
- What kind of group is most suitable for the task?
- How will the task be introduced and children's curiosity and enthusiasm aroused?
- Are the resources and materials suitable and sufficient?
- What is the teacher's role during the task?
- Are the children clear about the task in terms of process (how they are to work) and product (what they are expected to produce)?
- What response/feedback/reward will be given on completion of the task?

Table 4.3   Classification of group type, task and outcome

Type	Task demand	Intended outcome	Example
Seated group	Each pupil has a separate task	Different outcomes: each pupil completes a different assignment	Writing stories on themes chosen by the pupils
Working group	Each pupil has the same task	Same outcome: each pupil completes the same assignment independently	Mathematics worksheet
Cooperative group	Each pupil has a separate but related task	Joint outcome: each pupil has a different assignment	Making a map
Collaborative group	Each pupil has the same task	Joint outcome: all pupils share same assignment	Problem solving, e.g. discussing a social or moral issue

Source: Galton and Williamson (1992: 10)

Kinds of group

There are numerous kinds of group to serve different purposes. One way to ensure that successful interaction occurs is to make the group match the purpose. Galton and Williamson (1992) identify a variety of groups, as shown in Table 4.3.

Bennett and Cass (1988) and Bennett and Dunne (1992) found task-related talk to be highest in cooperative groups. The following types of group were used by teachers in the National Oracy Project:

- Friendship
- Mutual interest
- Mixed interest
- Targeted (jigsaw/rainbow)
- Mixed attainers
- Selected attainers
- Single gender
- Mixed gender

In the UK, Bennett and Cass (1988) studied the effects of group work on high, average and low attaining pupils and found that high attainers performed well, irrespective of the kind of group they were in. However, low attaining groups fared badly, confirming other research which suggests that low attainers seem to lack the necessary skills to interact and learn effectively in groups. Homogeneous grouping according to achievement is a feature of the NLSF that has drawn criticism from primary teachers, used to operating with heterogeneous groups. Such resistance is based largely on the suggestion that teachers who group children according to attainment create unequal social structures within their classrooms. Cairney and Langbien (1989) state that low achieving groups are *interrupted* far more frequently by teachers than are high achievers. The perception of teachers interacting with children and intervening in their learning as *interruption* is an unfortunate legacy of Piagetian thinking. The reason for grouping children according to their attainment and educational needs is so that learning objectives, resources and teacher input can be matched appropriately in order to meet those needs most effectively. It seems positively bizarre to recognize that children have different needs but not to differentiate in terms of teacher support. What teacher, with a class of beginning, intermediate and advanced swimmers, would not allocate them to different parts of the pool and provide differentiated activities and support? What is important is for groups to be organized flexibly and according to children's needs, rather than rigidly and as an organizational expediency.

Gender differences

They [pupils] should be taught to listen to others, questioning them to clarify what they mean, and extending and following up the ideas. They should be encouraged to qualify or justify what they think after listening to other opinions or accounts, and deal politely with opposing points of view.

(DfEE 1995a: AT1)

The National Oracy Project found gender differences between the discourse patterns of boys and girls, confirming the findings of other research (Galton *et al.* 1980; Swann 1992). Norman (1990: 22) claims that 'boys tend to talk more, interrupt more and be more aggressive while girls defer to others' ideas and are more tentative'. It was found that boys often speak in a challenging, confronting way and girls in a comforting reassuring way, indicating that girls tend to criticize others in more socially acceptable ways. Tann (1981) found that girls tended to be more consensus-seeking than boys and would refrain from challenging or critically evaluating each other's views. Phillips (1988) showed that while boys frequently deviated from a task, girls tended to remain on task and, in mixed gender groups, were often the ones to adopt a steering, focusing role. Moreover, Holden (1993) found that girls used a far higher proportion of abstract language when engaged in English tasks than did boys.

Gender differences are particularly noticeable when children work in pairs around a computer. Boys will tend to dominate an activity and assume control of the 'technology'. Video recording of children in National Oracy Project schools illustrated that, during computer-based activities, even where boys were contributing little to a discussion, they invariably took up a central seating position and retained ownership of the keyboard. Baddeley (1991) points to the danger of over-generalization with regards to gender issues and asserts that some boys will be quiet and unassertive and some girls will confidently hold their own. Nevertheless, the general decrease in quantity and depression of quality of girl's talk in mixed gender groups is a matter of concern.

Computers and group work

There is some evidence to suggest that computers can promote discussion and encourage collaborative learning (King 1989; Mercer and Fisher 1992; Fisher 1993; Hill and Browne 1994). However, such evidence is not conclusive. Although computers may have the potential for offering collaborative learning contexts, merely providing computers and software in classrooms will not automatically enhance the quality of children's interaction. While computers can generate a high level of on task talk, much of this talk reflects *procedural* ways of thinking. For example, Kumulainen (1994: 51) found that 'the Imaginative, Hypothetical, Experiential and Heuristic functions hardly occurred in children's language interactions at the word processor'. Fisher (1993) found that rather than redrafting significant features of their work, children focused mainly on editorial features of spelling and punctuation, while Mercer (1994: 29) suggests that 'discrete, serial, closed problem-solving tasks generate very little extended continuous discussion of any kind'. Computers, therefore, far from encouraging exploratory talk, can produce a didactic, instructional learning context, where children are offered a very limited set of feedback responses.

The Spoken Language and New Technology (SLANT) Project examined how primary children use talk when they are seated around computers. A major conclusion was that the success or failure of computer-based talk depends more on the quality of teacher–pupil interaction than on the nature of the software or on child–computer interaction. Mercer and Fisher (1992: 354) claim that although the quality of computer software is important, it is the joint activity of teachers and pupils that will determine the quality of the learning.

They suggest that:

the main defining influence on the structure and outcomes of a computer-based activity will be that of the teacher, through any initial 'setting up' of the activity, through the nature of the interventions he or she makes during the activity, and through the ways (before and after the time spent at the screen) that pupils are enabled to relate the activity to other educational experiences.

For computers to generate interactive discourse, teachers need to:

- choose software carefully to ensure that high quality feedback is offered to children;
- establish learning contexts which encourage exploration and collaboration;
- provide a seating arrangement that is likely to aid collaborative talk;
- ensure that children understand the ground rules for group work;
- develop discursive strategies so that children are able to hypothesize, reason and justify;
- make explicit the purpose and collaborative nature of the activity;
- intervene effectively once activities are under way.

The Talk, Reasoning and Computers (TRAC) Project (Wegerif and Mercer 1996) has confirmed that children who understand and can implement ground rules for collaborative discussion can use spoken language more effectively as a learning tool. My own experience confirms the view that the learning potential of computers for collaborative work is significantly diminished if children are unable to implement essential ground rules for cooperative learning. Computer activities do have the potential to generate talk, but work around a computer amplifies the need for children to possess essential group work strategies and metadiscoursal skills.

Group work strategies

Team–games–tournament (TGT)

TGT is a cooperative/competitive technique, where the purpose of the team is to prepare individual members for a tournament to be held later. Children are initially organized into heterogeneous, mixed ability home group teams. The groups are then provided with material to learn in preparation for the tournament. For the tournament, the class is reorganized into ability groups (ability is determined by past performance). Children compete in the tournament as representatives of their home group. The teacher aggregates tournament scores to find the highest scoring team and the highest individual scorers. Slavin (1983a) argues that because children are ability-grouped for the tournament they all have an equal chance of success.

Student teams achievement divisions (STAD)

STAD involves assigning children to heterogeneous groups or teams. A learning task is introduced to the whole class by the teacher and groups then work collaboratively. However, although the children collaborate in learning, the outcome is evaluated in terms of individual responses, which are then collated to gain a group score. Although this approach can raise motivation and encourage cooperation and interdependency, it can place undue stress on children and raise levels of anxiety.

The jigsaw technique

TGT and STAD are techniques that have been researched and used in American schools and have an element of competitiveness which many teachers have found to be counter-productive to collaborative group work in the long term. A variety of other organizational strategies were adopted and developed by teachers in the National Oracy Project. One of the most successful of these was the jigsaw technique. This is a method of working which helps to ensure that all group members participate in an activity by establishing three very important things:

- a group goal;
- individual targets;
- individual responsibility and accountability.

Children are organized initially into home groups. Each group member then takes responsibility for investigating a particular aspect of the task. The children are then reorganized into expert groups to focus on their specific area of work. This can take the form of fact finding, research or investigation, or it can be to discuss an issue from a particular perspective. The children eventually return to the home groups to report their findings and to offer individual contributions towards the group goal. The home group finally completes the task. The procedure is as follows:

- Organize the class into home groups, preferably of equal numbers.
- Number each child in the home group: for example, 1 – 2 – 3 – 4. If the numbers in a group are uneven, two children can be set the same individual task: for example, 1 – 2 – 3 – 4 – 4.
- Assign each child to one area for investigation. (This may be negotiated within the group, or the teacher may have to direct the children.)
- The children now form expert groups.
- Expert groups undertake investigations, discuss their work and agree on the main points to report back to the home group.
- Children reform into their home groups and each individual member reports back on the findings of the expert group.

An example of a jigsaw based around reading and writing non-fiction might be:

Task: to produce an information booklet about the Romans
Sources: James, S. (1994) *Ancient Rome* (Eyewitness Guide). London: Dorling Kindersley.

Marsden, B. (1994) *Roman Invaders and Settlers*. Hove: Wayland.

Whittock, M. (1996) *Living in Roman Britain*. London: Heinemann.

Williams, B. (1994) *Roman Britain 55BC–AD406*. London: Hamlyn.

Possible areas for investigation might be:

- Emperors and army
- Houses, homes and family life
- Roads, transport and trade
- Food, pastimes and entertainment
- Gods, worship and burial
- Citizens and slaves

The jigsaw technique has proved popular in the UK because it offers structure to investigative learning and, while demanding individual responsibility, it stresses cooperation rather than competition. The process also helps to consolidate individual learning by requiring children to report on their findings. It is often said that 'to teach is to learn' and in having to explain to peers, children have to clarify and organize or reorganize their thoughts and evaluate what they know and understand. Webb (1989) found that in reporting to peers and having to respond to questions, children are encouraged to reflect on their own learning and to evaluate their own understanding. The work of Lyle (1993) supports the results of the National Oracy Project, which reported that 'group talk can place pupils where they represent and make explicit their thinking to others; encouraging pupils to cross question each other about their work may result in a clearer definition of meanings' (Des Fountain and Howe 1992: 146).

Snowballing

Children are organized to discuss something or to investigate an issue in pairs. The pairs then join another pair to form a group and to share their findings. The small groups then join together to make a larger one: for example 2 – 4 – 8 – 16 – whole class plenary. This approach can be useful when controversial material is being read and evaluated, perhaps for bias or for portraying stereotypical images.

Think–pair–share

Children are asked to consider an issue or problem individually. They then explain their ideas to a partner. After the pairs have discussed the issue, they may join another pair, share views and emerge with a group conclusion or perspective. This approach can be used effectively for activities such as reading and preparing a response to an information text, or preparing a news item to be read aloud.

Rainbowing

Each member of a working group is given a colour. When the group task is complete the children form new groups according to their colours. Within the colour groups, children compare findings/discuss what they have achieved. This is a useful way of disseminating and sharing ideas. As with the jigsaw technique, it also helps children to clarify their own understandings and provides an opportunity for them to question others and to seek justification for any viewpoints. This technique can be useful for reading and critical evaluation of interpretative material, such as a poem or extract from a text. It can also be used for drafting and redrafting. For example, children can work on the beginning of a story in one group and then in their colour group, pool ideas and draw out the best features. The process can then be repeated for the next phase of a story.

Dyads

Working in pairs is particularly useful for young children who may find group work too demanding. Teachers in the National Oracy Project found that Year R and Year 1 children usually worked more effectively in pairs than in groups. Pair work can take place within group work as a means of division of labour, where the group subdivides in order to investigate a particular aspect of a topic. Each pair then feeds their information into the group effort.

Triads

Children work in threes, with each person taking on the role of either talker, questioner or notetaker. The talker expounds on an issue or explains some work that may have been undertaken either individually, with a partner or within a group. The questioner helps the talker by prompting, through seeking expansion, clarification and so on. The notetaker records the main points to emerge and reports back to the talker and questioner. This can often help to crystallize issues and enable talkers to consolidate their own learning.

Envoys

This is a method of disseminating ideas and information which can overcome the more laborious and repetitive procedure of having each group 'report back' to the whole class. Each group sends out one person as an envoy to another group. Envoys move from group to group explaining/sharing ideas gathered from each group they have visited.

Developing metadiscoursal skills

General rules for group work need to be supplemented by developing children's awareness of the roles they can play in discussion and the features of talk which are helpful and productive or unhelpful and unproductive. An essential element of successful group work therefore is the development of children's metadiscoursal awareness: that is, their understanding of group interaction and their ability to monitor, control and reflect on their own use of language. Unfortunately, ground rules often remain implicit, possibly as a result of primary teachers' unwillingness to 'impose' on the children's understanding of the world. However, as Edwards and Mercer (1987: 59) argue, 'there is no reason why children's acquisition of the modes of discourse and thought required by education should entail their loss of other, "real world" perspectives'. Hardman and Beverton (1993: 147) argue for the development of a metalanguage, which they say will enable children to 'reflect upon and evaluate their own discussions and increase their understanding of what the characteristic features of talk are and how they contribute to discussion'. According to Bruner (1986) it is this process of objectifying in language what we have thought, and then turning around on it and reconsidering it, that allows us to develop our understanding.

As a National Oracy Project coordinator, I worked with a teacher and her class of 39 Year 3 children in a city primary school. The class could euphemistically be described as 'challenging' and the teacher was concerned that the children might not possess the necessary social skills to enable them to engage in effective discourse. We embarked on a consciousness raising exercise and undertook the activities described on pages 88–9 to develop the children's understanding and appreciation of group work. They had tape-recorded themselves during discussions and critically evaluated the results. With the help of the teacher, the children had then drawn up their own set of ground rules. The following extract is a two-minute snapshot taken from a total discussion which lasted for 18 minutes before the teacher intervened, and continued for a further 16 minutes following her intervention. The children have been looking at various interpretations of *The Three Little Pigs* story. The class has been organized into small groups and each group has been given the task of discussing and designing a house to be built in a particular material. The material this group has to work with is straw.

Activity

- Read the transcript individually and make notes on anything you find interesting.

- Discuss with a colleague or colleagues what you think these children have learned about working in a group.
- Discuss Martin's role in the discussion.
- Identify any utterances that you feel are particularly significant.

1	*Kerry:*	The door's here like this . . . the straw's got to go round the window.
2	*Leslie:*	The straw's got to go round it hasn't it 'cos it isn't a square door.
3	*Carl:*	Yeah . . . no . . . but . . . [all the children start to talk at once].
4	*Martin:*	Just wait a minute and listen to Carl's advice.
5	*Carl:*	Well . . . the door'll have to be that high and then the window'll have to come about there [indicates on the drawing].
6	*Katy:*	I haven't had a speak yet.
7	*Martin:*	Right . . . Kate . . . see what you can say.
8	*Katy:*	Well do you want me to tell you what you can do for the knob . . . just curl some of the straw around tight and put it in . . . make a space . . . [all the children start to talk at once].
9	*Martin:*	Come on . . . let's listen to Kerry.
10	*Kerry:*	Could've been a bit of wool there rolled up.
11	*Leslie:*	Or we could have a piece of cotton wool.
12	*Sarah:*	Cotton wool . . . cotton wool's better.

[The discussion continues until the children's attention is focused on the roof.]

13	*Sarah:*	What we could do round there is get a piece of straw and make it stronger . . . right?
14	*Leslie:*	Show us.
15	*Martin:*	Straw . . . you mean tons of straw just bungled together?
16	*Sarah:*	No . . . I mean like a piece of strong straw that isn't bent and we can tie it round with the straw on the roof.
17	*Kerry:*	Like that [demonstrates with a piece of straw]?
18	*Leslie:*	Yeah . . . I've got a book . . . she's right . . . she's right . . . it is like that.
19	*Kerry:*	It's not very good for tying round is it?
20	*Sarah:*	Yeah but you could get a long piece of paper and colour it an orange brown and tie it round.

[The teacher now joins the group.]

21	*Teacher:*	How are you doing?
22	*Martin:*	We're still thinking about the door handle.
23	*Leslie:*	Because we don't know if it's card or wood.

24	*Sarah:*	We could have a bit of tissue paper or straw.
25	*Teacher:*	What do you think about a wooden door?
26	*Leslie:*	Oh yeah, a wooden door.
27	*Carl:*	A wooden door . . . how'd we do that?
28	*Teacher:*	Do you want to have a look in the books we took the story from?
29	*All:*	Yeah.
30	*Teacher:*	Sit where you are and I'll bring them to you.

Martin is obviously playing a leading role in the discussion. When the teacher and I first viewed the video recording, our initial thoughts were that Martin was dominating the discussion. However, after we had analysed the entire transcript, it became clear that he was actually preventing another group member (Leslie) from doing just that. Most of Martin's gatekeeping utterances are not to hold the floor for himself, but to let others in. Without his intervention it is likely that some group members, such as Carl and Kerry, would have been marginalized if not excluded. The maturity of Martin's interjections is impressive: for example he brings the group to order and offers the floor to Carl (4). He brings in Kate (7) and Kerry (9) and invites Sarah to expand on her idea (15). The teacher's intervention is also interesting. She recognizes the children have reached a point in the discussion where they need some guidance. She identifies the problem, ascertains their need, and with the minimum of fuss, equips them with the necessary resources to continue unaided for a further extended period.

It is worth reiterating that this group of Year 3 children were part of a class of 39 pupils in a city school. The class included one statemented child and a number with special educational needs. Small group interaction in this classroom is successful because the teacher:

- negotiates with her class the ground rules for group work;
- develops children's metadiscoursal skills and awareness;
- presents the group with appropriate tasks which require collaboration;
- is aware of group dynamics in formulating groups;
- makes the purpose of tasks explicit to the children;
- provides adequate resources;
- intervenes appropriately and effectively.

Small group work within a constructivist framework for learning

Building upon the work of others (Reid *et al.* 1982; Scott *et al.* 1987), the National Oracy Project adopted a useful theoretical framework in which individual, pair, group and whole class work all had a part to play:

- *Engagement or orientation:* arousing interest and establishing the topic, issue or problem to be investigated. Teacher and children establish existing knowledge and understandings. New information and stimulus is provided.

- *Exploration or elicitation:* relating existing knowledge and understanding to new information and stimulus. Clarifying existing beliefs, feelings and understandings.
- *Transformation or restructuring:* engaging in activity in which the learners extend their knowledge and understanding. Investigating, exploring and evaluating ideas.
- *Presentation and review:* Offering new knowledge and understanding to a critical audience. Reviewing and evaluating the learning experience.
- *Reflection and application:* Thinking and talking about what has been learned and considering how previous understanding has changed. Considering ways in which new understanding will impact on future learning.

It was recognized that at each stage the children may be working individually, in pairs, in small groups or as a whole class. The stage of engagement refers to the initial focusing of attention on a particular topic, issue or problem. During the exploration stage the children will be having their attention focused on the subject to be studied. They may be sharing a common experience which could involve listening to the teacher, watching a video, or going on a visit. At the transformation stage, children may be organized in several ways depending on the nature of the task. The teacher's main purpose should be to provide an opportunity for children to use the ideas and concepts that have been explored and to share their understanding of these in some way, perhaps through a jigsaw activity. It is at the exploration and transformation stages that the kind of investigative, hypothetical language, so crucial to the construction of meaning, is most prominent. The presentation stage offers children a chance to gain feedback through constructive criticism and evaluation. This can occur on a one-to-one basis between children, between teacher and child, within a whole class scenario, or through the envoy system. During the reflection stage, children need to be given space and time to consider their own learning and to identify areas for clarification and development. Table 4.4 shows pupils going through the different stages as they investigate the language of advertisements.

This learning framework proved to be of immense value when members of the National Oracy Project were attempting to analyse audio and video recordings of small group interactions and teacher intervention. Initially the general focus of attention was on the nature of activities and children's interaction, either without the teacher's presence or with minimal teacher intervention. However, it became increasingly clear that the teacher has a crucial and central part to play in scaffolding children's learning. As children's needs are diverse and dependent on their stage in the learning process, appropriate teaching roles will vary, with different roles being 'more' or 'less' appropriate at any particular time. Failure to recognize this repertoire of roles and to intervene, as and when necessary, limits teachers' effectiveness as enablers of children's learning.

Table 4.4 Example of learning stages in developing knowledge about the language of advertising

Learning stage	Explanation	Example
Engagement or orientation	Pupils encounter new information or material. This could be through teacher talk, reading, listening to radio or watching TV extracts, examination of texts from a variety of sources, a field trip or a visiting speaker.	Teacher introduces the idea of examining radio advertisements. Pupils record examples of radio advertisements on tape in order to investigate and evaluate the persuasive language used.
Exploration or elicitation	This involves giving pupils time and a structure to enable them to make sense of the information for themselves. Small group discussion is vital at this stage.	In groups pupils listen to their recorded advertisements. They discuss and evaluate the language used. Pupils choose one example to play to the other groups giving reasons for their choice.
Transformation or restructuring	Pupils are required to focus their thinking, sort out their ideas, make decisions and use their knowledge.	In the same groups, and bearing in mind the radio advertisements they have heard, pupils decide on an imaginary item to sell, its uses and sales points. Pupils produce a radio advertisement for their product.
Presentation and review	This is the stage when ideas are presented to an interested audience. It could be a presentation to the whole class or it could be pairs, pairs–groups, groups etc.	Each group plays its advertisement to other groups and answers questions from peers about the product and the way they chose to advertise it.
Reflection and application	This is a time for considering what groups have been doing, how the work went and the final outcome. Decisions may be made about follow-up work.	The teacher discusses with each group how they collaborated, the nature of their advertisement and how each person contributed to it. The teacher also explores with the group reasons for language choice and register.

Conclusion

In this chapter I have looked at issues relating to small group interaction and examined some techniques for developing cooperative group work. Ways of structuring activities to ensure maximum pupil participation and motivation have been explored. However, although the planning and structuring of activities is important, it is how teachers establish reciprocal climates for learning and how they interact with pupils during activities that significantly affects processes and outcomes. The roles that teachers play and the way their own use of language impacts on the learning context is examined in Chapters 5 and 6.

⑤ ○ The role of the teacher

Teacher dominated discourse

Barnes (1976) illustrated the importance of pupils being allowed to use spoken language to orientate existing knowledge to new observations, and he showed how the nature of tasks and audiences shaped pupils' responses. However, numerous studies (Bellack *et al.* 1966; Amidon and Hunter 1967; Sinclair and Coulthard 1975; Hargie 1978; Edwards 1980) have revealed the predominance of an asymmetrical discourse sequence in the classroom, with the teacher occupying the dominant role of expert. The teacher *initiates* the discourse with a question, the student *responds* with an answer and the teacher provides feedback in the form of an *evaluation*. It is the tendency of teachers to make the first and third moves in the (I-R-E) exchange that makes classroom discourse so distinctive.

In the following example, the children's answers are characteristically short as they attempt to guess what the teacher has in mind:

1   *Teacher:* So what do we call this?
2   *David:* Ermm . . . a slab.
3   *Teacher:* No, not a slab.
4   *Rachel:* A rafter.
5   *Teacher:* Not quite.
6   *Anna:*   A tile.
7   *Teacher:* So what do we call it? It's a corner . . . ?
8   *Helen:* A corner tile.
9   *Teacher:* A corner tile. Well done Helen.

When the pupil's response is well outside the teacher's acceptable parameters, she evaluates with an emphatic 'no' (3). If the answer is a little closer to what she will accept, she provides feedback in the form of a prompt such as 'not quite' (5), or by providing a starter for the pupil to complete such as 'So what do we call it? It's a corner . . . ?' (7). When the answer is acceptable, the teacher provides a positive evaluation through praise (9).

This kind of interaction has been contrasted with that of open group discussions which are reflective and hypothetical, where speech is tentative and exploratory and where pupils are prepared to take risks and to share their thoughts. Barnes argues that pupils in small group learning situations are more likely to enter into the heuristic mode of speech identified by Halliday (1969). The deficiency of an I-R-E pattern is that the exchange does not encourage active engagement in the learning process. Children become passive recipients and do not use language to explore, investigate, challenge, evaluate and actively engage in the construction of meaning. The I-R-E teacher–pupil exchange is a major feature of 'transmission' teaching (see Table 1.1, Chapter 1, p. 6), where there is closed rather than open discussion and where teachers are concerned with the acquisition of 'school knowledge'. Barnes describes school knowledge as that learned for a school purpose such as a test and quickly forgotten, in contrast to 'action knowledge', which is incorporated into a pupil's existing model of the world and which can be used to construct new meaning.

Progressive ideology

In Chapter 1 it was suggested that primary school pedagogy has been shaped by a Piagetian perspective which places the child at the centre of learning. The term 'child centred' has been used to describe individualized, investigative learning, emanating from a progressive educational philosophy. The term is plausible and attractive, since few people are likely to suggest that children are not at the centre of their own learning or that we should have a regressive educational philosophy. Thus began the marginalization of the teacher in primary education and a belief that children will develop knowledge and understanding most effectively if 'left alone' to explore, hypothesize, investigate and discover things for themselves. As Piaget (1970: 715) said: 'Each time one prematurely teaches a child something he could have discovered himself, the child is kept from inventing it and consequently from understanding it completely'. Throughout the 1970s and 1980s, primary teachers became 'facilitators'. The explicit and systematic teaching of English became taboo, with, as Barton (1998: 110) says, 'even the best English teachers discussing grammar teaching as if confessing a shameful act'. However, the ascent of Vygotskian theory and constructivist principles in the 1990s has helped to reassert the position of the teacher, not as a transmitter of information or a filler of empty vessels but as a significant participant, working and interacting with children in the learning process. This view is supported by research in Britain and the USA which has examined the efficacy of the teacher's role in primary practice, and raised concern over the quality of teacher–pupil discourse.

The ORACLE Project (Galton *et al*. 1980) found that pupils gave limited responses to the mainly closed questions posed by teachers and rarely initiated their own questions or explored issues. The survey did find the organization of the primary classroom had changed from the traditional organization of rows to small groups. However, work was largely undertaken individually and independently, with teacher intervention normally restricted to the provision of information or correction of work. The 1999 survey (see Galton *et al*. 1999) reports that, rather than finding an improvement in the quality of teacher–pupil interaction, there is now less emphasis on active learning and more time spent on direct instruction.

Edwards and Mercer (1987) set out to investigate classrooms which claimed to be influenced by progressive child-centred pedagogy and discovered that although many teachers espoused Piagetian theory their practices did not reflect this position. Teachers had their own agendas in terms of the knowledge they wished to transmit, but these were concealed behind 'pseudo-discovery' activities. This created an ambivalence which often resulted in inefficient and ineffective teacher–pupil discourse and a lack of shared understanding between teachers and pupils about the purpose of activities:

> Teachers may not be completely unaware of ground rules, nor be keeping them tacit in order to maintain authority, but instead they believe that a good teacher should not need to make such things explicit, and will gain nothing by doing so. According to this ideology, successful teaching is the creation of successful learning environments; if tasks, activities and lessons are well conceived, then children will learn. What is more, they will learn as is appropriate to their developmental stage; the activities will 'bring out' what they have. Meta-level discussions of what is the purpose of it all, or in which specific concepts are abstractly defined, will constrain or confuse them.
>
> (Edwards and Mercer 1987: 60)

Social constructivism: a way forward

Social constructivism offers a way out of the entrenched polarized positions of transmission and progressive approaches (the 'ideological tightrope' described by Alexander (1988)). Between the traditional teaching role (with the teacher as instructor–transmitter) and the progressive role (with the child as explorer–discoverer), there is a range of potential teacher–pupil relationships that elicit different teacher–pupil responses and engender different discourse patterns. Wells and Chang (1988) refer to the need for teachers to 'act contingently', which means being prepared and able to adopt appropriate teaching roles and to interact with children according to their learning needs on different occasions. This preparedness to act contingently is the essence of constructivist learning, and is absolutely essential if teachers are to scaffold children's learning successfully. However, acting contingently does not mean responding instantly to every pupil's immediate request. Individualized teaching and learning is practically unworkable and theoretically undesirable. The essence of constructivist learning is that pupils will gain through social interaction with others, where they share perceptions, extend their knowledge base and develop conceptual understanding through being exposed to other, sometimes conflicting, views of the world.

Intervention in teaching literacy

> Successful teaching, whether with the whole class, smaller groups or individuals, depends on certain essential factors. These include the quality of the teacher's explanations, clarity and structure of speech, the skilled construction and use of questions, and the ability to engage children in intensive discussion of increasingly complex ideas.
>
> (HMI 1990: 32)

Research by Mortimore *et al.* (1988) and Tizard *et al.* (1988) found that schools tended to be effective or ineffective, irrespective of children's home backgrounds. Their findings that school and teacher variables appeared to be more important in determining achievement suggest there are 'more' or 'less' efficient teaching strategies and that teacher intervention plays a significant role in determining children's progress. Such evidence would support the need for a carefully planned and structured approach to teaching, where children are made aware of the nature and purpose of activities, and where the learning is systematic and well-managed to ensure effective progress. Studies in the USA have also focused on the role of the teacher in scaffolding children's learning. McMahon and Goatley (1995), commenting on the Book Project, point to the importance of skilled teacher intervention during group reading while Palinscar and Brown (1984) demonstrate the potential of structured intervention in developing children's reading comprehension.

To summarize, therefore, evidence from HMI surveys and classroom research has illustrated the need for:

- carefully planned, focused activities;
- effective interactive discourse;
- skilled teacher intervention;
- systematic diagnosis and evaluation.

The dilemma facing many teachers is of maintaining some notion of child-centredness when teaching within a structured literacy hour, which requires them to focus their time and energy in a systematic way. The issue is not irreconcilable. In a social constructivist model of teaching and learning, the child lies at the heart of the process and must develop knowledge and understanding in relation to existing conceptions. For effective teaching and learning to occur, teachers need to:

- identify children's current levels of understanding;
- determine appropriate next steps in the learning process;
- plan suitable activities (learning experiences);
- scaffold the learning through quality interaction and skilled intervention;
- consolidate and reinforce learning;
- monitor progress.

The fact that children occupy a central position does not mean that teachers should abdicate responsibility, refrain from having an agenda, or be afraid to interject. Rather than thinking in terms of teachers having to suppress their expertise, it is more useful to consider ways in which teachers can best use their expertise to develop that of the children. The term 'child centred' has polarized opinions, aroused emotions and hindered rational thinking. It has focused attention on teaching styles rather than effective practices and strategies. Teaching is not merely about transmitting information, nor is it about standing back while children struggle to discover things for themselves. It is about understanding how children learn, creating interactive learning environments and intervening appropriately. As Edwards (1992: 240) states, 'the empowering of pupils is obviously not all or nothing, but temporary and provisional'. My work with teachers, both during and since the National Oracy Project, indicates that when expertise is dispersed a wide range of roles and relationships become possible.

As Table 5.1 indicates, effective teaching and learning requires teachers to move in and out of different roles. In looking at early literacy and the teacher, Fisher (1992) suggests that we should not ignore the role of the teacher as instructor, and she identifies the additional roles of facilitator, model, manager and assessor. The non-statutory guidance in *English in the National Curriculum: Key Stage One* (DES 1989) outlines a variety of roles when teaching reading and writing. For reading, the teacher should be:

- a responsive and interested listener to children's reading of their own writing and chosen texts;
- an organizer of opportunities to read with other adults and children;
- a partner/guide in discussion of reading experience;
- a reader of books and children's own stories, in order to provide an example and encourage interest;

Table 5.1 Appropriate teacher intervention

Learning stage	Use of language	Appropriate teaching roles may be
Engaging with new information, experiencing new stimuli	Recalling Recounting Connecting	Expert Announcer Director Manager Negotiator Conductor
Exploration of new information, interaction of stimuli with existing knowledge/understanding	Exploring Expounding Questioning Speculating Hypothesizing	Facilitator Provider Collaborator Arbitrator Chairperson Learner
Reshaping existing knowledge/understanding	Arguing Challenging Reasoning Justifying	Counsellor Scaffolder
Overt representation of new learning	Explaining Narrating Describing	Evaluator Critic
Reflection and self-analysis	Evaluating	Consolidator Confidant

- a support, helping children to use all the available cues to making sense of their reading;
- a monitor of reading development;
- a recorder of progress.

For writing, the teacher should be:

- an organizer of adults other than teachers who can work alongside children, 'scribing' for them, or using a keyboard, enabling them to compose at greater length than they could on their own;
- an editorial consultant;
- a praiser of achievement;
- an example of adult writing behaviour;
- a setter of standards;
- a recorder of progress;
- a monitor of learning development.

Teacher as expert: the importance of subject knowledge

In Chapter 4 it was suggested that active participation and the posing of questions by pupils is a key feature of critical reading and writing. However, the teacher has a major part to play in nurturing such productive discourse and facilitating pupil participation. Following the work of the Writing, Oracy and LINC Projects in England and Wales (1987–93) and that of Palinscar and Brown (1984) and Graves and Graves (1994) in the USA, the teaching strategies of modelling and demonstrating as ways of drawing children's attention to the structures and organizational features of language have become more prominent. Other research (Bennett and Carre 1993; Wray 1993; Wragg 1994) has indicated that for such support strategies to be effectively implemented, teachers need to possess a level of subject knowledge that will enable them to:

- diagnose difficulties or misconceptions and areas for clarification;
- identify teaching points and areas for development;
- make informed choices in terms of content and presentation of knowledge;
- devise appropriate activities;
- engage in productive interactive discourse.

The success of the NLS depends heavily on the skills and knowledge of primary teachers: 'The ability of primary teachers to teach literacy is by far the most important factor in whether or not children read and write well. If all primary school pupils are to read and write well, then all primary teachers need to learn how to teach literacy well' (DfEE 1997: 19). The DfEE (1998a: C9) emphasizes the need for primary teachers to have a sufficient grasp of subject knowledge in English to enable them to 'feel confident in those aspects of English which they have studied and which they are required to teach'. The document (*Teaching: High Status, High Standards*) is explicit in detailing the knowledge about language that trainee teachers should have before they may attain qualified teacher status. The National Curriculum (DfEE 1995a) and the NLSF (DfEE 1998b) have increased the demand for an adequate level of subject knowledge, particularly in regard to aspects of grammar, standard and non-standard English and language study. However, various reports (Ofsted 1993, 1995, 1996a; DfEE 1995b) have suggested that the inadequate subject knowledge of many primary teachers is a matter of concern. This concern was shared by Raban *et al.* (1994: 106–25) in their evaluation of the implementation of English in the National Curriculum. They found that teachers were uncertain about what the term *knowledge about language* actually meant, and many expressed a lack of confidence about teaching theoretical aspects of language, saying that they lacked the necessary expertise. For example, more than half the Key Stage 2 teachers in Raban *et al.*'s inquiry did not have an informed understanding of the concept of spoken formal English. Ofsted (1996a) confirmed that the inadequate level of teachers' subject expertise constitutes a serious problem.

Pedagogical subject knowledge

If teachers are to be successful in developing children's explicit awareness of knowledge about language and their understanding of the functions of parts of language, it seems desirable for them to possess that knowledge and explicit understanding themselves. HMI has consistently reported that in lessons where high standards are achieved, teachers have sound or good knowledge of the subject they are teaching (see Ofsted 1997: 6).

Although there is no automatic relationship between knowledge of a subject and the ability to teach it successfully, teachers do need to have a grasp of a subject in order to understand it in ways that will help their pupils learn. Shulman (1986) refers to this application of subject knowledge to the classroom as *pedagogical subject knowledge*. This includes an understanding of what makes the learning of specific topics easy or difficult; of how teachers can represent the subject in ways that make it comprehensible to the pupils; and of how they can diagnose the nature and source of misunderstandings. Most teachers possess an intuitive knowledge which may allow them to function adequately, but which does not equip them to analyse the reasons for errors in children's work or to offer adequate and appropriate support. It is the successful transformation of subject knowledge, for the purpose of teaching, that lies at the heart of pedagogical subject knowledge. As Chen and Ennis (1995: 389) point out, 'subject content knowledge is not taught in its original form'. During the process of transformation, the teacher may make choices, emphasize certain points and elaborate on others, reshape the knowledge to present it to the pupils in a manageable form, sequence it in particular ways and relate it to existing knowledge and understanding. Effective teaching therefore requires teachers to be able to make the transition from personal knowledge and understanding of a subject to the representation of that subject to their pupils.

It is generally recognized that children's knowledge about language should be developed explicitly and systematically. *Teaching: High Status, High Standards* (DfEE 1998a) stresses the need for planned activities which require pupils to be articulate, coherent and effective in standard English. The development of pupils' vocabulary is also a major concern, with an emphasis on the acquisition of subject-specific terminology and the ability to understand grammatical structures, to create coherent and cohesive texts and to discuss and evaluate different types of fiction, poetry and non-fiction texts. Having an adequate level of personal subject knowledge is not merely a matter of being informationally ahead of the pupils but of familiarity with the structure and processes which characterize English as a subject. Cox (1989: 6.3) argued that 'substantial programmes of teacher training are required if teachers are themselves to know enough to enable them to design with confidence programmes of study about language'. The confidence that would accrue from a sound subject knowledge base should equip teachers with the ability to make informed choices, to be creative and to develop stimulating learning environments. Without a fundamental grasp of those elements of language study that are expected to be taught in primary schools, there is a real danger of teachers relying on 'off the shelf' textbook activities and returning to the kind of arid decontextualized exercises described by the Bullock Report (DES 1975).

Carter (1990: 120) makes the point that 'a return to grammar is to be welcomed. But it will need to be a new-style grammar teaching, not an old-style grammar teaching'. If teachers are to deconstruct texts and develop children's knowledge and understanding of language during the literacy hour they need to be confident in their own subject knowledge. Excellent texts and material for professional development are now adding to the officially banned, but widely available, LINC resources (see Bunting 1997; NATE (National Association for the Teaching of English) grammar books, UKRA (United Kingdom Reading Association) publications and professional journals such as *Literacy & Learning* and *Primary English*). An analysis and evaluation of literature and an examination of the structure and organization of texts lies at the heart of the NLSF searchlight model. This offers a contextualized approach to the teaching of grammar where language is seen in use. Children are presented with models of texts which they can explore and interrogate. Working collaboratively with teachers and peers, pupils can examine the ways that authors use language and literary devices to create atmosphere, stimulate readers' interest and develop aspects of setting, character and plot. They can evaluate the accuracy and precision of texts, discuss irony, or detect bias.

Teachers using their expertise: scaffolding writers

Drawing on over ten years research, Bereiter and Scardamalia (1987) affirm the notion of 'reflective activity' in successful writers. Such writers, they argue, think aloud and:

- elaborate and reformulate their writing purposes and their plans for achieving these purposes;
- critically examine and revise their writing decisions;
- anticipate potential difficulties;
- make judgements and reconciliation between competing ideas;
- show an alertness to the needs of their potential and actual readership.

However, Bereiter and Scardamalia (1987) suggest that this kind of reflective activity is uncharacteristic of most primary age children, who tend not to explore options and possibilities, rarely place themselves in the reader's position and limit revisions to surface features. Fitzgerald (1987: 484) suggests that revision involves 'deciding what could or should be changed in the text and how to make desired changes, and operating, that is, making the desired changes'. Wells *et al.* (1990: 63) propose that 'by writing, reading and revising, and by discussing one's text with others, one can extend and refine one's knowledge in a conscious and deliberate manner'. They argue that the very act of composing requires children to systematically confront their own knowledge and to organize and shape the content of their work appropriately for the intended purpose and audience. Hayes *et al.* (1987) (cited in Wray 1994: 100), identify a range of revising strategies open to writers:

- ignore the difficulty, either because it is judged to be trivial or too difficult to overcome;
- suspend dealing with the problem until a later time as, for example, when a writer reads through a text to check specific details and notices a different kind of problem, making a mental note to deal with it later;
- look for further information, either in the text or in memory, in order to be able to deal with the identified problem;
- rewrite the text in order to preserve the idea expressed but not the means of its expression;
- revise the text to keep whatever can be saved.

Teachers need to help children develop a greater degree of conscious awareness of their thought processes while reading and writing. Explicit awareness raising and instructional practice (as demonstrated in the case study in Chapter 3) should be an essential ingredient of literacy teaching where children:

- are exposed to a range of good literary models;
- are made explicitly aware of the composing process;
- participate in focused discussion of texts (including their own and those of peers);
- develop process writing strategies;
- reflect on their own knowledge and strategies and evaluate their own progress.

And where teachers:

- model thinking and talking processes;
- demonstrate composing and redrafting processes;
- scaffold the learning through effective interactive discourse.

Scaffolding writers: case study

The NLSF (DfEE 1998b: 7) reiterates the National Curriculum (DfEE 1995a) requirement for children to be 'taught the underlying organizational ideas and terminology for talking about literature'. In this case study, the teacher is working with a Year 6 class to see if he can enable children to transfer the knowledge gained from the critical evaluation of texts during shared and guided reading sessions to their own writing. The development of a linguistic metalanguage enables the children to gain control over their own writing process. They move beyond description to analysis and conceptualization. They are able to discuss what they have written, how they have written it and what they might do to improve it.

Writing workshops (described in Chapter 3) have been organized to provide an environment where interactive peer–peer and teacher–pupil discourse can occur, and where children can draft and redraft work after gaining consultation and advice. Harris (1989: 8) suggests that 'the writing process can, in a simple way, be characterized as having three parts, bearing in mind, that these do not necessarily proceed in a linear way':

• pre-writing, involving research and planning;
• writing;
• revising and editing.

Successful writers will tend to:

• plan flexibly;
• review constantly;
• revise their original plan as they proceed;
• make more radical changes to their texts when revising.

Harris offers an applied model for process writing in the classroom:

Assembling strategies:	listing questions
	brainstorming
	mindmapping
	using grids
	plotting (narratives)
	diagramming, creating flowcharts and sketching
	researching and note-taking
Developing the text:	drafting
	revising (cut and paste)
	discussing collaboratively with peers/teacher
	reviewing text

Editing and proofreading: editing in groups
editing by self
proofreading

The suggestions that Harris (1989: 24) makes for developing writing indicate the value of collaboration and highlight the importance of interactive discourse between peers and between pupils and teachers. He suggests that 'a classroom in which the processes of writing are given due emphasis is likely to be a place in which many opportunities will occur or can be structured for valuable collaboration'. The teacher in this case study has established a system of response partners and editorial groups. This has encouraged productive peer–peer interaction and teacher–pupil conferences that provide an opportunity for valuable teacher–pupil discourse. Conferences allow the teacher to intervene effectively to support and extend the children's reading and writing. It is also through conferencing that the children can exhibit their current understanding.

Teacher–pupil conference

The extent of children's metalinguistic awareness becomes most apparent during teacher–pupil conferences when the teacher is able to make direct reference to specific stylistic choices children have made or to literary devices discussed in shared and guided reading sessions. In the following example Gareth is in the process of writing a story involving an animal as one of the main characters. He has written one draft and had a response from his response partner. The teacher recognizes that his intervention, at this stage, will probably prove useful in helping Gareth to develop his work.

Gareth is familiar with the story *Fair's Fair* (Garfield 1981) and in shared and guided reading time he has examined some of the literary devices used by Garfield. During these sessions, attention has been drawn to story openings and to different direct action and dialogue description techniques used by authors. During the conference, Gareth clearly transfers the knowledge and understanding acquired from his analysis of *Fair's Fair* and other texts to his own writing (see Figures 5.1–5.4).

> [The teacher reads the work.]
> *Teacher:* This is really good . . . what do you think . . . are you
> pleased with it?
> *Gareth:* Yeah it's OK but I think it's a bit short . . . I need more in it.
> *Teacher:* Which parts are you most pleased with?
> *Gareth:* The opening . . . how I've got the character right at the
> beginning . . . described him . . . a direct description right at
> the start.
> *Teacher:* Yes, it gets the reader's attention straight away, sort of
> grabs hold of you.

The opening of *Fair's Fair*

Jackson was thin, small and ugly and stank like a drain. He got his living by running errands and doing a bit of scrubbing on the side.

The opening of Gareth's story

'Grymer was short, round like a ball and had bandy legs that seemed to bend under his weight. He wore a scowl at all times and smoked a foul smelling pipe.

Figure 5.1 Story openings

Gareth: And then you can tell what he's like . . . from how he spits and he never says anything nice . . . and he's horrible to Patch . . . this bit here.

He spit all the time and never had a nice word to say about anyone. When he could not steal enough he had to work on the market carrying big pieces of meat on his back. Thats is why he always smelled so rotten.

There was a small black dog with a white patch over one eye who used to live around the market. People called him Patch and no one owned him but everyone used to give him bits of meat. Gymer pretended to give Patch some meat but would snatch it away at the last minute and Patch would go mad and start crying. The more patch cried the more Gaymer laughed

Figure 5.2 Story development

Teacher: I don't think you need to change the beginning . . . maybe . . . what about adding to the action description by having him talking to someone . . . you know . . . some dialogue description like Leon Garfield does in *Fair's Fair* with Jackson and Growler and Roald Dahl does with Mr and Mrs Twit?

Gareth: Mmm . . . you mean like showing he's horrible by saying
             something really nasty . . . mmm . . . like he calls her an old
             hag . . . yeah.

Following the discussion Gareth develops his story and uses dialogue description and colloquial language to develop Grymer's character (see Figure 5.3).
Gareth feels that his story is too short but he realizes that the answer is not
simply to write more. During shared and guided reading time the children
have examined different models of narrative schema, based for example on
those of Labov, Longacre and Hoey (see Harris 1993: 34–6). Because of
this, Gareth is not only aware of the need for a more complex schema, he is
also able to articulate his view and to discuss it with the teacher during the
conference.

'Give us a penny for the guy mister?" said Rosa.
'Whaddaya think my name is . . . Muggins?' snorted Grymer.
'Go on mister, its worth summat.'
'Shove off before I kick it.
'Let loose!' cried Rosa, it took me ages to make did this.'
Grymer's mouth twisted and he sneered, 'Well I'll
soon unmake it?

Figure 5.3   Developing Grymer's character

Gareth: Mmm . . . it's too short . . . there's not enough in it yet.
Teacher: What do you mean by enough?
Gareth: Mmm . . . it's got a good beginning but there's only one
             main thing that happens . . . only one happening.
Teacher: Yes there's just one main event at the moment . . . so you've
             got a simple story structure of beginning, middle and end.
Gareth: Yeah . . . I need some more events . . . more than just the
             one problem for solving.
Teacher: Yes, but not just a series of events . . . they need to be a
             gradual build up to the end don't they?
Gareth: Yeah . . . to a big ending . . . a climax.
Teacher: Leading finally to a resolution?
Gareth: Yeah, and then that's the end.

The discussion then focuses on Gareth's use of a particular literary device
which he has borrowed from Garfield.

'I'll get you', said Grymer, not in words but with his staring eyes and horrible mouth. ____
'Just you try', said patch, not in but with the way he growled

Figure 5.4 Use of literary devices modelled in *Fair's Fair*

Teacher: I like this . . . 'not in words but with his staring eyes and horrible mouth'.
Gareth: It's like . . . how the dog . . . talks to Jackson.
Teacher: Growler . . . yes.
Gareth: Yeah . . . 'cos animals don't really talk . . . like it says . . . not in words but . . . what it does . . . by what it does . . . by what it looks like.
Teacher: Through its actions and expressions you mean?
Gareth: Yeah . . . so you can believe it more than if it was an animal what talked.
Teacher: And you've used that for Grymer as well?
Gareth: Yeah, don't you think that's good? . . . I do.

Gareth now demonstrates his knowledge of different types of story. During an earlier shared reading session, pupils' attention had been drawn to the distinctive features of different kinds of narrative texts.

Teacher: So your story isn't anthropomorphic then?
Gareth: Emm . . . no 'cos it's an animal really . . . just an animal in the story . . . it isn't supposed to be like . . . a person . . . not like the animals in Farthing Wood . . . what's that called?
Teacher: Anthropomorphic.
Gareth: Yeah, mine's not that kind of story.
Teacher: No.
Gareth: No . . . mine's more like *Fair's Fair* . . . my story has to be read out loud . . . it's for telling . . . a person telling it . . . a storytape . . . I could do a storytape.

Making the implicit explicit

Bereiter and Scardamalia (1987) and Cairney (1990) found that primary age children were able to make intertextual links, or to borrow ideas and plots from literature, but were less likely to transfer more subtle stylistic elements into their own writing. However, through structured work during a literacy hour, where the teacher draws attention to the literary devices used by adult authors, children's writing skills can be developed. With direction from the teacher, providing models, demonstrating and drawing attention to the features and characteristics of a variety of stories, and through well-managed, focused group discussion, children can begin to develop their awareness of how texts are constructed. They can be familiarized with the literary devices used by successful adult authors and encouraged to adopt them in their own writing. A form of author mentorship can develop where children gradually come to internalize the scaffolding and transfer their new knowledge and understanding of texts and compositional techniques to their own writing.

One of the most striking features to emerge from this work was the way that children gradually developed a metalanguage and were able to use it effectively when discussing their own writing. The National Curriculum for English (DfEE 1995a: 14) requires that 'pupils should be introduced to the organizational, structural and presentational features of different types of text, and to some of the appropriate terms to enable them to discuss the texts they read, e.g. author, setting, plot, format'. The command of a metalanguage enabled children to identify, illuminate and focus on issues that were relevant to their writing. They were able to discuss their own work, relate it to texts they had experienced and discuss the appropriateness of using particular devices to extend and enhance their own work. The use of subject-specific terms helped the children to clarify their thoughts, identify issues and engage in lucid, focused discourse with each other and with the teacher. As Barnes and Sheeran (1992: 91) point out, 'If what distinguishes a subject is its distinctive conventions of thought and particular conceptions of phenomena, the task for teachers is to communicate those conventions as useful . . . ways of understanding the world'.

Gareth has clearly demonstrated:

- an explicit knowledge and awareness of literary devices;
- the use of a metalanguage to critically evaluate texts and to discuss his own writing;
- an ability to use literary devices consciously and appropriately in the creation of his own texts.

Scaffolding readers

Listening to children reading has, for many years, been common practice in primary schools. However, research (Lunzer and Gardner 1979; Arnold 1982; Ofsted 1996b) shows that it is more effective for teachers to allocate their time to listen to children read less often but with real purpose and with an emphasis on the quality of the experience rather than the quantity. Ofsted (1996b: 8–9) observed 'many sessions devoted to free reading with little or no intervention by the teacher which did not contribute much, if anything, to pupils' progress yet were lengthy, regular occurrences'. The report is critical of the daily ritual of listening to children read, stating that 'in general, teachers set too much store by this activity' (p. 15). It concludes that listening to children read is most successful when it is 'diagnostic and related to an effective recording system designed to correct pupils' errors through planned sequences of work' (p. 16).

Discourse in developing children's metacognitive awareness

If children are to become independent readers, they need to develop an explicit awareness of the processes and procedures they are going through as they read. Brown (1987) suggests that the acquisition of skills is not enough: children need to develop an understanding of when and how to apply various strategies. Shared and guided reading sessions offer teachers the opportunity to demonstrate reading strategies and model metacognitive processes. Paris *et al.* (1984) (cited in Wray 1994: 112) argue that children should have reading strategies explained to them. Five techniques for teaching are identified:

- *Informed teaching:* teachers explicitly told their children what a strategy involved, how it could be used and when and why they might use it.
- *Metaphors for strategies:* teachers compared particular reading strategies to other, real life activities; for example, preparing to read a passage was compared to planning a trip.
- *Group dialogue:* teachers encouraged groups of children to discuss what they were learning from particular texts and how they were approaching the reading.
- *Guided practice:* introduction of particular strategies was followed up by specially written worksheets in which children were asked to use the strategies.
- *Bridging:* teachers periodically led lessons in which strategies they had taught were applied to other kinds of text, drawn from a range of curriculum areas.

Palinscar and Brown (1984) looked at ways of improving text comprehension through 'strategy instruction'. They devised a system for encouraging children to interrogate text through a series of focusing steps which, in effect, help children to monitor their own learning:

- *Summarizing:* a self-review where children are asked to read (or reread) and summarize a text and to identify the main ideas and check their own understanding.
- *Questioning:* getting children to ask questions about the text, which encourages them to reread and to check their understanding of the content and the main ideas.
- *Clarifying:* children are asked to identify any problem areas or parts of a text they didn't understand and to take appropriate action; for example, rereading, reading 'around' the problem area, asking for assistance.

- *Predicting:* children are asked to make predictions based on their under-standing of the text they have read.

These structured teaching procedures are based on a Vygotskian apprentice-ship model of learning (see Chapter 1, Figure 1.1, p. 6). In this model the pupil moves from novice to expert through receiving explicit instruction in techniques that, when successfully applied, lead to independence. Rather than simply listening to children read, the teacher takes an active and positive approach. However, this does not elicit passive learning. On the contrary, through quality discourse, teacher and learner engage in a dynamic inter-active process, where the teacher's aim is not merely to teach the use of reading strategies but to develop an understanding of when and how to apply those strategies appropriately and effectively.

Shared reading

Shared reading can be done with an individual child, a small group or a whole class. There is nothing particularly innovative about the procedure. Holdaway (1979) advocated shared reading and it is what many parents have been doing for years. However, it is *how* the adult intervenes that really matters and Bruner's notion of scaffolding is central to the process of shared reading. With very young children, the adult may act as a model for reading and a child may simply follow the story, joining in occasionally. Stories which contain a repetitive element are especially useful because the child can hear particular sounds being repeated, see the word shapes and letter patterns, and predict – on the basis of a pattern that is repeated with only one or two words changed. Adults may also encourage and guide children as they attempt to read, or may explicitly point out certain features of the text. As children develop and become increasingly more independent, adults should gradually withdraw and allow the children to take over. Intervention might then take the form of a discussion or a simple appreciat-ive comment. Guppy and Hughes (1999: 49) discuss this gradual move towards independent reading. They refer to *cue talk*, which is described as the pivotal stage where 'the weight of responsibility tilts from adult to child', and to *assisted reading*, where the adult guides the child's choice of cues. Shared reading can also occur where one child who is a proficient reader scaffolds another.

Paired reading

Paired reading is a more structured form of shared reading with an indi-vidual child. It follows a definite procedure which both the adult and child agree to follow:

- choose a book that the child wants to read;
- before reading the general content might be discussed;
- the adult and child agree on a prearranged signal, such as a tap on the table, or a touch of an arm;
- the adult and child begin reading aloud together;
- when the child wishes to take over she or he gives the prearranged signal;
- the adult stops reading aloud;
- when the child makes an error (miscue) the adult says the correct word;
- the child repeats the word and then continues;
- if the child hesitates or struggles with a word the adult waits for about five seconds before supplying it;
- the adult and child then read together again until the child gives the signal for the adult to remain quiet.

A reading conference

Sometimes called a 'reading interview', a reading conference is where the teacher spends time with individual children to discuss their reading. It may involve listening to a child read and possibly conducting a running record or miscue analysis. However, its main purpose is to keep track of a child's reading development, to show a genuine interest and to offer guidance and assistance where necessary.

To conduct a reading conference:

- arrange a time with the child in advance;
- organize the class so that the conference can take place without interruption;
- arrange an area in the classroom for the conference to be held;
- try to familiarize yourself with some of the books the child has read;
- try to have some books the child has read at hand;
- prepare the resources, if you wish to conduct a running record;
- talk to the child in general about the books, their favourite authors, how they feel they are reading and so on;
- focus on particular books and ask questions about them;
- ask the child to choose a particular part of a book to read to you;
- offer guidance on further reading/recommend new authors;
- keep a record of the conference in the child's reading profile.

Example of a reading conference

Samantha is 9 years old but has a reading age of around 7. Given a free choice, she will select books well within her comfort zone. Her reading record shows a predilection for the *Postman Pat* series and for stories that contain animals, especially cats. The teacher has arranged to do a reading conference and has brought along some of the books Samantha has read. The teacher wants to induce Samantha to read a broader range of more challenging books that will develop her vocabulary, extend her reading skills and introduce her to different writing styles and story structures. However, Samantha does not find reading easy so the teacher has chosen texts that will interest Samantha and that she will be able to read with a little support.

T: What are you reading now Sam?
S: Postman Pat.
T: Which one this time? I should think you've read them all by now.
S: *Foggy Day.*
T: Pat's foggy day. Haven't you read that one before?
S: Mmm. I like it.
T: I like the way the cat . . . what's its name?
S: Jessie.
T: Yes, Jessie. The way Jessie hangs onto the inside of the door.
S: She sits on the seat in the front.
T: Oh yes, she does that as well. And I like Mrs Goggins and the farmer . . . um . . .
S: Alf Thompson.
T: Yes, Alf Thompson . . . why do you like Postman Pat stories so much Sam?
S: Mmm . . . don't know.
T: I like them because everything turns out right in the end.
S: Mmm.
T: Let's see, what did you read before that? [teacher looks at Samantha's record]
S: *The Beast in the Bathtub.*
T: What sort of a beast was it?
S: It's a . . . um . . . like a big green dragon . . . not a dragon but big and green and it was fat and it had a long tail and a funny face.
T: And what did it do?
S: It wasn't real . . . the story . . . it's about this little boy named Lewis and he makes it up.
T: He makes up the beast?
S: Yeah, he makes it up 'cos he doesn't want a bath . . . so he says there's a beast in the bath.
T: I've got the book here somewhere. What was your favourite bit in the story?
S: The pillow fight . . . where they had a pillow fight on the bed.
T: Can you find that bit and read it to me? [Samantha reads the page.] You read that really well Sam. Was that easy for you to read?

S: Yeah.

T: Yes, you read it beautifully. Then you read *The Post Office Cat* I see. What was that like? Did you read that OK?

S: Yeah . . . OK . . . some words were hard but it was OK.

T: Another story with cats in . . . do you like cats?

S: Mmm . . . we've got two cats . . . Tigger and Sprat.

T: Tell me about the *Post Office Cat* then. What's its name?

S: Clarence.

T: And what happens to Clarence? [Samantha tells the teacher the story.] That's a lovely story . . . I like that. Did you enjoy it?

S: Mmm . . . yeah.

T: I know a good story about a cat. His name is Sampson and he lives in a church. I think you'll enjoy it. I want you to read it for me and tell me what you think. Do a report on it for me. Will you do that?

S: Mmm.

T: Good girl. OK, here it is. That's Sampson . . . and the mouse . . . that's Arthur. [The teacher reads the first two pages aloud.] Now, you read for me. [Samantha reads the next two pages.] The teacher tape-records the reading to do a miscue analysis later.] OK Sam . . . thanks. Do your best to read the rest on your own now but I'll help you if you need me to.

Following the conference, the teacher was able to recommend other books and Samantha eventually progressed from the *Postman Pat* series by Cunliffe to read *The Railway Cat* by Phyllis Arkle (1987), *Olga Takes Charge* by Michael Bond (1983), *The Disappearing Cat* by Thelma Lambert (1986) and *The Bureaucats* by Adams (1986).

Group reading

Chambers (1993: 44) claims that: 'In any group of children, no matter what their supposed cleverness or lack of cleverness, we find that if they begin by sharing their most obvious observations they soon accumulate a body of understanding that reveals the heart of a text and its meaning(s) for them all'. Ofsted (1996b: 25) found that 'the small number of sessions of group reading where the pupils were able to read and discuss the same text were generally effective'. Research in Australia, the UK and the USA has shown how the learning potential of group reading is significantly enhanced by skilful teacher intervention. Applebee and Langer (1983) refer to 'instructional scaffolding' where teachers and pupils collaborate to:

- determine the difficulties that a new task is likely to pose;
- select strategies that can be used to overcome the specific difficulties anticipated;

- structure the activity as a whole to make those strategies explicit (through questioning and modelling) at appropriate places in the task sequence.

Graves and Graves (1994) describe activities for supporting readers which they call the 'scaffolded reading experience' (SRE). Their strategy is based upon Bruner's notion of scaffolding the learner and on the premise that, in order to develop as readers, children need to be challenged but they also need to be given the scaffolding necessary to meet those challenges. Considerations for the teacher are identified and related to planning and implementation phases (see Graves and Graves 1994: 31–3 for a more detailed account of each option).

In group reading teachers can:

- model the reading process demonstrating the range of cueing strategies;
- demonstrate the use of reading strategies such as skimming, scanning, using contents and index, extracting main points, summarizing, evaluating and reading for bias;
- explore with children literary devices and stylistic choices;
- draw attention to the language and organizational features of different genres.

Conclusion

Polarized conceptions of traditional didactic teaching and progressive child-centred learning have either overemphasized or marginalized the teacher's role. Effective teaching and learning occurs when, through interactive discourse, teachers and pupils collaborate in the construction of meaning. Ways of developing exploratory talk in the classroom are explored in Chapter 6.

(6) ○ Exploratory talk

Questions and questioning

Questioning is 'the predominant technique for initiating, extending and controlling classroom discourse' (Dillon 1982: 128). Research has demonstrated the prevalence of teacher dominated discourse and shown that the majority of questions asked by teachers do not elicit exploratory activity or encourage pupil participation. The I-R-E exchange pattern, where pupils attempt to guess what teachers have in mind, is a major characteristic of classroom discourse. Young (1984: 230) describes how teachers 'regularly and routinely channel pupils' ideas'. Hughes and Westgate (1988: 11) discovered the persistence of this pattern and report that, when teachers were talking to pupils, 'whether the groups consisted of as many as six pupils, or as few as two, seemed to make little difference'. Research (Galton *et al.* (ORACLE) 1980; Alexander *et al.* 1991; Alexander 1995) shows that most of the questions asked by teachers are of a closed, low cognitive level which require a limited response. Galton *et al.* (1999: 63) found that although since the ORACLE 1980 (Galton *et al.*) survey there had been an increase in the percentage of teacher questions, 'it was factual and closed questions which dominated and accounted for the greatest part of the increased proportion of questioning'. They conclude that a large proportion of teacher–pupil talk is devoted to telling pupils facts or giving them directions and that although individualized teacher–pupil interaction has decreased, and group and whole class teaching has increased, the quality of interaction has remained largely unchanged.

Interactive discourse is the 'power source' for constructivist learning, and if shared and guided reading is to be effective teachers need to find ways of moving beyond the I-R-E pattern. Hughes and Westgate (1988: 15) suggest that the most productive talk requires not only an adult's presence and instructional skills but also an adult's skills in listening and drawing pupils into more even-handed exchanges: 'This kind of talk permits a "negotiation" of meanings – by which is implied openness on the teacher's part to stimulate, take seriously and even challenge a framework in which this expression can be refined and extended'.

Question types

A distinction has been made between lower order factual questions, requiring pupils to recall or report information, and higher order interpretative questions, requiring opinion, judgement, reasoning, analysis and evaluation. A further distinction has been made between closed questions, where there is one acceptable answer, and open questions where there are several responses that would be acceptable. The typology showed in Table 6.1 has been developed from the work of Barnes *et al.* (1969).

Morgan and Saxton (1991: 41–50) classify questions according to general function. First are questions which elicit information and draw out what is already known in terms of information and experience. Such questions are used to:

• establish procedure;
• establish discipline and control;
• unify the class;
• focus on the recall of facts;
• supply information and suggest implications;
• reveal experience.

Second are questions which shape understanding and help teachers and pupils to sort out, express and elaborate their thoughts and feelings. Such questions are used to:

• focus on making connections;
• press pupils to rethink or restate more specifically;
• promote expression of attitudes, biases and points of view;
• demand inference and interpretation;
• focus on meanings that lie behind actual content.

Third are questions which press for reflection and challenge children to think critically and creatively. Such questions are used to:

• develop suppositions or hypothesis;
• focus on personal feelings;
• focus on future action/projection;
• develop critical assessment/value judgements.

Table 6.1 Question types

Question type	Explanation and example
Data recall	Requires the pupil to remember facts, without putting the information to use. For example: Where do badgers live?
Naming	Asks pupils to simply name an event, process or phenomenon without showing insight into how the event is linked to other factors. For example: What do we call this kind of word?
Observation	Asks pupils to describe what they see without attempting to explain it. For example: What is Max doing in this picture?
Control	Involves the use of questions to modify pupils' behaviour. For example: Will you stop that and sit down?
Pseudo	Constructed to appear that the teacher will accept more than one response, when in fact this is not the case. For example: Do you think it was right for Marv to bully Mouse?
Speculative/ hypothesis-generating	Asks pupils to speculate about the outcome of a hypothetical situation. For example: Imagine if the Grolle had not been friendly, what do you think might have happened in the story?
Reasoning or analysis	Asks pupils to provide reasons to justify ideas. For example: You've said these newspaper reports are very different. What makes you think that?
Evaluation	Makes pupils consider all aspects of a situation. For example: What evidence is there to suggest that this text is fictional rather than factual?
Problem solving	Asks pupils to construct ways of finding out answers to questions. For example: Suppose we wanted to discover if dragons really did exist in the past, how could we go about it?

Alternatives to direct questions

Active participation and the raising of questions by pupils is a feature of successful shared and guided reading. However, work in the USA and UK by Dillon (1988, 1994) and Wood and Wood (1984, 1988) indicates that asking direct questions is not an effective way to elicit or sustain interactive discourse. Dillon argues against the use of questions which, he says, will foil discussion processes and will not stimulate pupil thinking or encourage participation. Wood and Wood (1988: 285) support this view and argue that if teachers ask questions to encourage questions from children it will not happen. They suggest that by asking questions teachers 'get only what they ask for'. If shared and guided reading is to be successful, pupils need to display the kind of behaviour described by Tizard and Hughes (1984), where they:

- ask questions;
- participate in extended discussions;
- consider issues of how, why, when and where.

Wood (1992) claims that teachers who use alternatives to direct questions are more likely to create classroom climates where children are encouraged to speculate and hypothesize. This is not to suggest that control questions serve no purpose. After all, a teacher interacting with 30 pupils operates in a very different context than a parent indulging a single child. The management issues are different and so are the personal relationships. Teachers are responsible for the education and welfare of all the pupils in their care and classroom management is a fundamental issue, not only for learning but also for children's safety. Children are educationally, socially and physically at risk in uncontrolled classrooms. Moreover, Hargreaves (1984) notes how open questions can pose management problems for the teacher since they authorize pupils to indulge in long and sometimes irrelevant answers. This will no doubt strike a familiar chord with most teachers. Wood (1988) also identifies the dilemma of wanting to encourage exploratory talk but simultaneously needing to manage discussion in a disciplined way. Rather than jettisoning the use of questions, teachers need to develop a repertoire of alternative strategies to complement a range of different types of question. Dynamic interactive discourse and effective teaching and learning will result from teachers making appropriate choices. As Wood (1992: 209) says:

> If the aim of a lesson or teacher–pupil interaction is simply to establish whether or not facts have been learned and committed to memory, then talk which is rich in teacher questions and high in control will probably achieve the result intended. If, however, the aim is to discover what pupils think, what they want to know, or what they are prepared to share with their peers, then such lessons will prove self-defeating.

Dillon (1985) and Wood and Wood (1988) studied classrooms where teachers used alternatives to direct questions. Their findings that pupil response and initiative is greater after these alternatives have been used, were confirmed by the National Oracy Project (1987–93). Alternative strategies are, for example:

- increasing thought-provoking rather than factual recall questions;
- raising queries;

- making a declarative statement/stating own opinions or interpretations;
- redirecting (ricocheting) questions to other pupils;
- increasing the length of pauses after questions;
- tolerating periods of silence and allowing time for pupils to think and reflect;
- summarizing what has been said;
- seeking clarification;
- inviting elaboration;
- encouraging other pupils to question, probe, and seek clarification and elaboration.

It seems that when teachers use alternatives to questions pupils tend to:

- pose their own questions and make suggestions and evaluations;
- explore, speculate and hypothesize;
- share personal knowledge, beliefs and experiences;
- contribute to discussions and participate more freely;
- respond and refer to other pupils' contributions;
- display more initiative and contribute ideas spontaneously.

Gender differences

Although both ORACLE surveys (Galton *et al.* 1980; Galton *et al.* 1999) report no discernible difference between the time teachers give to boys and girls during whole class interaction, other research in the UK (Swann and Graddol 1988), and in the USA (Sadker and Sadker 1985) found that boys contributed far more to classroom talk in whole class contexts. Questions addressed to boys were usually of a more open and challenging nature than were those addressed to girls, which were more often rhetorical or requiring only a yes/no answer. After studying six classes of children from ages 3 to 11, Redpath (1989) found that boys took more turns than girls in a ratio of 3:1. Bousted (1989) also found whole class discussion dominated by boys and she confirms the claim by French and French (1984) that some boys use particular strategies to gain and keep the teacher's attention, to hold the floor and monopolize discussion. They found that what should have been whole class discussions often developed into small group discussion between the teacher and a few dominant boys. Holden (1993: 184) found that the quality of talk in small group work was influenced by gender balance and, most significantly, that not only did girls use far more abstract talk when working on English tasks, but the proportion of girls' talk was twice as high as the boys, indicating that 'in group work girls do get a chance to develop their language skills in a way that does not happen in whole class discussion'. Holden concludes that the amount of talk from girls in language tasks when they are involved in cooperative group work is evidently far greater, in both quality and quantity, than the talk elicited from them in whole class discussions. The implication is that, in order to provide equality and to elicit effective interactive discourse in whole class contexts, teachers need to be aware of the factors which encourage female participation in small group work and to extend this to whole class discussions. Moreover, if girls engage in more abstract language in English work, it would also seem profitable to create whole class contexts where such a level of discourse could be facilitated by the girls rather than depressed by the boys' tendency to use action talk: that is, talk restricted to the activity of the moment.

Exploratory talk

Exploratory language appears to develop if open contextual contexts are created by teachers and subsequently perceived as such by pupils. To encourage a more interactive discourse pattern, National Oracy Project teachers developed open questioning techniques. They applied strategies such as making a statement rather than asking a question, diverting a question or an answer from one student to another, remaining silent, and resisting the urge to direct and inform. Teachers found that, by applying the following strategies, they were able to elicit more extensive and educationally productive responses from children.

The teacher might *initiate* through:

- *Challenging:* 'I'm not sure that you have enough evidence to say that.'
- *Directing:* 'If you look at the title it might suggest something to you.'
- *Enquiring:* 'How do you think you'll go about doing that?'
- *Inviting:* 'Would you like to tell me about how you did that?'
- *Stating:* 'That was difficult to write.'
- *Suggesting:* 'It might be a good idea to look in the index.'
- *Modelling:* 'I'm not sure but I think what I might want to ask myself is . . .'
- *Listening and encouraging:* 'That sounds really interesting, go on.'

The teacher might provide *feedback* by:

- *Appraising and praising:* 'That would make sense, good thinking.'
- *Encouraging exploration:* 'You might take that argument even further.'
- *Focusing/orienting:* 'So consider what your next step might be.'
- *Helping the child to reflect:* 'Let's just think about what we've discussed.'
- *Offering hypotheses:* 'Suppose you applied that principle to another situation.'

- *Providing information:* 'Yes, what you're talking about is called alliteration.'
- *Relating to own experience:* 'I felt exactly the same way about that.'
- *Relating to the child's experience:* 'I think you found that Betsy Byars had a similar style.'
- *Seeking clarification:* 'I'm not clear about what you're saying.'
- *Urging amplification:* 'I'd like to know a little more about that.'

After watching video recordings and evaluating their classroom practices, my teaching colleagues in the National Oracy Project stated that, because pupil–teacher interaction varied according to the stage in the learning process, there was no one discourse pattern that was appropriate for all occasions. However, they were able to identify a general approach to teaching and learning that helped avoid a closed response and initiated a mental process more commensurate with a constructivist view of learning. This may be illustrated in the following way:

- *Initiate:* teacher introduces an issue, stimulates interest, relates to current experience.
- *Delegate:* pupils assume responsibility for their learning as individuals and as a group.
- *Explore:* pupils investigate and interrogate.
- *Appraise:* pupils and teacher reflect on the learning.
- *Launch:* reflection operates as a launch pad to determine further initiatives.

This general approach facilitated a learning process where students challenged assumptions, posed questions, interrogated texts, sought interpretations, examined different perspectives and actively engaged with problems and issues.

Encouraging exploratory talk in group discussions

Even when teachers are not directly involved in discussion, they are nevertheless exerting considerable influence over language patterns. Some researchers have illustrated how pupils' traditional conceptions of school learning contexts and acceptable discourse patterns can inhibit their capacity for collaborative discussion (Edwards and Mercer 1987; Barnes and Sheeran 1992; McMahon and Meyers 1993). Ground rules for learning in particular contexts are influenced by historical and contemporary factors. The culturally based definitions and attitudinal baggage that pupils bring to lessons can shape their use of language in group discussions. Discourse patterns are affected not merely by the nature of the task but also by pupils' conception of prevailing contextual conditions.

Pupils' perceptions of tasks: closed or open contextual conditions

National Oracy Project teachers I worked with felt that pupils' use of hypothetical, exploratory language and their reasoned evaluation of texts were the most significant features of successful group discourse in literacy lessons. *Desultory talk* (random exchanges which contribute little to the task in hand) and *disputational talk* (where participants disagree and take decisions individually without constructive dialogue) were seen as features of unsuccessful group interaction. Discourse in small group work was therefore evaluated according to the distribution of:

- hypothetical/exploratory utterances;
- evaluative/reasoning utterances;
- disputational utterances;
- desultory utterances.

In comparing pupil discourse it is tempting to look no further than the most obvious variables, such as the nature of the task and its relevance to the students. However, the two transcripts I present here are selected from a range of 40 discussions and illustrate wide differences in children's use of language during small group work on identical tasks. The group discussions arose out of similar and deliberate teaching strategies. They followed a pattern of teacher-led preparation and culminated in a task to be carried out through small group talk. In these, as in other lessons, the talk processes and the value attached to them by the teacher were emphasized in more or less explicit ways. The discussions involve the same teacher, the same class and the same group of children. They usefully illustrate the point that it is not necessarily the nature of a task itself which determines the interaction and its outcomes, but the children's conceptions based upon their perception of teacher expectations and ground rules or contextual conditions. These emerge not only from the nature and structure of the task but also from the teacher's introduction and the subsequent interaction of the pupils once the task is under way.

The teacher in the transcripts considers the tasks to be similar and he believes he has established identical ground rules for learning. He feels he has provided a learning context where, using a broad set of questions as a guideline, pupils will read and collaborate in a critical discussion of texts. The teacher directs attention particularly towards aspects of style and encourages the pupils to discuss the authors' use of language and literary devices. In the first discussion pupils are examining *Conrad's War* by Andrew Davies (1978), and in the second discussion *London Snow* by Paul Theroux (1982). The teacher's common practice is to follow a period of shared whole class reading with directed group work. During group work sessions, pupils are provided with copies of texts or photocopies of extracts from texts to examine and discuss. In the first example the teacher has read the opening two chapters from *Conrad's War* to the whole class and pupils have been asked to work in small groups to evaluate the story according to aspects of setting: plot, characters, style and theme.

It is possible to identify a series of phases in the following transcript as the pupils' talk evolves. It begins semi-collaboratively with Beckie attempting to explore the characters of Conrad and his father.

Beckie: Conrad seems a bit spoiled I think . . . I wouldn't talk to my dad like that . . . he's . . . sort of
Jay: He's horrible to his dad.
Beckie: . . . got no respect.
Shabina: Yeah like he calls him a tramp . . . says his friends think he's a tramp.
Jay: He's nutty . . . nutty . . . [reading from the text] 'mad decrepit old tramp'.

Kirsty now attempts to develop group collaboration by suggesting a collective interrogation of the text and a gathering of evidence, but this meets with limited success.

Kirsty: So shall we read through and make a note of all these first?
Shabina: Yeah he thinks he's useless . . . he says [reading from the text] 'why are you so useless?'
Kirsty: OK . . . if I write all this down for now then and
Jay: He calls him Fuzz [laughing].
Kirsty: . . . then we can talk about it.
Shabina: You what . . . why?
Jay: Dunno . . . 'cos he's got a beard I suppose.

Shortly, what proves to be a decisive transition takes place as Jay signals an independent approach to the work.

Jay: I'm gonna say Conrad doesn't respect his dad . . . thinks his dad is a nut . . . a nutty old tramp.
Beckie: Conrad does not think much of his dad . . . he thinks his dad is useless [writes this down].
Jay: Is that what you're putting?
Shabina: I'm putting that he doesn't have any respect for his dad.

These last two utterances mark the onset of much more individualized work. From this point on and for some minutes, the talk involves little more than minor associated transactions.

Beckie: Shab, are you writing out bits from the book?
Shabina: Yeah some bits like where Conrad or his dad say things to each other.
Jay: This is daft . . . as if you could make a tank.

When Kirsty does attempt to initiate some collaborative discussion she is rejected.

> *Kirsty:* But do you think he's really going to make a tank or is he just going to imagine it ... [reading from the text] ... it says 'Somewhere out there in his imagination'.
> *Jay:* Well just put what you think ... I think it's daft.

Some other potentially collaborative moves are made but get nowhere and the talk eventually subsides into a sporadic and mainly off-task mode.

> *Shabina:* Did you see whatsit last night?
> *Jay:* *Home and Away?* No ... missed it.
> *Shabina:* Oh ... have you got a ruler?
> *Kirsty:* What do you want a ruler for?
> *Shabina:* I'm underlining bits. ...
> *Jay:* You'll get done.
> *Shabina:* Only in pencil ... I can rub it out after.

The pupils believed the activity to be a conventional comprehension exercise where they were expected to read a text and demonstrate their understanding of it by answering questions. They felt that the onus was on each individual *product* which the teacher would assess rather than on the *process* of working collaboratively: 'Well ... we could talk ... if we wanted ... we knew Mr Crawford wouldn't mind us talking ... but so long as we all got on with it ... wrote something down ... like ... got the answers'.

The contrast between the talk in the activity on *Conrad's War* and that arising through the same pupils discussing *London Snow* could hardly be sharper. The girls begin their discussion by focusing on the main characters in the story. The talk evolves in a fully collaborative manner and could be described as truly exploratory, with a hypothetical mode of language indicated by linguistic markers such as '*What if*', '*Suppose*', '*I reckon*', '*But don't you think*', '*So are you saying*', '*Yeah but*', '*How do you know*' and '*Perhaps*'. The talk is also naturally but deliberately managed by the group so as they clarify the task, exchange views, challenge, reason, justify and extend ideas.

> *Beckie:* I think he's made Snyder seem more nasty by how he's made the others.
> *Shabina:* Yeah like the others are ... nice ... nicer.
> *Kirsty:* Like Mrs Mutterance ... [reading from the text] 'she was white haired and small and entirely round'.
> *Jay:* Yeah and she wore funny fingerless mittens and sucked sweets.

Shabina: Yeah it's how he's described them . . . but he's made
Mrs Mutterance and Amy both small and I reckon he's
done that on purpose.

Beckie: That's what I mean . . . to make Snyder seem more
horrible . . .

Jay: To make Snyder seem more threatening . . . more scary . . .
'cos . . . yeah . . . here it says her face was white and
solemn.

Kirsty: [reading from the text] 'A kittenish concern in the large
dark eyes'.

Shabina: Suppose he's saying she's just like a kitten . . . like a kitten
is . . . small

Kirsty: But not just small.

Shabina: . . . like . . . a kitten . . . because anything can hurt a kitten.

Jay: Not anything.

Kirsty: No but kittens trust people don't they . . . I think he's
trying to make Amy seem like someone who you could
hurt dead easy.

Beckie: Yeah . . . oh yeah . . . 'cos look . . . Wallace . . . he calls
Snyder an old monster man . . . so don't you think that's
good . . . he's making Amy a little kitten and Snyder a
monster.

Jay: And here . . . back here it says he was like a bear . . .
[reads from the text] 'his shadow a bear on the wall'.

The pupils go on to discuss Mrs Mutterance. One pupil (Beckie) feels that
like Amy, Mrs Mutterance is projected by the author as weak and vulnerable
to contrast with Snyder and make him appear more menacing.

Beckie: She's like an old mother cat . . . all fat and cuddly.

Jay: So are you saying she's weak and scared as well . . . she
wouldn't

Shabina: But don't you think she does

Jay: . . . be able to defend Amy.

Shabina: . . . she's not scared of Snyder.

Kirsty: How do you know that . . . how do you know she's not?

Jay: She never tells him to bog off or anything does she?

Kirsty: Yeah if she wasn't scared of him she'd tell him to get lost
and she never does.

Shabina: Oh I think she does though . . . she doesn't tell him . . .
like . . . say get out or get lost . . . bog off or anything . . .
not in those words but she

Beckie: Puts him in his place . . . yeah makes fun of him.

Shabina: . . . makes fun of him . . . so she can't be scared of him.

Kirsty: How do you mean?

Beckie: She tells him she can do what she wants . . . [reading from the text] 'I own this entire premises'.
Shabina: And when he asks for fudge she tells him he can have a mint lump or nothing . . . but earlier on when they're talking about it snowing she tells him off for boasting and she makes fun of him . . . she says . . . where is it . . . oh yeah [reading from the text] 'I've never heard such a lot of old rope in all my life it's just gas and goose feathers'.
Beckie: Right . . . and as well she ignores him when he thinks he's got something really important to tell them . . . she carries on talking to Amy and Wallace about sixpences.
Shabina: Perhaps . . . maybe she knows something about the shop he doesn't . . . so she doesn't take him seriously . . . just makes fun of him . . . like she says [reading from the text] 'that's no smile his shoes are too tight'.

The discussion demonstrates both effective social interaction and cognitive engagement as the children collaboratively interrogate the text. They show no evidence of producing answers merely to gain teacher approval. The children said they felt that, although the task was focused, the process of discussion and investigation was as important as the outcome or product. They believed the teacher wanted them to use the broad questions as a basis for sharing ideas and opinions in order to interrogate the text collaboratively: 'It didn't have to be what he thought if you know what I mean . . . if we could . . . like say we thought Amy was made timid 'cos . . . whatever . . . to make Snyder more horrible and that . . . if we could say why . . . if we could say why we thought that . . . right . . . it was OK'.

The difference in pupils' understanding of contextual conditions for each task significantly affected their use of language and the distribution of utterances (see Table 6.2).

It is easy with hindsight to see how the teacher's pre-task directions for the discussion of *Conrad's War* were likely to elicit a more muted response from pupils than the directions for *London Snow*. The teacher said that in

Table 6.2 Distribution of utterances

Conrad's War (closed contextual conditions)		London Snow (open contextual conditions)	
Hypothetical/exploratory	10	Hypothetical/exploratory	31
Evaluative/reasoning	27	Evaluative/reasoning	78
Disputational	32	Disputational	21
Desultory	38	Desultory	12

the *Conrad's War* task he had assumed the children were familiar with the ground rules for critical reading sessions and understood the importance of reasoned explorative discourse. However, in the teacher's directions this remained implicit. The teacher revealed that his intention was not to encourage independent work but merely to ensure the children justified their views by reference to the text: 'I just took it for granted they understood . . . you know, that I expected them to work together and share ideas . . . but I wanted to make sure they based what they were saying on evidence . . . to support their ideas by reference to the text'.

The teacher's directions for *Conrad's War* were:

Now when you move into groups remember to look at the questions. I don't mind which aspects you look at but maybe at this stage you might want to look at the main characters. What are they like? What is their relationship? How does the author tell you about them, the kind of people they are, their personalities, appearance, habits and so on? Right, any questions about anything before you start? OK then let's see what you can make of Conrad and Co. But remember I don't want silly answers that can't be justified. You have to show evidence from the text to support what you say. Right, let's see what you can come up with.

In the *London Snow* task the teacher's intention was the same but the ground rules for collaborative interaction were made more explicit. His directions were:

Before you move into group work I want to remind you of the purpose of the discussion framework – that is, it is a framework to help you discuss as a group, all of you cooperating and giving views and listening to the views of others. And when I say your views I mean your views based on some kind of reasoning with some kind of reference to the text. I want you to justify what you say by referring to the text, giving evidence to support your views. So it doesn't matter what you think about the characters or whatever. The main thing is that you work together and discuss and evaluate each others' ideas before you reach any final decisions. OK? Right, I just wanted to make that clear. Right? OK then let's see what you can do.

Exploratory language is used most frequently when pupils hold a shared understanding of contextual conditions and when this corporate perspective places a higher value on the cognitive process (investigation and interrogation) than the managerial product (finding correct answers). When pupils perceive a task as having open contextual conditions, discourse is characterized by tentative exploration and propositional extension. Their learning is enhanced as they manage conflict, identify problems and issues, order and develop their thoughts, monitor their own progress, display tolerance of others' views and practise turn taking in the discussion process. A significant feature of the collaborative process, in the two example transcripts, is the way children consider and evaluate each other's contributions and adapt their own views accordingly. The perception of the teacher in a supportive, facilitating role helps pupils to develop a learning context or 'climate of reciprocity' as noted by Howe (1990). The children do not only consider and evaluate material presented to them, they also formulate questions for themselves.

It seems that, when pupils collectively perceive the teacher in a non-evaluative role, they are more likely to use exploratory language and interrogate texts collaboratively through an exchange of diverse and often conflicting ideas. When children have a shared understanding of open contextual conditions, they exercise self-regulation, display self-determination and a desire to persevere with a task. However, simply organizing pupils in small groups does not mean they will automatically adopt a propositional style of speech or engage in collaborative discourse. As McMahon and Goatley (1995: 24) suggest, changes in instructional material are important but 'the oral discourse patterns prevalent in many classrooms also need modification'. Unless teachers are very explicit in establishing the ground rules, pupils tend to assume that normal rules of product assessment apply.

Conclusion

How tasks are introduced and the activities designed by teachers to lead into group discussions are especially important. It is at the phase of introducing group tasks that children's expectations and understandings of contextual conditions are confirmed. Classroom research has, for some time, recognized the significance of pupils' contextual perceptions and expectations about their roles as learners (Mercer 1992; Westgate and Corden 1993; Edwards and Westgate 1994). Pupils tend to resist new ways of interacting and often fail to engage in dynamic discourse during group discussions. However, when pupils perceive teachers in a non-evaluative role and recognize the task as having open contextual conditions, they are able to overcome inhibitions formed through previous expectations and preconceived ideas about the required output. Unless teachers make clear to pupils that the process of discussion has priority, there is correspondingly less chance that pupils will feel able to talk collaboratively or explore and critically evaluate texts. Creating the circumstances where critical reading and group discussion can flourish involves more than organizing classrooms into small groups. Collaborative discourse must be seen as a complex task involving, for instance, discussion between pupils and teachers of the ground rules which are to apply and of the pupils' own perceptions of their roles, the learning task and its purpose.

As Barnes (1976, 1992) has argued, teachers might teach but it is always the pupils who have to do the learning. However, he also points out that teachers cannot assume this learning will take place simply because pupils are allowed to talk:

> The quality of the discussion – and therefore the quality of the learning – is not determined solely by the ability of the pupils. The nature of the task, their familiarity with the subject matter, their confidence in themselves, their sense of what is expected of them, all of these affect the quality of the discussion and *these are all open to influence by the teacher.*
>
> (Barnes 1976: 71, emphasis added).

The success of the NLS, the development of interactive discourse and the effectiveness of large and small group work demands adequate resources and careful planning but, most of all, it requires knowledgeable, skilful teachers.

Speaking and listening to reading and writing: story making, storytelling

Stories stories everywhere

Narrative is described by Hardy (1977) as a primary act of mind. She suggests that stories are made up about every conceivable aspect of life, from the past, present and future. Andrew Wilkinson (in Wilkinson *et al.* 1990: 30) writes:

There are those [stories] which retrieve and construct the history of the family, and those which go back beyond it; there are stories which envisage the future – what we will do when . . . There are stories of humorous, scurrilous, pathetic incidents, polished by constant retelling. There are garrulous, reiterant, obsessive stories. There are stories which originally belonged to other people which subtly pass into our own family history. There are stories which are retellings from books; there are stories read from books, fairy stories, nursery rhymes – but even in the most literate of homes these do not constitute the majority of stories. These are stories made up to amuse children on a wet day, which once started continue week after week, even month after month till their originators are heartily sick of them, though the children never tire. There are stories children themselves tell.

Listening to stories

The DfEE (1995a: 3b) suggest that children should be encouraged to explore the 'characteristic language in storytelling'. The positive impact of young children having stories read to them is well documented (Hewison and Tizard 1980; Topping 1985; Dombey 1988; Dickinson 1995). Wells (1985, 1987b) and Olson (1984) believe that through listening to stories being read to them young children learn about the features and organization of language, and begin to assimilate and understand the more abstract mode of representing experience through writing. Both Dombey (1988) and Heath (1983) note how parents mediate between authors and children by applying oral markers, such as stress and intonation, to denote syntactic forms, while Bus (1994) shows how children develop concepts about print, or 'book knowledge', which provide them with a springboard for learning to read in school. Wells (1987b: 194) found a correlation between preschool experiences and measures of literacy on school entry. He concludes that 'children who grow up in a literate environment where reading and writing are naturally occurring, daily activities have a distinct advantage when they start their formal education'. Fox (1993) traces one child's book knowledge and shows how, over time, it becomes absorbed and incorporated into his own personal narrative. She illustrates how children's conception of story develops from an awareness of character and plot, to aspects of style and discourse, leading eventually to a full understanding of narrative conventions.

Storytelling

> As tunes of the tale are twirled on the tongue, the storyteller shares his words and simultaneously hears these words. So there is more than one kind of active listening happening as the teller relives the tale in a creative community of listeners.
>
> (Grainger 1997: 41)

I once asked a storyteller to explain the difference between story reading and storytelling. 'Storytelling is atavistic,' he replied, 'it links to some kind of primeval human need to hear and experience and make sense of the world through word of mouth.' Storytelling is personal and intimate, it derives from a time before books and the written word. An oral story can be told and retold, and each time it can be changed, embellished, elaborated or simplified. Storytelling is a dramatic improvisation, a symbiosm, where speakers and listeners construct and occupy worlds of their own creation. Through voice and eye and gesture, the listener is drawn into a story, woven into the tale as a participant, to feel anger, fear, despair and joy. Storytelling is interactive: it moves the listener back and forth from spectator to participant. The storyteller achieves this through inflection, emphasis, cadence, pace, pause and register.

Children possess an implicit knowledge of grammar, gained through living and communicating in a social world. Storytelling builds on this implicit knowledge and helps to make explicit some of the differences between spoken and written language. Most specifically, it draws attention to the way that language varies according to context, purpose and audience. In making and telling stories to each other, or in retelling tales, children develop their understanding of how language works. They learn how words fit together most effectively, which words are more or less appropriate, weak or powerful, when to raise or lower the voice, change pace or pause for effect. Although the details of retold stories may differ, the essential structure will act as a basis for performance and improvisation. Differentiating between narrative voice and dialogue in a story can develop children's awareness of differences in standard and non-standard English and can lead to discussions about colloquial and idiomatic language. As Wells and Nicholls (1985: 15) claim:

> Just as important as recognising and valuing diversity between speakers is the encouragement of versatility within speakers . . . for all speakers, even the monolingual, there is a range of varieties, or registers, that have to be mastered in order to communicate effectively in the various social situations that they are likely to encounter. Some of these varieties are acquired as part of growing up in the local community, but others need to be the subject of conscious attention at school.

I once read (or performed) *Wolf Pie* by Matthews and Ross (1989) to some children. After listening to the story they discussed the author's style and use of language and decided that it was an oral tale, intended to be read aloud. In groups the children wrote their own oral stories and these were clearly influenced by hearing *Wolf Pie*, for example:

Narrator: Once – I'm not sure when – there lived a kind old woman.
Woman: 'Hey up me duck . . . have an apple,' she said.

Howe and Johnson (1992) argue that teachers need to consider how a wide range of story types containing different language styles might be harnessed in the classroom as a means of learning. Although Howe and Johnson make the point that storytelling should not be seen as an alternative to reading, they show how storytelling can enhance and develop children's knowledge about language. They suggest (1992: 8) that listening to and telling oral stories will focus children's attention on aspects of spoken language such as:

- Language diversity (the possibility of including dialect or different languages in a telling).
- Change and consistency in language. (What happens to your language when you 'update' a traditional tale? What differences can be detected between successive tellings to different audiences and why? What features of a story remain constant? Why?)
- The differences between oral and written versions of the same story.
- The structures and conventions of oral narrative (e.g. such aspects as formal beginnings and endings – how many variations on 'once upon a time' can pupils find?)
- Developing the use of one's voice as a storyteller; experimenting with different pitch, or the effects of pausing; whispers, shouts, other accents, mimicry and so on.

From listening and reading to talking and writing

The National Curriculum for English (DfEE 1995a) states that children should 'be given extensive experience of children's literature' (p. 6), 'be encouraged to respond imaginatively to the plot, characters, ideas, vocabulary and organisation of language in literature' (p. 13) and 'be taught to use the characteristics of different kinds of writing' (p. 15). *The National Literacy Strategy Framework for Teaching* (DfEE 1998b) reiterates the requirement for children to be 'taught the underlying organisational ideas and terminology for talking about literature' (p. 7). One way of helping children to develop critical reading and creative writing skills is to make them aware of the literary models that surround them and which they can emulate when composing their own writing. The influence of literature on young writers has long been recognized, and there is now substantial evidence to suggest that a form of mentor relationship can develop between authors and children (Taylor 1986; Hansen 1987; Rosenblatt 1989; Harwayne 1992; Fox 1993; Mallett 1997). Lancia (1997: 471) shows how children 'spontaneously borrow ideas temporarily as they develop their own writing craft'. After reading *Cops and Robbers* (1977) and *Burglar Bill* (1977) by the Ahlbergs, Rahsmi (aged 7) wrote a story about Robber Roberta, the 'lady robber'. The following conversation took place between Rashmi and her friend Kirsty:

Kirsty: Ahh you . . . you've copied you have.
Rashmi: No I haven't then.
Kirsty: You have . . . you . . . that's . . . Mr Ahlberg . . . He could get the police on you for that.
Rashmi: [very concerned now] Roy . . . Mr Ahlberg won't will he?
Roy: No, he's a very nice man.
Rashmi: Do you know him?
Roy: Well, I've met him and he's a very good friend of my friend.
Rashmi: Will you ask him if it's OK?

It is thought that through listening to the language of stories being read to them, children learn about the language features and organizational aspects of written texts (Perera 1987; Meek 1988; Tannen 1989). This important link between oral language and writing is explored by Rosen. He comments: 'Many young children, or older semi-literate children and adults, do not really know that everything that they say can be represented in writing. They do not realise that their noises, grunts, shouts, whispers, slang, rude words, dialect phrasings and the like can actually be all written down' (1998: 22). He suggests that it is through writing that we can celebrate and record the variety and richness of oral language:

It [writing] can record playground songs, stories my granddad told me, a tongue twister my friend told me, funny things our dads say when they stand in front of the mirror. It can represent dialect, monologue, dialogue, jokes, commands, pleadings, intimate chats and gossip. Much of this is a highly undervalued, uncherished area of human creativity. It exists as a main carrier of our culture and identity, and yet children in schools get few chances to record it and celebrate it. Writing it does give them that possibility.

(Rosen 1998: 23)

Although Rosen is critical of the sharp distinction made between children's oral (subjective) language and the formal (objective) language often required in school work, he emphasizes the need to develop children's awareness of reading–writing connections. Children, he says, 'know that dialect exists as "this stuff we're saying" but don't know that it *can* be written down' (1998: 65). The notion of a writing repertoire is important, because it suggests there are many kinds of writing to communicate ideas and information and to represent a range of human experiences. Genre theory is useful in identifying predominant language and organizational features of different kinds of text but it must be remembered that the more creative we are with language and the more we manipulate it, the more blurred become the boundaries.

However, the successful manipulation of language requires conscious awareness, reflective thinking and a degree of control over the writing process. For example, after visiting a biscuit factory children who are asked to write about 'biscuit production' may want to include in the text a worker's personal feelings about working on an assembly line (it pays peanuts, bores you and makes your back ache), but the purpose of the writing and its intended audience needs to be considered. Writing is not good or bad *per se*: it is effective or ineffective, elegant or inelegant, powerful or puny in relation to its purpose and audience. To be literate is to be able to identify one's purpose, to recognize predominant social conventions and expectations and to use language in order to achieve a desired outcome: whether this is to inform, direct, persuade, entertain, shock or challenge conventions and overturn the status quo. Including a worker's personal thoughts about life on an assembly line is fine, if the inclusion is the result of conscious choice rather than due to lack of knowledge or because of misunderstanding.

Developing metacognitive awareness

Bereiter and Scardamalia (1987) point to the need for children to develop metacognitive understandings of their own writing processes. They explore the kinds of learning which young writers must undertake in order to develop the writing skills associated with mature authors. They differentiate between what they call 'knowledge telling' and 'knowledge transformation'. The former refers to writing where little planning, drafting or revision occurs, and where the work lacks reflection or ongoing evaluation but merely represents existing knowledge or understanding. The latter refers to a more dynamic process of writing where drafting and revision takes place and the writer is constantly reflecting on the content, coherence, form and style.

Rosenblatt (1989: 154) refers to the interrelationship between reading and writing as 'transactional' rather than 'interactional'. She points out that 'reading and writing obviously differ in that the writer starts with a blank page and must produce a text, while the reader starts with what is already written and must produce meaning', but suggests that each conditions and is conditioned by the other. Reading therefore, rather than being a related but separate process that interacts with writing, is actually an integral part of the composition of text, with the writer interacting (as a reader) with the text as it is being produced. The quality of interaction will clearly depend on children's metalinguistic awareness and their ability to be critical readers/respondents.

Bereiter and Scardamalia (1987) suggest that a notable feature of compositional maturity is the way that children are able to talk about their stories in a way which indicates knowledge transformation. This transformation, they argue, manifests itself in children's ability to reflect on choices that have been made in a piece of writing, either about content, or aspects of style beyond the surface features of handwriting, punctuation and spelling. They claim (1987: 266–7) that the (compare, diagnose, operate) process (CDO), which is a part of the composing process that is involved in revising text and in rethinking rhetorical choices, 'provides a strong indication of increasing compositional maturity'. They conclude that 'under ordinary circumstances the CDO process is not run through by children at all' (p. 284), because normally the complex task of managing the multiple tasks of writing tends, in most children of this age, to be overwhelmed by the need to deal with surface features.

Explicitly raising children's awareness of the language and organizational features of texts may help to move their attention beyond secretarial aspects of writing and encourage them to pay more attention to compositional features. Focusing on the structures of language through examining and discussing literature may not only develop children's critical reading skills but may also help them to write more effectively, since they will begin to integrate the language structures they encounter into their own writing repertoire (Kress 1986; Bearse 1992; Currie 1997). The development of a metalanguage, therefore, would seem to be a crucial element in enabling children to communicate effectively when they discuss and evaluate the texts of others and also compose texts of their own.

Case study: critical reading, group discussion and composition

Active participation and the posing of questions is a key feature of critical reading and writing. How texts are examined, and the ways that children are organized within the classroom to explore and interrogate literature, are important. The value of group reading and discussion to develop children's reading skills and critical faculties has been well documented (Wells and Chang 1988; Wells 1989; Wells *et al.* 1990; Corden 1996; Ewing and Kennedy 1996). Referring to discussion groups at Key Stage 1, Ofsted (1996b) states: 'at their best, these groups enabled pupils who had just shared part of a text to consider together common points about the narrative, characterisation and plot' (p. 22); and at Key Stage 2, 'questions about details of the text and plot arose from the pupils themselves as well as from the interventions of the teacher' (p. 25). The importance of interactive teacher–pupil and peer–peer discourse in making reading–writing connections is illustrated in Table 7.1.

Table 7.1 Making reading–writing connections through interactive discourse

Reading (NLS framework Year 6, Term 1)	Interactive discourse
Be familiar with the work of some established authors and know what is special about their work.	Teacher provides comparative texts, leads whole class discussion and draws attention to literary devices.
Explain preferences in terms of authors' styles and themes.	Teacher and pupils discuss texts in small groups.
	Pupils evaluate texts and discuss aspects of language, setting, character, plot, style, mood and theme.

Writing (NLS framework Year 6, Term 1)	Interactive discourse
Plan quickly and effectively the plot, characters and structure of own narrative writing.	Teacher provides model drafts for discussion.
	Teacher demonstrates the drafting process, adapting/modifying authors' texts.
	Teacher and pupils compose texts collaboratively.
	Pupils gain response partner feedback and discuss their independent writing (drafting).
	Teacher conferences and scaffolds during independent writing (drafting).

In Chapter 3 I presented a case study describing activities undertaken by one Year 6 class during shared and guided reading time and writing workshop sessions. I now want to focus on the work of those children whose writing was influenced by group discussions of Leon Garfield's book, *Fair's Fair* (1981). I present extracts taken from transcripts of group discussions, along with examples of children's written work produced during writing workshop sessions. The spoken extracts and written examples have been chosen to illustrate how, having had their attention drawn to specific literary devices, the children were able to discuss and critically evaluate texts, and to transfer the knowledge and insights they gained to their own writing. To stimulate discussion the group used question cards produced either by the teacher or by other children (see Figure 7.1).

Activity

- Read each group discussion.
- Read the corresponding example of children's written work.
- Discuss any links between the spoken discourse and the written text.

Group discussion 1

In the following extract, the children are examining the book for examples of non-standard English and discussing its appropriateness.

1	*Ailsa:*	Some of the words he uses are dead odd.
2	*Nicky:*	What . . . . like 'spifflicating'?
3	*Ailsa:*	Yeah that's one time and like . . . 'shove off I got no food'.
4	*Nicky:*	That doesn't seem right does it?
5	*Shaun:*	My mum'd tell me off if I said that . . . She's say our Shaun speak proper.
6	*Ailsa:*	Yeah but he does it a lot in this book . . . he says like . . . ain't and that.
7	*Satvinda:*	[reading from the text] 'And them what lives' . . .
8	*Nicky:*	'It were late' he says . . . it 'were' late.
9	*Shaun:*	It's how they'd speak though isn't it?
10	*Ailsa:*	I don't . . . I'd say 'was late'.
11	*Shaun:*	No but it's how Jackson would . . . 'I brung back your dog'.
12	*Nicky:*	Yes it's how they'd speak then and Jackson's poor isn't he . . . he wouldn't say things like, 'Oh I say I've brought back your dog' . . . it wouldn't sound real.
13	*Satvinda:*	The characters seem more . . .
14	*Nicky:*	Lifelike.
15	*Satvinda:*	More for real don't they?

Setting	Character
What do you think about the opening to the story?	Who are the main characters in the story?
Did the opening of the story grab your attention?	What are the main characters like?
Did the opening make you want to read on?	How does Leon Garfield bring the characters to life?
If the opening did make you want to read on, what did Leon Garfield do to make you feel like this?	Can you find examples in the book where Garfield shows you what the characters are like through their appearance, or how they behave, or through what they think, or what they say?
If the opening didn't grab your attention, what might Leon Garfield have done to make it more interesting?	

Plot	Style
What do you think are the main events in the story?	Is there anything about Leon Garfield's writing style that is interesting or unusual?
What do you think is the high spot (climax) to the story?	Is there anything he does that you think you would like to do in your own writing?
Do any characters behave in unexpected ways in the story?	Can you find any places in the book where people or places are described very well?
Why were you surprised by any of the characters' behaviour?	Has Garfield used any special words or done anything to help you imagine people and places?
Are there any unexpected events or twists in the story?	
Why were you surprised by any events in the story?	
Did the story end as you thought it would or not?	
Were you satisfied with how the story ended, or would you have changed the ending?	
What changes might you have made? Why?	
What type of story is *Fair's Fair*?	
Is it easy to fit into a category? Why or why not?	

Figure 7.1 *Fair's Fair* question cards

Ailsa (1) draws attention to the colloquial language used by characters in the story and she and Nicky (2, 8) clearly feel this is rather unusual and are not entirely comfortable with it. Shaun however, feels that it is entirely appropriate for the characters and context. Although Ailsa (10) remains sceptical, Nicky and Satvinda (12–15) show that they understand how Garfield has used non-standard English to make his characters appear realistic.

Writing example 1: Satvinda's story

Using a wordprocessor, Satvinda has written a story about a boy who has witnessed some older boys breaking into a car. The boys have seen him and given chase.

Ja went home the long way so Nathan wouldn't get him.

He went along by the canal and over the fields. He knew about a broken bit in the fence he could get through. But when he got there the three boys were waiting for him.

'Lemme through or I'll tell!' Ja shouted.

'You ain't goin nowhere.'

'You ain't sayin nuffin.'

Ja was scared because they were much bigger than him and tough looking.

He looked around for another way to escape.

Satvinda demonstrates a conscious decision to use non-standard English in the dialogue, in contrast to the adoption of standard English for the narrative voice.

Group discussion 2

These children are examining *Fair's Fair* and have focused on the author's use of tense.

1	*Adrian:*	It's best when it's read out isn't it?
2	*Gemma:*	Yeah for telling . . . it's best for storytelling.
3	*Mike:*	It'd be good on cassette . . . as a story tape . . . 'cos it sounds like it's happening.
4	*Gemma:*	Yeah . . . 'big as the night it comes straight at him'.
5	*Josie:*	'He gets his hand round its tree of a neck'.
6	*Adrian:*	Yeah . . . 'Jackson stares at it'.
7	*Mike:*	Yeah so it's happening right now . . . Jackson's staring at the dog right now . . . this second.

Adrian, Gemma and Mike (1–3) all conclude that the story is written in a particular way which makes it good to read aloud. Gemma, Josie and Adrian (4–6) read extracts from the book to illustrate the point and Mike (7) identifies the effect that Garfield's use of the present tense has on the reader.

Writing example 2: Josie's story

Josie's story is about Clare and Michelle who are exploring a cavern (see Figure 7.2). Josie has used the present tense to give immediacy and excitement to her story. In order to depict the anxious, frantic fumbling of one of her characters, she has also adopted Garfield's strategy of using the semi-colon as a cohesive tie to connect clauses.

clare and michelle Scramble to there feet and stare into the darkness. Something Shuffles towards them! There is Something there but the darkness hides it. Then they Can See a Shape. Two fierce red eyes stare at them and they Scream in terror. "Yikes it's a giant Vampire bat", Shouted clare.
"No it's a giant Spider" Said michelle. There legs turn to jelly and there mouths go dry. Then clare remembers the matchis in her packit. She is scared; she fumbles She nearly drops the box. At last She lights a match and the cave is filled with light. The Spider is nowhere to be Seen

Figure 7.2 Josie's story

Group discussion 3

The following extract shows the discourse of a group that has focused on Garfield's use of similes.

1   *Alex:*   Jackson stank like a drain . . . he does that a lot . . . he
            uses a lot of that whatsits . . . what are they?
            [The children can't remember the word and ask the teacher.]
2   *Shabina:* I think that's wicked how he does that.
3   *Faye:*   Yeah like Growler with 'eyes like street lamps'.
4   *Shabina:* 'And jaws like an oven door'.
            [The children now examine the text for further examples.]
5   *Rachel:*   'Doors with panels all over like a poacher's buttons'.
6   *Faye:*   'An iron letterbox as thin as a miser's mouth' . . . that's
            brilliant that is.
7   *Shabina:* Yeah you could just say like an iron letterbox with a
            thin opening but it wouldn't be anywhere near as good.
8   *Alex:*   Yeah . . . similes . . . they're good they are.
            [The children notice how Garfield uses repetition of simile and
            metaphor to make a point.]

9   *Shabina:* He puts two for some things.
10   *Rachel:* How do you mean?
11   *Faye:*   Oh yeah.
12   *Shabina:* 'Dreadful weather with snowflakes fighting in the
               wind'. 'Dreadful weather as hard and bitter as a
               quarrel'.

Alex (1) identifies the preponderance of simile in the story but he's not quite sure of the technical term for it. Shabina, Rachel and Faye (2–6) show their appreciation and explore the text for examples to read aloud. Shabina's evaluative comment (7) demonstrates a thorough understanding of the concept and she articulates Alex's feelings (1, 8). Shabina then draws the group's attention to another prominent strategy that Garfield has used throughout the story, which is the parallel phrasing and repetition of metaphor.

Writing example 3: Shabina's story

Shabina is writing a fantasy story based on the model of a questor tale. The children have examined the framework of a questor tale and watched a schools television broadcast about questor tales (see Figure 7.3). Later in the story Shabina goes on to describe a storm at sea (see Figure 7.4). This is a clear demonstration of the transfer of knowledge and insight gained through group discourse and the children's evaluation of *Fair's Fair*. Shabina has used the technique of parallel phrasing that she particularly noted during the group discussion.

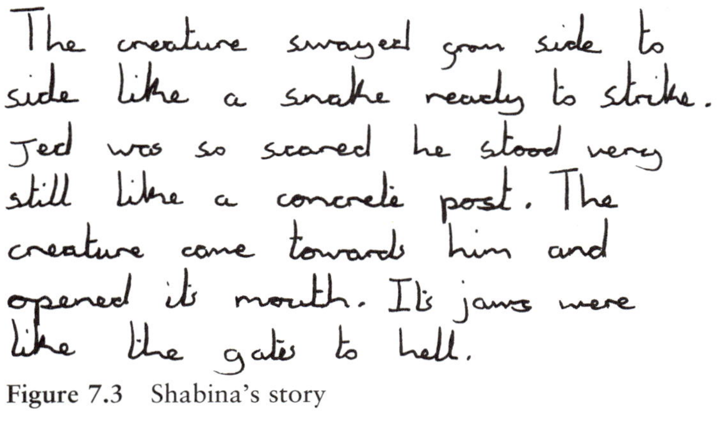

The creature swayed from side to side like a snake ready to strike. Jed was so scared he stood very still like a concrete post. The creature came towards him and opened it mouth. Its jaws were like the gates to hell.

Figure 7.3 Shabina's story

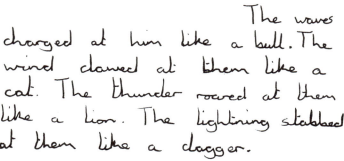

The waves charged at him like a bull. The wind clawed at them like a cat. The thunder roared at them like a lion. The lightning stabbed at them like a dagger.

Figure 7.4   Shabina's story, continued

Developing a sense of narrative structure

Vygotsky (1978: 116) notes that 'make believe play, drawing and writing can be viewed as different moments in an essentially unified process of development of written language'. Meek (1991) argues that, through narrative play, children learn to locate imaginative thoughts and events according to the conventions of narrative. Children develop an understanding of narrative genre from an early age as they have stories read to them and begin to read for themselves. However, they need to develop their use of a more sophisticated story structure than a simple beginning, middle, end model. Getting children to draw out the schematic structure of a story, such as *Fair's Fair*, can be used to illustrate this point and help extend the quality (not just the quantity) of children's own narrative writing. Having examined the structure of a particular text, children can be encouraged to adopt a similar pattern as they engage in a variety of storytelling and story making activities, as demonstrated below:

- Tell the story of Jackson/Lillipolly/Mr Beecham up to the beginning of *Fair's Fair*.
- Tell or rewrite the story through Growler's eyes.
- Retell or rewrite the story, changing some of the characters.
- Retell or rewrite the story using the characters in a different situation.
- Use the repetitive theme of the story using the structure and literary devices in an entirely new way.
- Retell or rewrite the story, making personality changes to the characters.
- Retell or rewrite the story, changing selected parts to alter the plot.
- Use the characters and situation to write a sequel.

Various narrative structures have been offered, and attempts made, to describe children's conceptual understanding and progression in writing stories. Christie (1989) describes the movement from simple *chronicle* to

Table 7.2   Story schemas

Hoey (1983)	Labov (1972)	Martin and Rothery (1980)	Longacre (1976)
	Abstract		Aperture
Situation	Orientation	Orientation	Exposition
Problem	Complicating action Evaluation	Complication	Inciting movement Developing conflict Climax
Solution	Resolution Evaluation Coda	Resolution	Denouement Final suspense Conclusion

well developed *story* in the written narratives of children aged 7–13. She distinguishes between chronicle, which is characterized by mundanity and predictability, and well-developed story, which is characterized by unpredictability and disruption of probability. Others have developed models based on Aristotle's sequence of complication–crisis–solution. These models can be presented as shown in Table 7.2.

After hearing or reading a story the structure can be tracked on a frame, as in the example for *Fair's Fair* shown in Figure 7.5.

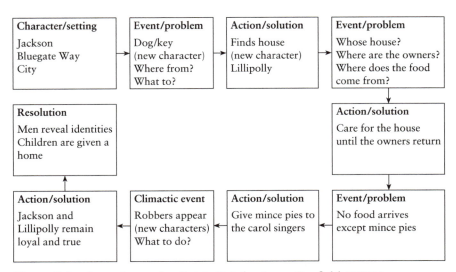

Figure 7.5   Story frame for *Fair's Fair* by Leon Garfield (1981)

Table 7.3   Questor tale frame

Character/s	Setting/s	Strengths	Weaknesses	Quest	Trials

Children might also discuss particular types of story and attention might be focused on tales that follow similar patterns and share common features. The frame shown in Table 7.3 could be used to identify the common features of a questor tale such as *Odysseus*.

Providing story frames for discussion

Pair or group discussions and collaborative story making can be facilitated through the provision of story frames. These should be adapted according to the age and competence of the children. For example, the following framework might be suitable at Key Stage 1:

> Once/One day/Once there was/Once upon a time/In the time
> before . . .
> Everyone was happy until . . .
> Along came . . .
> . . . thought to herself . . .
> And so it was that . . .
> But . . .
> After a while . . .
> Eventually . . .
> What could she do?
> After that . . .
> In the end . . .

The story frame shown in Table 7.4, which poses a series of questions, might be more suited to children in the upper years of Key Stage 2.

Posing questions: providing a reader audience

Children's narrative is often action orientated and has little character development, as evidenced in the following story written by a 7-year-old:

The Pirate Advenchar

> Once upon a time there lived a pirate he saw my gold he chased
> me and trid to kill me and my friends didnt no he was comeing and

Table 7.4 Key Stage 2 story frame

Event/question	Response
Story opening	The letter arrived just in time to stop Clare and Michelle from being bored to death
What was Clare like?	Description
What was Michelle like?	Description
How did they get on?	Relationship, interaction
Where did they live?	Setting
What was the letter?	An invitation to go somewhere/do something (or what?)
Where did they go?	A village, town, country, island, friend's house, on holiday (or what?)
What was this place like?	Description
What happened?	They found a map, explored some caves, discovered underground passages beneath a house (or what?)
Then what happened?	They got lost, found something or someone living there (creature, alien, ghost or what?)
How are they threatened?	Held captive, taken away to another planet (or what?)
How do they escape?	Found a way out, made friends with/trick the creature or alien (or what?)

he killed them and then chased me again and I just rimemberd the magic key and rubered it but it did not work and I ran one before he got near me and his parrot flew in the sky. then I found it then I rub the magic key and it worked and I went home. Wow what a advenchar

There is much to be said for this piece of work. The writer provides an appropriate opening and introduces one of the main characters. He provides a sequence of events and the text is written fairly consistently in the past tense. There is a combination of simple, compound and complex sentences. The story has a beginning, a middle and an end. A problem is posed and a resolution is found. This structure may be a useful fundamental framework but it is somewhat limited and doesn't allow for the development of a more sophisticated plot. In *The Pirate Advenchar* we are left with an unsatisfactory image of the pirate and the reader might also want to know more about the writer's friends. By probing and posing a number of questions it may be possible to help the child to extend the text. Questions might include: Tell me more about this pirate, who is he? What's his name? Where is he from? What does he look like? Does he have any friends? What are they like? Does he have a ship? Shall we draw the ship? In adopting this strategy, teachers can help to make explicit the kinds of question readers might pose.

Talking about characters

Children need to understand the importance of character and to develop their awareness of character as the 'psychological spring' which sets the action into motion. Since pupils will be familiar with the formulaic nature of children's TV programmes this can be a focal point for discussion. For such formulaic narratives to work, there have to be correlative formulaic (or archetypal) character roles. Children can develop their understanding that the kinds of character they create will determine the ways in which they are likely to behave, and that from this behaviour will stem the action of the story. For example, in *The Twits* by Roald Dahl (1982), the disgusting personalities of Mr and Mrs Twit lead to them being nasty and cruel, not only to each other but also to the monkeys and birds. The whole story is, therefore, based upon the characteristics of the Twits, which triggers and sustains the action (see Figure 7.6). Drawing attention to the way that popular authors organize their writing offers children models for their own writing.

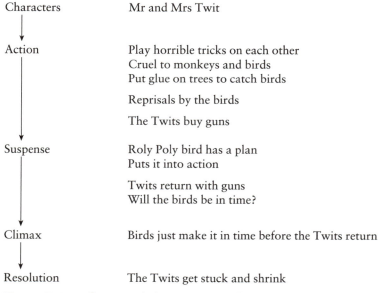

Characters	Mr and Mrs Twit
Action	Play horrible tricks on each other
	Cruel to monkeys and birds
	Put glue on trees to catch birds
	Reprisals by the birds
	The Twits buy guns
Suspense	Roly Poly bird has a plan
	Puts it into action
	Twits return with guns
	Will the birds be in time?
Climax	Birds just make it in time before the Twits return
Resolution	The Twits get stuck and shrink

Figure 7.6   Influence of characters on plot in *The Twits*

Talking about names and images

Names play a vital part in creating character in a story. Charles Dickens provides many examples of names used for connotative effect. For example, *Squeers, Gradgrind, Boffin, Smike, Barnacle, Chuzzlewit.* Children can engage in activities where their attention is drawn to the importance of names and the kinds of image they create. Names evoke images and elicit connotations in the reader. Dickens used names to signify archetypal characteristics, and although the postmodern perspective would challenge such a direct interrelationship, many popular children's authors continue to employ the strategy with success. Their work offers a useful focal point for classroom discussion. Children can be asked to discuss the kinds of image particular names conjure up in their minds. For example:

Gizzardgulper	Mrs Mutterance	Fidget Wonkham Strong
Gowie Corby	Voldermort	Bilbo Baggins
Aunt Spiker	Snyder	The Jigaree
Tyke Tyler	Mrs Pepperpot	Princess Smartypants
Mouse	Augustus Gloop	The Trunchbull

Children can be asked to draw up a list of characters and to discuss what names might be appropriate for them in a story. For example:

A hero/heroine	A pet dog	A school bully
A lively gran	A spiteful adult	An eccentric lollipop lady
An alien	A spoilt child	An unusual teacher

Children can then be asked to choose a number of names from the list and to weave them into a story. When a group has completed a story, the children could ask another group to compile a set of illustrations to accompany the text. An interesting exercise is to see how the illustrators' perceptions of the characters match those of the writers. This again can lead to useful discussion. The children can read their stories out loud, each taking a different part or parts, or they can record their stories on cassette. My pupils occasionally produced story tapes for partially-sighted children. Having such an audience made the writers think very carefully about bringing their characters to life through the sounds and connotations of words.

When children are watching cartoons, or playing video games, what they probably don't realize is that the characters involved are actually caricatures, where the features of a person or creature have been exaggerated purposefully. Authors like Dickens and Hardy used hyperbole in order to create such caricatures – not only to represent individual characters, but to represent general human qualities and social and political codes. A useful way of getting children to develop their powers of focalization (to focus on the detail of their characters) is to characterize them. Again, drawing attention to the way in which successful writers have done this provides children with a

Table 7.5 Frame for *Cobblewok the Shortsighted Cobra*

Character	Name	Form and peculiarities	Consequences
Owl	Ollie	Wicked	Frightening
Gorilla	Godzilla	Wise	Adventurous
Cat	Silas	Forgetful	Thrilling
Eagle	Ellie	*Kind*	*Humorous*
Fox	Anniah	*Rheumatic*	*Outrageous*
Snake	*Cobblewok*	*Short-sighted*	*Slapstick*
Crocodile	Brian	*Clumsy*	Romantic
Lioness	Asimar	Elegant	Sad
Badger	Khan	Gangling	Tragic
etc.	etc.	etc.	etc.

useful model. In the following poem, 'Song of the City', Gareth Owen (1985) has brought someone he remembers from his past to life by relating her to the comic strip character *Desperate Dan*:

> Anna Mae Chip Shop O'Sullivan
> Ran a shop from a dormobile van,
> Served cod wrapped in last week's Beano
> Had a chin like Desperate Dan.

> Anna Mae Chip Shop O'Sullivan
> Built like a battle ship,
> Smoked a pipe like a skull and crossbones
> And talked like a comic strip.

Making choices: locating characters in a story frame

Making a frame can help children to develop characters by considering the importance of names, attributing particular characteristics and considering possible consequences that such choices might have. In the example shown in Table 7.5 one pupil has decided that his main character will be a shortsighted cobra named Cobblewok. The pupil wants Cobblewok to have certain characteristics and for the consequences (plot) to be humorous.

Group story making

The advantages of group story making are that it:

- provides a secure context for interactive discourse;
- encourages collaboration, sharing and exploration of different ideas;

- encourages reflection, evaluation and analysis;
- provides opportunities for more reticent speakers to contribute;
- allows children to draw on the knowledge and experience of others;
- develops skills in oral drafting and redrafting;
- provides an opportunity to practise and develop discursive skills and strategies.

Group story making ideas

Headlines

In this activity, each group is presented with a headline. Some headlines may be of a sensational or unusual variety. Groups are asked to tell the story which goes with the headline, or to invent one. The activity could lead to a discussion of the style found in different kinds of newspaper. The oral activity could be used in conjunction with a word processor and desktop publishing program. Having told, taped, written or word processed the newspaper article, children may then choose to write a script of the events which led to the newspaper article. This could be taped for others to listen to before they read the newspaper account.

Radio plays and talking stories

Making a radio play or a story tape focuses children's attention on the need for clarity and also emphasizes the differences between various kinds of written and spoken text. When the children I taught made story tapes for partially sighted and blind children, the need for clarity of expression and differentiation of voice and register became of paramount importance. In making a radio play children have to rework a text into a script and provide directions and sound effects. Including advertisements in the radio broadcast provides an additional dimension and requires a change of language and register.

Using illustrations and photographs

Asking children to make drawings, or providing them with a set of drawings can stimulate discussion and encourage them to think more carefully about characters. A discussion point can be for children to decide what kind of action is likely to occur as a result of making particular choices. Photographs or illustrations can be used to help a group of children create and narrate a story to the class. Four to six illustrations or photographs should encourage children to organize the story into a series of events, leading to a climactic point and a resolution. Illustrations or photographs need not always be placed in the same order, and using the same resources with a whole class

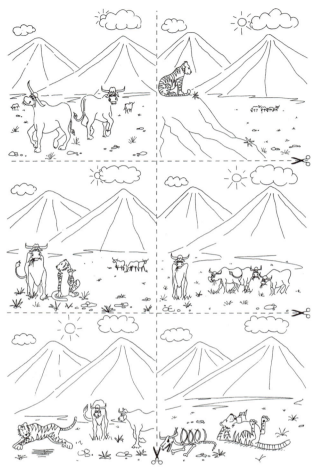

Figure 7.7   Fable illustrations

can result in an interesting variety of group stories. The set of illustrations shown in Figure 7.7 could be used to stimulate work on fables.

Clues

In this activity, children work in groups of three or four. Each group is given several items which they are told were found at the scene of a crime, for example: bus/rail ticket, charred note, unfinished letter, receipt, key, diary entry and so on. The group's task is to decide what the crime was and how the clues fit into the picture. Having decided on the scenario, the group can present its story in different ways. For example:

- newspaper report of the crime, giving details of the crime and the police's suspicions;
- newspaper report after the crime has been solved, showing how the police traced and arrested the criminals;
- narrative account of the crime;
- 'crimewatch' report, using studio presenter and interview with police investigator;
- taped radio report with interviews.

Before the groups start it can be useful for them to consider some clues. For example, a train timetable with one journey ringed. What conclusions could they draw from this? Could it belong to the criminal or the victim? Did the person catch the train or not? What was the timetable doing at the scene of the crime? Could they use it to dramatic effect in their account?

Twinning

This is a way of making a story with a partner. Each person says one word at a time so the story is continually passed from one to the other. The activity encourages careful listening and focuses attention on the need for coherence. For example:

Once/there/was/a/queen/who/wanted/to/fly/so/she/sent/ for . . . and so on.

Glove puppets and shadow theatre

Simple puppets can be used by children to tell stories. Providing a cassette recorder while children are rehearsing or developing the script with their puppets allows children to go through an oral drafting process and enables them to record their first and subsequent attempts at developing the story, refining it until they are satisfied. It also encourages them to reflect on the language being used and on the use of different voices.

Transforming genre

Children can be provided with a poem, diary entry or letter. In pairs or groups children can discuss what story may lie within or beyond the content. For example: a diary entry might read, 'this was the day I had been dreading'. Newspaper articles can be presented as a basis for stories. Children might take characters from poems and locate them in stories.

Just suppose?

Children are given 'Just suppose?' situations, either all the same one or different ones to different groups, for example:

- You became very small.
- You can see through the back of your head.
- You find a magic box full of . . .
- You can turn into any shape.
- You develop extraordinary powers.
- You can become someone else for short periods of time.

Groups should record their thoughts and then be given an opportunity to share their ideas with the rest of the class. Where all the children are thinking about the same situation there could be a pooling of ideas with the teacher writing them up on the board or overhead projector. Where each group has a different situation it might be that the rest of the class can add to a group's ideas. This sharing session is important as it gives children the chance to explain their ideas to the rest of the class and enables them to receive feedback from the teacher and their peers. Time should be provided for planning a story with a particular audience in mind. The story might be told, written or put on cassette. Tape recording a story is particularly helpful for children who find writing so difficult that it can arrest the flow of ideas.

Person, place, object, event

Each group is given four cards, preferably of different colours:

1 Person
2 Place
3 Object
4 Event

On the appropriate card pupils write down a person, place, object or event. The cards are collected in and redistributed so that each group has one of each card but not a card they have written on. Using the cards the group plan out a story. After 10–15 minutes each group shares its ideas with the rest of the class. It is also useful, at this stage, to focus the group's attention on the type of story being created and the likely audience. After the feedback session the groups re-form and develop their stories. The stories can be written, told or tape recorded.

Variation using jigsaw technique

Groups of four children are given a set of cards (one of each). Each child chooses a card and then all the children with 'place' cards form a new group and so on. The new group has a joint responsibility to produce as much information as possible about the area for which they are responsible. After ten minutes or so the children return to their home groups as the experts in that particular area. For example: the child from the *place* group is responsible for bringing back the information and sharing it with the home group. This method of working means that every child is involved in the activity and has the role of 'expert' for some of the time. Once together, and having shared their information, the children rejoin home groups and start to make their story, which could be written, tape recorded or told. It is interesting how the same pieces of information can generate very different stories, depending on the story genre chosen by the home group.

Recipe for a story

A book with a well-illustrated jacket is chosen. The teacher and children discuss what information can be gleaned from the jacket. The beginning of the story should be read aloud as a means of stimulating further discussion and gathering more clues. A short section about halfway through the book might then be selected, read aloud and discussed. The children should then form small groups to construct the complete story. The end result can be told or written collaboratively.

Knock, knock stories

Reading this kind of story to a group of young children can lead to the idea of pictures with opening doors and different characters behind the doors. Each of the characters behind the doors can be presented and the children encouraged to tell their story. This might be taped or written for another audience. Older children might draw pictures or use photographs of people and place them behind the doors with information about them on the opposite page, or they might choose to tell the story of one person, using photographs, adding drawings and using a tape recording to tell the story which could go with the book.

Story box or bag

While telling a story, the teacher should have a box or story bag containing several articles relevant to the tale. This can be developed for generating further story making ideas, with the children collecting together different objects to place in boxes and using these as the basis for other stories. The idea of boxes containing different objects can provide a stimulating focus for instant storytelling, encouraging children to develop ideas and create characters.

Character boxes

The teacher places in a box several objects which relate to the same person and asks children to describe the person. Working in pairs or groups, children can use the objects to make a story. They can then tell their story using the objects as a guide. For example: old photograph, scarf, medal, tools, pen, perfume bottle, purse, old bus ticket, empty book of stamps and so on.

Story trays

The teacher provides plastic tidy trays containing, for example, soil, sand or wood shavings. The children can use play people or simple cardboard cut-out characters and build up a scene for a story. This can then be used for storytelling by the children or story making with the teacher acting as scribe.

Story maps

Working in pairs or groups and using large sheets of sugar paper, children can design the background or setting for a story. For example: forest, village, town and so on. Simple cardboard cut-out characters can be made and mounted on blobs of Plasticine or menu holders. Using the completed map and characters, children can tell their story using the props.

Plasticine story making

Children can create characters out of Plasticine and use them to tell a story. The children can work individually and tell their stories to the teacher, or may work collaboratively and tell their stories to other pupils. Having the Plasticine characters helps the children to sequence the events in their stories.

Computer stories

There are computer programs (see NCET 1992) which enable pupils to create their own stories, selecting from a number of characters and objects found in particular kinds of tale. Children are able to create stories using the characters they have chosen, producing the text and adding graphics as features or border prints. The stories created can be printed out and made into books.

Is anyone there?

In this activity, the teacher talks to the class about places they visit on a regular basis such as school, supermarket, library, railway station, sports centre, playground, park. The children have to imagine that they turn up and find the place deserted. They have to describe a scene and provide a number of items that may act as cues for a story. A poem, such as 'Flannan Isle' (Gibson cited in Blishen 1963) might be read. Groups can discuss possible events and write a story about what happened. This could be dramatized/made into a radio play.

The connectives game

This activity is particularly useful for developing children's awareness and use of connectives. The activity can be done as a whole class or in small groups. A range of connective cards are drawn to 'frame' a text and provide cohesive ties to elaborate and extend the story. With a whole class, large cards are needed and the teacher might choose from a set of opening cards, such as 'On a dark night long ago', to establish a setting. This would be followed by selection from another set of character cards, such as 'there lived' or 'there was'. The action or events would then be stimulated by offering each child, in turn, a connective card, such as 'one morning' or 'without warning'. The story could be developed as each child offers a response. The teacher can keep the story flowing by choosing suitable connectives and can bring the story to an end with a concluding connective, such as 'eventually' or 'finally'.

Babble gabble

This activity encourages both speaking and listening skills. The teacher tells the children they are going to listen to a story and afterwards are going to work in pairs and to retell it. After the initial telling one child begins to retell the story to a partner as fast as she or he can but with as much attention to detail as possible. After a minute the teacher shouts 'change!' and the listener now has to continue with the tale. This pattern continues for as long as necessary. It is important to let the children know that they do not have to retell the story in exactly the same words as the teacher. However, they do have to listen carefully in order to remember the plot and the general sequence of events.

Special powers

In this activity, children look at characters with special powers, such as Superman/woman. The teacher might read an extract from a story, such as *The Ogre Downstairs* by D. Wynne-Jones (1974). This may be followed by a brainstorming session where children think up ideas for special powers such as X-ray vision, invisibility, mind reading, time travel, a magic ring/sword/charm, the ability to foretell the future or change shape/age. The class can make packs of 'special powers' cards and character cards. Each group then selects a card from each pack and uses this as the basis for a story. For example: a cat that can see into the future.

Tall stories

Tall stories such as Michael Rosen's Lollipop lady, The loaf and the knife and The Bakerloo flea (1982) can be read. Children can take an everyday situation and make it unusual. Alternatively, they can take unusual characters and make them ordinary, as Raymond Briggs does with *Father Christmas Goes on Holiday* (1977).

Literature circles

Not exactly a storytelling activity, the purpose of literature circles is to provide a secure, supportive small group environment where children can discuss and evaluate texts orally without the pressure of having to write a 'report' or 'book review'. However, in their different interpretations of a text, children are 'telling their stories'. I have found that literature circles work best if children have read a text independently, perhaps during quiet reading time or at home. They then come to the literature circle prepared to discuss their thoughts and feelings. However, younger readers will benefit from teacher support, and in such cases a corporate shared reading of a text is preferable. Literature circles encourage active reading and critical discussion.

Story-drama

> Story drama can present text as "earprint". Some print longs to be said aloud.
>
> (Booth 1994: 128)

Story-drama may be seen as an extension to story making and storytelling. However, story-drama is not simply the enacting or presentation of story, but the investigation and interrogation of texts *through* dramatization. Through drama and role play, texts can be deconstructed, characters examined and relationships explored. Layers of text can be revealed and subtle agendas unveiled. Drama, like group work, is a social activity. It can promote collaborative talk through the need to identify purposes, present interpretations and take account of audiences' needs. Moffett (1968), in his theory of discourse, points to the power of dialogue or collaborative discourse in developing thought and language. Story drama offers contexts and opportunities for such interactive discourse to occur as children create, speculate, reflect, share and evaluate ideas in their search for meanings and interpretations. Through story drama, children can predict, hypothesize, imagine, empathize and consider various standpoints. They can deconstruct, manipulate and create texts and engage emotionally with issues, characters and events. As Grainger (1998: 35) suggests, 'children move in and out of the text, and in and out of the felt experience. Such moves and the drama conventions which shape them, illuminate the reader's engagement, and mediate, develop and transform their meaning making'.

Children bring to drama their own knowledge and experiences, which in turn impact on the drama and their interpretation of events and relationships. Bruner (1986) claims that narrative occupies two landscapes at the same time: a landscape of action, with participants' intentions and goals, and a landscape of consciousness, relating to what participants know, think and feel, based on their values, attitudes and beliefs. The latter stimulates an emotional response and draws us into the narrative. In story-drama children can go through the dialectical process of experiencing real and imaginary worlds simultaneously.

The move from drama as performance art to drama as a tool for learning can be traced to the work of Dorothy Heathcote. Her emphasis was on encouraging children to explore feelings and personal interpretations, and transform them into external action. Booth (1994: 118–19) sees story-drama as a complex interrelationship between reading, interpreting, exploring and enacting, as the child moves between spectator and participant roles and brings different perspectives to bear:

> The relationship between the two learning areas of drama and reading lies in the world of meaning. It is the idea of symbolisation and its role in the discovery and communication of meaning that connects drama and reading. Both areas are concerned with interaction. In story drama, the children enter into a dialogue, modifying and exploring symbols by changing and challenging each other's contributions. When reading, they enter at first into a dialogue with the author, then with other readers and finally with themselves. Through discussion and analysis, they modify and develop their understanding of the author's meaning, as well as absorbing the diversity of meanings their classmates have taken from the text. In both cases, children are negotiating at the symbolic level.

Full circle: the important role of the teacher

The real challenge is, as Grainger (1998: 35) says, 'to help the learners make more conscious use of their reading journeys in the imaginary world of drama'. Eisner, in *The Mythology of Art Education* is critical of the notion that all children need to develop the arts are materials, motivation and encouragement. He argues that 'the ability to use [an art form] as a vehicle for expression is in large measure a learned ability and the teacher has a much more complex task than simply providing materials and encouragement' (cited in Booth 1994: 27).

In discussing the role of the teacher and highlighting the importance of effective teacher planning, preparation and skilled intervention, we seem to have come full circle, returning to the theories of Piaget and Vygotsky discussed in Chapter 1. Students on teacher education courses often dismiss the understanding of theoretical concepts as an instrumental but professionally irrelevant course requirement. Teaching is perceived as a practical activity, largely concerned with the provision and organization of resources, and 'enthusiasm' is seen to be the most important teaching quality. However, the most effective students and teachers recognize that enthusiasm needs direction, and that classroom practice must be underpinned by sound theoretical principles and informed by research evidence. In this book I have explored the learning potential of exploratory talk and examined the view that the introduction of the NLS and a dedicated literacy hour need not be incompatible with constructivist learning or result in arid, decontextualized teaching. I have argued that children learn most effectively through a process of collaborative interaction, where teachers demonstrate, model and scaffold the learning, and where both teachers and learners engage in interactive discourse to construct knowledge and develop understandings.

Children's literature

Adams, R. (1986) *The Bureaucats*. London: Young Puffin.
Ahlberg, J. and Ahlberg, A. (1977) *Burglar Bill*. London: Heinemann.
Ahlberg, J. and Ahlberg, A. (1978) *Cops and Robbers*. London: Heinemann.
Ahlberg, J. and Ahlberg, A. (1981) *Peepo*. London: Picture Puffin.
Ahlberg, J. and Ahlberg, A. (1986) *The Jolly Postman, Or Other People's Letters*. London: Heinemann.
Anholt, L. (1999) *Camille and the Sunflowers*. London: Frances Lincoln.
Arkle, P. (1987) *The Railway Cat*. London: Young Puffin.
Avery, G. (1978) *Mouldy's Orphan*. London: Puffin.
Ball, B. (1989) *Stone Age Magic*. London: Corgi.
Berg, L. (1979) *My Dog Sunday*. London: Young Puffin.
Bond, M. (1983) *Olga Takes Charge*. London: Young Puffin.
Briggs, R. (1972) The three little pigs, in *The Fairy Tale Treasury*. London: Picture Puffin.
Briggs, R. (1977) *Father Christmas Goes on Holiday*. London: Picture Puffin.
Browne, A. (1986) *Piggybook*. London: Julia Macrae.
Byars, B. (1976a) *The Eighteenth Emergency*. London: Puffin.
Byars, B. (1976b) *The Midnight Fox*. London: Puffin.
Chambers, S. (1998) *Barty's Scarf*. London: Picadilli.
Conlon-McKenna, M. (1990) *Under the Hawthorn Tree*. Dublin: O'Brien.
Cunliffe, J. (1982) *Postman Pat* from the BBC TV series. Hippo: Scholastic.
Dahl, R. (1982) *The Twits*. London: Puffin.
Dahl, R. (1984) *Revolting Rhymes*. London: Puffin.
Dahl, R. (1989) *Matilda*. London: Puffin.
Davies, A. (1978) *Conrad's War*. London: Blackie.
Dickens, C. (1979a) *Great Expectations*. Glasgow: Collins Graded Readers.
Dickens, C. (1979b) *Oliver Twist*. Glasgow: Collins Graded Readers.
Discovery World. (1997) London: Heinemann (series).
Doherty, B. (1995) *Street Child*. London: Heinemann.
Edwards, D. (1993) *A Strong and Willing Girl*. London: Mammoth.
Foreman, M. (1972) *Dinosaurs and all that Rubbish*. London: Picture Puffin.
Garfield, L. (1968) *Smith*. London: Puffin.

Garfield, L. (1981) *Fair's Fair*. London: Macdonald.

Garfield, L. (1984) *Six Apprentices*. London: Heinemann.

Garfield, L. (1986) *The December Rose*. Harmondsworth: Puffin.

Garfield, L. (1988) *The Stolen Watch*. London: Puffin.

Gates, S. (1994) *Beware the Killer Coat*. London: Walker.

Gibson, W. (1963) 'Flannan Isle', in E. Blishen, *The Oxford Book of Poetry for Children*. Oxford: Oxford University Press.

Hoban, R. (1974) *How Tom Beat Captain Najork and his Hired Sportsmen*. London: Jonathan Cape.

Hughes, T. (1968) *The Iron Man*. London: Faber and Faber.

Impey, R. and Porter, S. (1988) *A Letter to Father Christmas*. London: Orchard.

Kilner, J. (1979) *Joe Burkinshaw's Progress*. London: Methuen.

Lambert, T. (1986) *The Disappearing Cat*. London: Young Puffin.

Matthews, A. and Ross, T. (1989) *Wolf Pie*. London: Mammoth.

Murphy, J. (1978) *The Worst Witch*. London: Puffin.

Nicholls, H. and Pienkowski, J. (1972) *Meg's Eggs*. London: Piper.

Oakley, G. (1972) *The Church Mouse*. London: Macmillan.

Owen, G. (1985) *Song of the City*. Glasgow: Collins.

Pearce, P. (1970) *Tom's Midnight Garden*. London: Oxford University Press.

Pfister, M. (1995) *The Rainbow Fish*. London: North–South Books.

Root, B. and Hughes, M. (1994) *Animal Homes*. Aylesbury: Ginn & Company.

Rosen, M. (1982) 'The loaf and the knife,' 'Lollipop Lady', and 'The Bakerloo flea' in *Nasty*. London: Longman Knockout.

Rosen, M. (1987) The three bears, told as 'Goldisocks and the Wee Bears' in *Hairy Tales and Nursery Crimes*. London: Young Lions.

Rosen, M. and Oxenbury, H. (1989) *We're Going on a Bear Hunt*. London: Fontana.

Ross, T. (1976) *Goldilocks and the Three Bears*. London: Andersen Press.

Russell, C. (1990) *Geordie Racer*. London: BBC Publications.

Scieszka, J. (1991) *The True Story of the Three Little Pigs*. London: Puffin.

Sefton, D. (1995) *The Day the Smells Went Wrong*. London: Puffin.

Speare, E.G. (1983) *The Sign of the Beaver*. Glasgow: Collins.

Stolz, M. (1990) *Cat Walk*. London: Fontana Young Lions.

Theroux, P. (1982) *London Snow*. London: Puffin.

Tolstoy, A. and Oxenbury, H. (1972) *The Great Big Enormous Turnip*. London: Pan.

Tomlinson, T. (1987) *The Flither Pickers*. London: Julia Macrae.

Trivizas, E. (1993) *The Three Little Wolves and the Big Bad Pig*. London: Heinemann.

Walsh, J.P. (1986) *The Butty Boy*. London: Puffin.

Walsh, J.P. (1995) *Thomas and the Tinners*. London: Macdonald.

White, E.B. (1963) *Charlotte's Web*. London: Puffin.

Wynne-Jones, D. (1974) *The Ogre Downstairs*. London: Macdonald.

References

Adams, M. (1990) *Beginning to Read: Thinking and Learning about Print*. Cambridge: MIT Press.

Alexander, P., Schallert, D. and Hare, V. (1991) Coming to terms: how researchers in learning and literacy talk about knowledge. *Review of Educational Psychology*, 51: 170–86.

Alexander, R. (1988) Garden or jungle? Teacher development and informal primary education, in A. Blyth (ed.) *Informal Primary Education Today*. Lewes: Falmer Press.

Alexander, R. (1992) *Policy and Practice in Primary Education*. London: Routledge.

Alexander, R. (1995) *Versions of Primary Education*. London: Routledge.

Alexander, R., Rose, J. and Woodhead, C. (1992) *Curriculum Organisation and Classroom Practice in Primary Schools: A Discussion Paper*. London: DfEE.

Amidon, E. and Hunter, E. (1967) *Improving Teaching: The Analysis of Verbal Interaction*. New York: Holt, Rinehart and Winston.

Applebee, N. and Langer, J. (1983) Instructional scaffolding: reading and writing as natural language activities. *Language Arts*, 60(2): 168–75.

APU (Assessment of Performance Unit) (1988) *Surveys of Language Performance Assessment Matters*. London: Department of Education and Science.

Arnold, H. (1982) *Listening to Children Reading*. Sevenoaks: Hodder and Stoughton.

Baddeley, G. (1991) *Teaching, Talking and Learning in Key Stage 2*. Sheffield: NATE/NCC Publications.

Baker, C. and Freebody, P. (1993) The crediting of literate competence in classroom talk. *The Australian Journal of Language and Literacy*, 16(4): 279–94.

Barber, M. (1997) *The Learning Game: Arguments for An Educational Revolution*. London: Indigo.

Barnes, D. (1976) *From Communication to Curriculum*. Harmondsworth: Penguin.

Barnes, D. (1992) The role of talk in learning, in K. Norman (ed.) *Thinking Voices: The Work of the National Oracy Project*. London: Hodder & Stoughton.

Barnes, D. and Sheeran, Y. (1992) Oracy and genre, in K. Norman (ed.) *Thinking Voices: The Work of the National Oracy Project*. London: Hodder & Stoughton.

Barnes, D. and Todd, F. (1977) *Communicating and Learning in Small Groups*. London: Routledge & Kegan Paul.

Barnes, D., Britton, J. and Rosen, H. (1969) *Language, the Learner and the School.* Harmondsworth: Penguin.

Barton, G. (1998) Grammar without shame. *The Use of English*, 49(2): 107–18.

Beard, R. (1998) *National Literacy Strategy Review of Research and other Related Evidence.* London: DfEE.

Bearse, C. (1992) The fairy tale connection in children's stories: Cinderella meets Sleeping Beauty. *The Reading Teacher*, 45(9): 688–95.

Bellack, A., Kliebard, H., Hyman, R. and Smith, F. (1966) *The Language of the Classroom.* Columbia: Teachers' College Press.

Bennett, N. (1985) Interaction and achievement in classroom groups, in N. Bennett and C. Deforges (eds) *Recent Advances in Classroom Research* (*British Journal of Educational Psychology* monograph series, no. 2).

Bennett, N. and Blundell, D. (1983) Quantity and quality of work in rows and classroom groups. *Educational Psychology*, 3(2): 93–105.

Bennett, N. and Carre, C. (1993) *Learning to Teach.* London: Routledge.

Bennett, N. and Cass, A. (1988) The effects of group composition on group interactive processes and pupil understanding. *British Educational Research Journal*, 15: 19–32.

Bennett, N. and Dunne, E. (1992) *Managing Classroom Groups.* Cheltenham: Stanley Thornes.

Bennett, N., Desforges, C., Cockburn, A. and Wilkinson, B. (1984) *The Quality of Pupil Learning Experiences.* London: Lawrence Erlbaum.

Bereiter, C. and Scardamalia, M. (1987) *The Psychology of Written Composition.* Hillsdale, NJ: Lawrence Erlbaum.

Biot, C. (1984) *Getting on Without the Teacher.* Sunderland: Centre for Educational Research and Development, Sunderland Polytechnic.

Blyth, J. and Hughes, P. (1997) *Using Written Sources in Primary History.* London: Hodder & Stoughton.

Booth, D. (1994) *Story Drama: Reading, Writing and Roleplaying Across the Curriculum.* Ontario: Pembroke.

Bossert, S., Barnett, B. and Filby, N. (1984) Grouping and instructional organisation, in P. Peterson, L. Wilkinson and M. Hallinan (eds) *The Social Context of Instruction.* Orlando, FL: Academic Press.

Bousted, M. (1989) Who talks? The position of girls in mixed sex classrooms. *English in Education*, 23(3): 41–51.

Britton, J. (1987) Vygotsky's contribution to pedagogical theory. *English in Education*, 21(3): 22–6.

Brown, A.L. (1987) Metacognition, executive control, self regulation and other mysterious mechanisms, in F. Weinert and R. Kluwe (eds), *Metacognition, Motivation and Understanding.* Hillside NJ: Lawrence Erlbaum.

Bruner, J. (1972) *The Relevance of Education.* Harmondsworth: Penguin.

Bruner, J. (1985) Vygotsky: a historical and conceptual perspective, in J. Wertsch (ed.) *Culture, Communication and Cognition: Vygotskian Perspectives.* Cambridge: Cambridge University Press.

Bruner, J. (1986) *Actual Minds, Possible Worlds.* Cambridge, MA: Harvard University Press.

Bruner, J. (1990) *Acts of Meaning.* London: Harvard University Press.

Bryant, P. (1989) Nursery rhymes, phoniological skills and reading. *Journal of Child Language*, 16: 407–28.

Bunting, R. (1997) *Teaching About Language in the Primary Years*. London: Fulton.

Bus, A. (1994) The role of social context in emergent literacy, in E.M.H. Assink (ed.) *Literacy Acquisition and Social Context*. London: Harvester Wheatsheaf.

Cairney, T. (1990) Intertextuality: infectious echoes from the past. *The Reading Teacher*, 43: 478–84.

Cairney, T. and Langbien, S. (1989) Building communities of readers and writers. *The Reading Teacher*, April: 560–7.

Cambourne, B. (1988) *The Whole Story: Natural Learning and the Acquisition of Literacy in the Classroom*. Auckland: Ashton Scholastic.

Carter, R. (1990) *Knowledge About Language and the Curriculum: The LINC Reader*. London: Hodder & Stoughton.

Central Advisory Council for Education (1967) *Children and their Primary Schools* (Plowden Report) (2 vols). London: HMSO.

Chambers, A. (1993) *Tell Me: Children Reading and Talk*. Stroud: Thimble.

Chen, A. and Ennis, C. (1995) Content knowledge transformation: an examination of the relationship between content knowledge and curricula. *Teaching and Teacher Education*, 11(4): 389–401.

Christie, F. (1988) Genres as choice, in I. Reid (ed.) *The Place of Genre in Learning: Current Debates*, Victoria: Deakin University Press.

Christie, F. (1989) *Writing in Schools, Vol. 1 Study Guide*. Victoria: Deakin University Press.

Clay, M. (1972) *The Early Detection of Reading Difficulties: A Diagnostic Survey*. Auckland, New Zealand: Heinemann.

Cohen, E. (1994) Restructuring classrooms: conditions for productive small groups. *Review of Educational Research*, 64: 1–35.

Comber, B. and Cormack, P. (1997) Looking beyond skills and processes: literacy as social and cultural practices in classrooms. *Reading*, 31(3): 22–9.

Cope, B. and Kalantzis, M. (1993) *The Powers of Literacy: A Genre Approach to Teaching Writing*. London: Falmer Press.

Corden, R. (1996) Talking into literacy. Paper presented at the 36th UKRA Conference, University of Northumbria, Newcastle upon Tyne, July 5–7.

Corson, D. (1988) *Oral Language Across the Curriculum*. Clevedon, OH: Multilingual Matters.

Cowie, H. and Ruddock, J. (1988) *Cooperative Group Work: An Overview*. London: B.P. Educational Service.

Cox, B. (1989) *English for Ages 5–16* (the Cox Report). London: Department of Education and Science.

Cripps, C. (1990) *A Hand for Spelling*. Poole: Learning Development Aids.

Croll, P. and Hastings, N. (eds) (1996) *Effective Primary Teaching: Research Based Classroom Strategies*. London: Fulton.

Croll, P. and Moses, D. (1985) *One in Five: The Assessment and Incidence of Special Educational Needs*. London: Routledge.

Crook, C. (1991) Computers in the zone of proximal development: implications for evaluation. *Computers in Education*, 17(1): 81–91.

Currie, L. (1997) Why use a novel? *Reading*, 3(1): 11–16.

Dawes, L., Fisher, E. and Mercer, N. (1992) The quality of talk at the computer. *Language and Learning*, October: 22–5.

Dearing, R. (1994) *The National Curriculum and its Assessment* (the Dearing Report). London: School Curriculum and Assessment Authority.

Deci, E. and Ryan, R. (1985) *Intrinsic Motivation and Self Determination in Human Behaviour*. New York: Plenum.

DES (Department of Education and Science) (1975) *A Language for Life* (the Bullock Report). London: HMSO.

DES (Department of Education and Science) (1988) *Report of the Committee of Inquiry into the Teaching of English Language* (the Kingman Report). London: HMSO.

DES (Department of Education and Science) (1989) *English in the National Curriculum: Key Stage One*. London: HMSO.

Des Fountain, J. and Howe, A. (1992) Pupils working together on understanding, in K. Norman (ed.) *Thinking Voices: The Work of the National Oracy Project*. London: Hodder & Stoughton.

DfEE (Department for Education and Employment) (1995a) *English in the National Curriculum*. London: HMSO.

DfEE (Department for Education and Employment) (1995b) *Teachers Make a Difference: A Research Perspective on Teaching and Learning in Primary Schools*. London: Teacher Training Agency.

DfEE (Department for Education and Employment) (1997) *The Implementation of the National Literacy Strategy*. London: DfEE.

DfEE (Department for Education and Employment) (1998a) *Teaching: High Status, High Standards*. Circular 4/98. London: Teacher Training Agency.

DfEE (Department for Education and Employment) (1998b) *The National Literacy Strategy Framework for Teaching*. London: Standards and Effectiveness Unit.

Dickinson, D. (1995) *Bridges to Literacy: Children, Families and Schools*. Oxford: Blackwell.

Dillon, J.T. (1982) The effects of questions in education and other enterprises. *Journal of Curriculum Studies*, 14(2): 127–52.

Dillon, J.T. (1985) Using questions to foil discussion. *Teaching and Teacher Education*, 1: 109–21.

Dillon, J.T. (1988) *Questioning and Teaching: A Manual of Practice*. London: Croom Helm.

Dillon, J.T. (1994) *Using Discussion in Classrooms*. Buckingham: Open University Press.

Dombey, H. (1988) Partners in the telling, in M. Meek and C. Mills (eds) *Language and Literacy in the Primary School*. London: Falmer Press.

Downing, J. and Valtin, R. (eds) (1984) *Language Awareness and Learning to Read*. New York: Springer Verlag.

Doyle, W. (1983) Academic work. *Review of Educational Research*, 53(2): 159–99.

Dyson, A. (1987) The value of time off task: young children's spontaneous talk and deliberate text. *Harvard Educational Review*, 57(4): 396–420.

Edwards, A.D. (1980) Patterns of power and authority in classroom talk, in P. Woods (ed.) *Teacher Strategies*. London: Croom Helm.

Edwards, A.D. (1992) Teacher talk and pupil competence, in K. Norman (ed.) *Thinking Voices: The Work of the National Oracy Project*. London: Hodder & Stoughton.

Edwards, A.D. and Furlong, V. (1978) *The Language of Teaching*. London: Heinemann.

Edwards, A.D. and Westgate, D.P.G. (1994) *Investigating Classroom Talk*. London: Falmer Press.

Edwards, D. and Mercer, N. (1987) *Common Knowledge: The Development of Understanding in the Classroom*. London: Methuen.

Elbers, E. and Kelderman, A. (1994) Ground rules for testing: expectations and misunderstandings in test situations. *European Journal of Psychology of Education*, 9(1): 111–20.

Ewing, J.M. and Kennedy, E.M. (1996) Putting co-operative learning to good effect. *Reading*, 30(1): 15–19.

Fisher, E. (1993) Characteristics of children's talk at the computer and its relationship to the computer software. *Language and Education*, 7(2): 97–114.

Fisher, R. (1992) *Early Literacy and the Teacher*, UKRA. Sevenoaks: Hodder & Stoughton.

Fitzgerald, J. (1987) Research on revision in writing. *Review of Educational Research*, 57(4): 481–506.

Flanders, N. (1970) *Analysing Teacher Behaviour*. Reading, MA: Addison Wesley.

Fox, C. (1993) *At the Very Edge of the Forest: The Influence of Literature on Storytelling by Children*. London: Cassell.

Frater, G. (1988) Oracy in England – a new tide: an HMI overview, in M. Maclure *et al. Oracy Matters*. Milton Keynes: Open University Press.

French, J. and French, P. (1984) Gender imbalances in the primary classroom: an interactional account. *Educational Research*, 22: 127–36.

Friere, P. (1972) *Cultural Action for Freedom*. Harmondsworth: Penguin.

Galton, M. (1989) *Teaching in the Primary School*. London: David Fulton.

Galton, M. and Willcocks, J. (eds) (1983) *Moving from the Primary Classroom*. London: Routledge & Kegan Paul.

Galton, M. and Williamson, J. (1992) *Group Work in the Primary Classroom*. London: Routledge.

Galton, M., Simon, B. and Croll, P. (1980) *Inside the Primary Classroom*. London: Routledge.

Galton, M., Hargreaves, L., Comber, C., Wall, D. and Pell, A. (1999) *Inside The Primary Classroom 20 Years On*. London: Routledge.

Garfield, L. (1984) *Six Apprentices*. London: Heinemann.

Garfield, L. (1986) *The December Rose*. Harmondsworth: Puffin.

Gee, J. (1990) *Social Linguistics and Literacies: Ideology in Discourse*. London: Falmer Press.

Goswami, U. and Bryant, P. (1990) *Phonological Skills and Learning to Read*. Hillsdale, NJ: Lawrence Erlbaum.

Graff, H. (1994) The legacies of literacy, in J. Maybin (ed.) *Language and Literacy in Social Practice*. Adelaide: Multilingual Matters.

Grainger, T. (1997) *Traditional Storytelling in the Primary Classroom*. Leamington Spa: Scholastic.

Grainger, T. (1998) Drama and reading: illuminating their interaction. *English in Education*, 32(1): 29–36.

Graves, M. and Graves, B. (1994) *Scaffolding Reading Experiences: Designs for Student Success*. Norwood, MA: Christopher Gordon.

Guppy, P. and Hughes, M. (1999) *The Development of Independent Reading: Reading Support Explained.* Buckingham: Open University Press.

Halliday, M.A.K. (1969) Relevant modes of language. *Educational Review*, 21(2): 26–31.

Halliday, M.A.K., McIntosh, A. and Strevens, P. (1964) *The Linguistic Sciences and Language Teaching.* London: Longman.

Hansen, J. (1987) *When Writers Read.* Portsmouth, NH: Heinemann.

Hardman, F. and Beverton, S. (1993) Co-operative group work and the development of metadiscoursal skills. *Support for Learning*, 8(4): 146–50.

Hardy, M. (1977) Narrative as a primary act of mind, in M. Meek, A. Warlow and G. Barton (eds) *The Cool Web: The Pattern of Children's Reading.* London: Bodley Head.

Hargie, O. (1978) The importance of teacher questions in the classroom. *Educational Research*, 20(2): 97–102.

Hargreaves, D. (1984) Teacher's questions: open, closed and half open. *Educational Research*, 26(1): 46–52.

Harris, J. (1989) *Writing in the Classroom: Drafting.* Sheffield: Sheffield Hallam University.

Harris, J. (1993) *Introducing Writing.* Harmondsworth: Penguin.

Harwayne, S. (1992) *Lasting Impressions: Weaving Literature into the Writing Workshop.* Portsmouth, NH: Heinemann.

Hastings, N. (1990) Questions of motivation. *Support for Learning*, 7: 135–7.

Hayes, J., Flower, L., Schriver, K., Stratman, J. and Carey, L. (1987) Cognitive processes in revision, in S. Rosenberg (ed.) *Reading, Writing and Language Learning.* Cambridge: Cambridge University Press.

Heath, S. (1983) *Ways With Words. Language, Life and Work in Communities and Classrooms.* Cambridge: Cambridge University Press.

Heath, S. (1986) Sociocultural contexts of language development, in M. Terpstra and S. Gieskes (eds) *Beyond Language: Social and Cultural Factors in Schooling Language Minority Students.* Los Angeles, CA: California State University.

Hertz-Lazarowitz, R. (1990) An integrative model of the classroom: the enhancement of cooperative learning, in R. Lazarowitz and N. Miller (eds) *Interaction in Cooperative Groups: Theoretical Anatomy of Group Learning.* London: Cambridge University Press.

Hewison, J. and Tizard, J. (1980) Parental involvement and reading attainment. *British Journal of Educational Psychology*, 50: 209–15.

Hill, A. and Browne, A. (1994) Talk and the microcomputer: an investigation in the infant classroom, in D. Wray (ed.) *Literacy and Computers: Insights from Research.* Widnes: United Kingdom Reading Association.

HMI (Her Majesty's Inspectorate of Schools) (1978) *Primary Education in England.* London: HMSO.

HMI (Her Majesty's Inspectorate of Schools) (1982) *Education 5–9.* London: HMSO.

HMI (Her Majesty's Inspectorate of Schools) (1985) *Education 8 to 12 in Combined Middle Schools.* London: Department of Education and Science.

HMI (Her Majesty's Inspectorate of Schools) (1990) *Aspects of Primary Education: The Teaching and Learning of Language and Literacy.* London: HMSO.

HMI (Her Majesty's Inspectorate of Schools) (1998) *Teacher Assessment in the Core Subjects at Key Stage 2: Policy and Practice.* London: Ofsted.

Hoey, M. (1983) *On the Surface of Discourse*. London: Allen & Unwin.

Hoggart, R. (1970) Culture – dead and alive, in *Speaking to Each Other: About Society*. London: Chatto and Windus.

Holdaway, D. (1979) *The Foundations of Literacy*. Auckland: Ashton Scholastic.

Holden, C. (1993) Giving girls a chance: patterns of talk in co-operative group work. *Gender and Education*, 5(2): 179–89.

Hood, S. (1975) Visual literacy examined, in B. Luckham (ed.) *Audio-Visual Literacy, Proceedings of Sixth Symposium on Broadcasting Policy*. Manchester: University of Manchester.

Howe, A. (1990) A climate for small group talk, in M. Brubacher, R. Payne and K. Rickett (eds) *Perspectives on Small Group Learning: Theory and Practice*, Ontario: Rubicon.

Howe, A. and Johnson, J. (1992) *Common Bonds: Storytelling in the Classroom*. London: Hodder & Stoughton.

Hoyles, C., Sutherland, R. and Healey, I. (1990) Children talking in computer environments: new insights on the role of discussion in mathematics learning, in K. Durkin and B. Shine (eds) *Language and Mathematics Education*. Buckingham: Open University Press.

Hughes, M. and Westgate, D.P.G. (1988) Re-appraising talk in nursery and reception classes. *Education*, 16(2): 9–15.

Hull, R. (1985) *The Language Gap*. London: Methuen.

Jackson, H. and Stockwell, P. (1996) *The Nature and Functions of Language*. Cheltenham: Stanley Thornes.

Johnson, D. and Johnson, R. (1990) What is cooperative learning? in M. Brubacher, R. Payne and K. Rickett (eds) *Perspectives on Small Group Learning: Theory and Practice*. Ontario: Rubicon.

Johnson, D., Maruyama, G., Johnson, R., Nelson, D. and Skon, L. (1981) Effects of cooperative, competitive and individualistic goal structures on achievement: a metaanalysis. *Psychological Bulletin*, 89: 47–62.

Johnson, D., Johnson, R. and Holoubec, E. (1988) *Circles of Learning: Cooperation in the Classroom* (revised edn). Edina, MN: Interaction Book Company.

Jones, A. and Mercer, N. (1993) Theories of learning and information technology, in P. Scrimshaw (ed.) *Language, Classrooms and Computers*. London: Routledge.

Kagan, S. (1985) Dimensions of cooperative classroom structures, in R. Hertz Lazarowitz, S. Kagan, S. Sharan, R. Slavin, C. Webb (eds) *Learning to Cooperate, Cooperating to Learn*. Netherlands: Kluwer Academic/Plenum.

King, A. (1989) Verbal interaction and problem-solving within computer-assisted cooperative learning groups. *Journal of Educational Computing Research*, 5(1): 1–15.

Kress, G. (1986) Interrelationships of reading and writing, in A. Wilkinson (ed.) *The Writing of Writing*. Milton Keynes: Open University Press.

Kumulainen, K. (1994) Word processors creating a social context for learning, in D. Wray (ed.) *Literacy and Computers: Insights from Research*. Widnes: United Kingdom Reading Association.

Labov, W. (1972) *Language in the Inner City*. Oxford: Blackwell.

Lancia, P. (1997) Literary borrowing: the effects of literature on children's writing. *The Reading Teacher*, 50(6): 470–5.

Latham, P. (1992) Oracy and the National Curriculum, in K. Norman (ed.) *Thinking Voices: The Work of the National Oracy Project*. London: Hodder & Stoughton.

Longacre, R. (1976) *An Anatomy of Speech Notions*. Lisse: Peter de Ridder.

Lotman, M. (1988) Text within a text. *Soviet Psychology*, 26(3): 32–51.

Luke, A. (1993) The social construction of literacy in the primary school, in L. Unsworth (ed.) *Literacy and Teaching: Language as Social Practice in the Primary School*. Melbourne: Macmillan.

Lunzer, E. and Gardner, K. (eds) (1979) *The Effective Use of Reading*, Schools Council Project. London: Heinemann.

Lyle, S. (1993) An investigation into ways in which children talk themselves into meaning. *Language and Education*, 7(3): 181–97.

McMahon, S.L. and Goatley, V.J. (1995) Fifth graders helping peers discuss texts in student led groups. *The Journal of Educational Research*, 89(1): 23–34.

McMahon, S.L. and Meyers, J.L. (1993) *What's Happening Here? A Comparison of Two Literature Discussion Groups*. Paper presented at the National Reading Conference, Charleston, SC.

Mallett, M. (1997) Developing learning: can you say a little more about that? Helping children make their response to fiction explicit. *Education*, 25(1): 11–17.

Martin, J. and Rothery, J. (1980) *Writing Project, Paper 1*. Sydney: Department of Linguistics, University of Sydney.

Martin, N. (1976) Encounters with models. *English in Education*, 10(1): 9–15.

Masterman, L. (1980) *Teaching About Television*. London: Macmillan.

Maybin, J. and Moss, G. (1993) Talk about texts: reading as a social event. *Journal of Research in Reading*, 16(2): 138–47.

Meek, M. (1988) *How Texts Teach What Readers Learn*. Stroud: Thimble Press.

Meek, M. (1991) *On Being Literate*. London: Bodley Head.

Meek, M. (1992) Literacy re-describing reading, in K. Kimberley, M. Meek and J. Miller (eds) *New Readings: Contributions to an Understanding of Literacy*. London: A. & C. Black.

Mercer, N. (1991) Computers and communication in the classroom, Unit 7, EH232. *Computers and Learning*. Milton Keynes: The Open University.

Mercer, N. (1992) Culture, context and the construction of knowledge, in P. Light and G. Butterworth (eds) *Context and Cognition*. London: Harvester Wheatsheaf.

Mercer, N. (1994) The quality of talk in joint activity at the computer. *Journal of Computer Assisted Learning*. 10: 24–32.

Mercer, N. (1995) *The Guided Construction of Knowledge: Talk Amongst Teachers and Learners*. Clevedon, OH: Multilingual Matters.

Mercer, N. and Edwards, D. (1981) Ground rules for mutual understanding: a sociopsychological approach to classroom knowledge, in N. Mercer (ed.) *Language in School and Community*. London: Edward Arnold.

Mercer, N., Edwards, D. and Maybin, J. (1988) Putting context into oracy: the construction of shared knowledge through classroom discourse, in M. Maclure, T. Phillips and A. Wilkinson (eds) *Oracy Matters*. Milton Keynes: Open University Press.

Mercer, N. and Fisher, E. (1992) How do teachers help children to learn? An analysis of teachers' interventions in computer-based activities. *Learning and Instruction*, 2: 339–55.

Michaels, S. (1985) Hearing the connections in children's oral and written discourse. *Journal of Education*, 167: 36–56.

Moffett, J. (1968) *Teaching the Universe of Discourse*. New York: Houghton Mifflin.

Moore, P. and Tweddle, S. (1992) *The Integrated Classroom: Language Learning and IT*. London: Hodder & Stoughton.

Morgan, N. and Saxton, J. (1991) *Teaching, Questioning and Learning*. London: Routledge.

Mortimer, P., Sammonds, P., Stoll, L., Lewis, D. and Ecob, R. (1988) *School Matters*. Wells: Open Books.

National Writing Project (1989) *Responding to Written Work*. London: Nelson.

NCET (1992) *Starting Stories*. Coventry: National Council for Educational Technology.

Norman, K. (1990) *Teaching, Talking and Learning in Key Stage 1*. Sheffield: NATE/ NCC Publications.

Norman, K. (ed.) (1992) *Thinking Voices: The Work of the National Oracy Project*. London: Hodder & Stoughton.

Ofsted (Office for Standards in Education) (1993) *The New Teacher in School*. London: Ofsted Publications.

Ofsted (Office for Standards in Education) (1995) *English: A Review of Inspection Findings: 1993/94*. London: Ofsted Publications.

Ofsted (Office for Standards in Education) (1996a) *Subjects and Standards: 1994/5 Inspection*. London: Ofsted Publications.

Ofsted (Office for Standards in Education) (1996b) *The Teaching of Reading in 45 Inner London Primary Schools*. London: Ofsted Publications.

Ofsted (Office for Standards in Education) (1997) *Using Subject Specialists to Promote High Standards at Key Stage 2*. London: Ofsted Publications.

Olson, D. (1984) See! Jumping! Some oral antecedents of literacy, in H. Goelman, A. Oberg and F. Smith (eds) *Awakening to Literacy*. Portsmouth, NH: Heinemann.

Opie, I. and Opie P. (1975) *Children's Games in Street and Playground*. Oxford: Clarendon.

Palinscar, A.S. and Brown, A.L. (1984) Reciprocal teaching of comprehension, fostering and comprehension monitoring activities. *Cognition and Instruction*, 2: 117–75.

Paris, S., Cross, D. and Lipson, M. (1984) Informed strategies for learning: a program to improve children's reading awareness and comprehension. *Journal of Educational Psychology*, 76: 1239–52.

Perera, K. (1987) *Understanding Language*. Sheffield: National Association for the Teaching of English.

Peters, M. and Cripps, C. (1983) *Catchwords: Ideas for Teaching Spelling*. London: Harcourt, Brace, Jovanovich.

Philips, S. (1983) *The Invisible Culture: Communication in Classroom and Community on the Warm Springs Indian Reservation*. New York: Longman.

Phillips, T. (1988) On a related matter: why 'successful' small group work depends upon not keeping to the point, in M. Maclure, T. Phillips and A. Wilkinson (eds) *Oracy Matters*. Milton Keynes: Open University Press.

Phillips, T. (1992) Why? The neglected question in planning for small groups, in K. Norman (ed.) *Thinking Voices: The Work of the National Oracy Project*. London: Hodder & Stoughton.

Piaget, J. (1970) *The Science of Education and the Psychology of the Child*. New York: Viking Press.

Pollard, A. (1985) *The Social World of the Primary School*. London: Holt, Rinehart & Winston.

Prentice, M. (1991) A community of enquiry, in *Talk and Learning 5–16: An In-service Pack on Oracy for Teachers*. Milton Keynes: The Open University.

QCA (1998) *Gathering Evidence of Children's Reading Through Talk*. London: Qualifications and Curriculum Authority.

Raban, B., Clark, U. and McIntyre, J. (1994) *Evaluation of the Implementation of English in the National Curriculum at Key Stages 1, 2 and 3 (1991–1993)*. London: School Curriculum and Assessment Authority.

Redpath, J. (1989) *Girls and Boys' Interaction in Primary Classrooms*. Ealing: Gender Equality Team.

Reid, J., Forrestal, P. and Cook, J. (1982) *Small Group Work in the Classroom*. Perth: Western Australia Education Department.

Robertson, L. (1990) Cooperative learning à la CLIP, in M. Brubacher, R. Payne and K. Rickett (eds) *Perspectives on Small Group Learning*. Oakville, Ontario: Rubicon.

Rohrkemper, M. (1985) Individual differences in students' perceptions of routine classroom events. *Journal of Educational Psychology*, 77(1): 29–44.

Rosen, C. and Rosen, H. (1973) *The Language of Primary School Children*. Harmondsworth: Penguin.

Rosen, M. (1998) *Did I Hear You Write?* (2nd edn). Nottingham: André Deutsch.

Rosenblatt, L.M. (1989) Writing and reading: the transactional theory, in J. Mason (ed.) *Reading and Writing Connections*. Boston, MA: Allyn & Bacon.

Sadker, M. and Sadker, D. (1985) Sexism in the schoolroom of the 80s. *Psychology Today*, March: 54–7.

Salomon, G. and Globerson, T. (1989) When teams do not function the way they ought to. *Journal of Experimental Social Psychology*, 26: 168–83.

SCAA (School Curriculum and Assessment Authority) (1997a) *Looking at Children's Learning: Desirable Outcomes for Children's Learning on Entering Compulsory Education*. London: School Curriculum and Assessment Authority.

SCAA (School Curriculum and Assessment Authority) (1997b) *Use of Language: A Common Approach*. London: School Curriculum and Assessment Authority.

Scott, P., Dyson, T. and Gater, S. (1987) *A Constructivist View of Learning and Teaching in Science: Children's Learning in Science Project*. Leeds: Centre for Studies in Science and Mathematics Education.

Sharan, S. (1980) Cooperative learning in small groups: recent methods and effects on achievement, attitudes and ethnic relations. *Review of Educational Research*, 50: 241–71.

Sharan, S. and Shaulov, A. (1989) Cooperative learning, motivation to learn and academic achievement, in S. Sharan (ed.) *Cooperative Learning: Theory and Research*. New York: Praeger.

Sharan, Y. (1990) Group investigation: expanding co-operative learning, in M. Brubacher, R. Payne and K. Rickett (eds) *Perspectives on Small Group Learning*. Oakville, Ontario: Rubicon.

Shulman, L. (1986) Those who understand: knowledge and growth in teaching. *Educational Researcher*, 15(2): 4–14.

Simon, B. and Willcocks, J. (eds) (1981) *Research and Practice in the Primary Classroom*. London: Routledge.

Sinclair, J. and Coulthard, M. (1975) *Towards an Analysis of Discourse: The Language of Teachers and Students*. London: Oxford University Press.

Slavin, R. (1983a) *Cooperative Learning*. New York: Longman.

Slavin, R. (1983b) When does cooperative learning increase student achievement? *Psychological Bulletin*, 94(3): 429–45.

Speare, E.G. (1983) *Sign of the Beaver*. London: Collins.

Stainthorp, R. (1999) The big national experiment: questions about the National Literacy Strategy. *The Psychology of Education Review*, 23(1): 3–8.

Stannard, J. (1998) *The National Literacy Strategy Trainer's Cassette 2*. London: Standards and Effectiveness Unit, DfEE.

Stanovich, K. (1986) Matthew effects in reading: some consequences of individual differences in the acquisition of literacy. *Reading Research Quarterly*, 21: 360–407.

Swann, J. (1992) *Girls, Boys and Language*. London: Blackwell.

Swann, J. and Graddol, D. (1988) Gender inequalities in classroom talk. *English in Education*, 22(1): 48–65.

Tann, S. (1981) Grouping and group work, in B. Simon and J. Willcocks (eds) *Research and Practice in the Primary Classroom*. London: Routledge.

Tannen, D. (1989) *Talking Voices*. Cambridge: Cambridge University Press.

Taylor, G. (1986) The development of style in children's fictional narrative, in A. Wilkinson (ed.) *The Writing of Writing*. Milton Keynes: Open University Press.

Tizard, B., Blatchford, D., Burke, J., Farquar, C. and Plewis, I. (1988) *Young Children at School in the Inner City*. Hove: Lawrence Erlbaum.

Tizard, B. and Hughes, M. (1984) *Young Children's Learning, Talking and Thinking at Home and at School*. London: Fontana.

Topping, K. (1985) Parental involvement in reading: theoretical and empirical background, in K. Topping and S. Wolfendale (eds) *Parental Involvement in Children's Reading*. London: Croom Helm.

Tough, J. (1977) *Talking and Learning: A Guide to Fostering Communication Skills in Nursery and Infant Schools*. London: Ward Lock.

Vygotsky, L.S. (1978) *Thought and Language*. Cambridge, MA: MIT Press.

Vygotsky, L.S. (1982) *On the Child's Psychic Development*. Copenhagen: Nyt Nordisc.

Webb, N. (1989) Peer interaction and learning in small groups. *International Journal of Educational Research*, 13: 21–39.

Webb, N. and Cullian, L. (1983) Group interaction and achievement in small groups: stability over time. *American Educational Research Journal*, 20(3): 411–23.

Wegerif, R. and Mercer, N. (1996) Computers and learning through talk in the classroom. *Language in Education*, 10(1): 47–64.

Wells, G. (1985) *Language Development in the Pre-School Years*. Cambridge: Cambridge University Press.

Wells, G. (1987a) Apprenticeship in literacy. *Interchange*, 18(1–2): 109–23.

Wells, G. (1987b) *The Meaning Makers*. London: Hodder & Stoughton.

Wells, G. (1989) Language in the classroom: literacy and collaborative talk. *Language and Education*, 3(4): 251–74.

Wells, G. (1992) The centrality of talk in education, in K. Norman (ed.) *Thinking Voices: The Work of the National Oracy Project*. London: Hodder & Stoughton.

Wells, G. and Chang, G. (1986) From speech to writing: some evidence on the relationship between oracy and literacy, in A. Wilkinson (ed.) *The Writing of Writing*. Milton Keynes: Open University Press.

Wells, G. and Chang, G. (1988) The literate potential of collaborative talk, in M. Maclure, T. Phillips and A. Wilkinson (eds) *Oracy Matters*. Milton Keynes: Open University Press.

Wells, G., Chang, G. and Maher, A. (1990) Creating classroom communities of literate thinkers, in S. Sharan (ed.) *Cooperative Learning: Theory and Research*. New York: Praeger.

Wells, G. and Nicholls, J. (eds) (1985) *Language and Learning: An Interactional Perspective*. London: Falmer Press.

Westgate, D.P.G. and Corden, R. (1993) What we thought about things: expectations, context and small group talk. *Language and Education*, 7(2): 115–26.

Wilkinson, A. (1965) *Spoken English (Educational Review* occasional publications no. 2). Birmingham: University of Birmingham.

Wilkinson, A., Davies, A. and Berrill, D. (1990) *Spoken English Illuminated*. Buckingham: Open University Press.

Willes, M. (1983) *Children into Pupils*. London: Routledge.

Wood, D. (1988) *How Children Think and Learn*. Oxford: Blackwell.

Wood, D. (1992) Teacher talk, in K. Norman (ed.) *Thinking Voices: The Work of the National Oracy Project*. London: Hodder & Stoughton.

Wood, D., Bruner, J. and Ross, G. (1976) The role of tutoring in problem-solving. *Journal of Child Psychology and Psychiatry*, 17(2): 89–100.

Wood, D. and Wood, H. (1984) An experimental evaluation of five styles of teacher conversation on the language of hearing impaired children. *Journal of Child Psychology and Psychiatry*, 25(1): 45–62.

Wood, D. and Wood, H. (1988) Questioning versus student initiative, in J.T. Dillon (ed.) *Questioning and Discussion: A Multidisciplinary Study*. Norwood: Ablex.

Wragg, E. (1994) Teachers' subject knowledge, in A. Pollard and J. Bourne (eds) *Teaching and Learning in the Primary School*. London: Routledge.

Wray, D. (1993) Student teachers' knowledge and beliefs about language, in N. Bennett and C. Carre (eds) *Learning to Teach*. London: Routledge.

Wray, D. (1994) *Literacy and Awareness*. London: Hodder & Stoughton (for United Kingdom Reading Association).

Young, R. (1984) Teaching equals indoctrination: the dominant epistemic practices of our schools. *British Journal of Educational Studies*, 32(3): 220–8.

Index

PRIMARY WRITING

Dominic Wyse

This book focuses on an approach to teaching writing in the primary school called the 'process approach'. The approach has been recognized internationally as an important method for the teaching of primary writing. In the UK it has become a focus particularly through the National Writing Project, the LINC project and more recently in the National Curriculum.

At a time of increasing traditionalism in primary education *Primary Writing* portrays an in-depth account of an innovative approach to the teaching of writing. *Primary Writing* is the first book length examination of the process approach in the UK and convincingly demonstrates its strengths and benefits. For any teacher who uses a 'mixture of methods' the process approach cannot be ignored.

The author has eight years experience as a primary teacher at KS1 and KS2 and as a language coordinator in inner-city and suburban schools. His experience of using the process approach in the classroom and sharing the approach with colleagues has resulted in a text that gives detailed and vibrant examples of practice alongside relevant research.

Contents
Introduction – Writing workshop – Emergent writing – The development of composition – Transcription – Interaction – Recording language development – The links with reading – Developing the process approach throughout the school – The process approach and the National Curriculum – The wider picture – Appendices – References – Index.

176 pp   0 335 19813 9 (Paperback)   0 335 19814 7 (Hardback)

THE DEVELOPMENT OF INDEPENDENT READING
READING SUPPORT EXPLAINED

Peter Guppy and Margaret Hughes

Listening to children read, both at home and at school, has long been regarded as a vital element in the teaching of reading. However, it is a practice which is rarely examined in any detail. This book shows why it is not enough just to 'hear readers' and demonstrates how adult interventions should change as children's reading develops through five distinct but overlapping stages.

The book explains the central importance of cues – those providers of the information which a reader uses to solve a problem word – and redefines 'the basics' by identifying the three permanent components of reading – Reading the lines, Between the lines and Beyond the lines. The authors outline practical classroom activities to help children develop competence in balancing cues, highlighting the integration of meaning and phonics.

This accessible book will be an invaluable resource for all adults involved in teaching reading. It provides a rationale for good practice and offers practical and adaptable materials which can be used to support initial training, INSET, workshops for classroom helpers, and parent-meetings.

Contents
Introduction – Rationale: the basics – Bookbinding – Chiming in – Cue talk – Assisted reading – Part 1: The nature of assisted reading – Part 2: The three reading levels – Part 3: Ingredients of an assisted reading session – Part 4: Ten supportive actions for a problem word – Part 5: Phonic knowledge within reading – Conclusion – Branching out – The team approach – teachers, parents and helpers – References – Related reading – Index.

192 pp   0 335 20152 0 (Paperback)

SUPPORTING LANGUAGE AND LITERACY DEVELOPMENT IN THE EARLY YEARS

Marian Whitehead

This book presents a developmental view of language, the emergence of literacy and the role of literature in the early years.

The age range covered is 0–6 years, a period characterized by unparalleled speed and complexity of growth in thinking, language, social and cultural awareness and physical skills.

Perspectives on language, literature and literacy in the early years are combined in one accessible volume. Chapters on communication, play, narrative and national literacy requirements provide a helpful way into some complex issues.

The book uses child observations and case studies to demonstrate the learning that goes on in a variety of homes and early years settings and challenges many current shibboleths in the field of early years language and literacy.

The book will be valuable reading for all adults seeking to support young children's language and literacy learning – parents, teachers, nursery nurses, childminders, playgroup leaders and other early years professionals.

Contents
Introduction – Great communicators – Play and language – Once upon a time . . . – Literacy begins here – Language, literature and literacy in two early years settings – National requirements and frameworks for language and literacy – Talking together – Bibliography – Index.

176 pp   0 335 19931 3 (Paperback)   0 335 19932 1 (Hardback)